HOLIDAYS IN HELL

Also by P. J. O'Rourke

Holidays
In
Hell

·······························

P. J. O'Rourke

GROVE PRESS
New York

Published simultaneously in Canada
Printed in the United States of America

Library of Congress Cataloging-in-Publication Data

O'Rourke, P. J.
   Holidays in hell / P .J. O'Rourke.
   ISBN 0-8021-3701-6
   1. O'Rourke, P. J. 2. Travel—Humor. 3. Vacations—Humor.
4. World politics—1975–1985—Humor. 5. World politics—1985–1995—
Humor. I. Title.
PN6162.O75   1988   818'.5402—dc19   88-17599

Designed by Laura Hammond Hough

Grove Press
841 Broadway
New York, NY 10003

03   10 9 8 7 6 5 4 3

To the memory of John Courteney Boot,
in Evelyn Waugh's *Scoop*,
who spent "some harrowing months
among the Patagonian Indians"
and wrote a book called *Waste of Time*.

• •

Often the more you understand, the less you forgive.
                    —Jillian Becker
                    Director, Institute for the
                    Study of Terrorism

Take up the White Man's burden—
    The savage wars of peace—
Fill full the mouth of Famine
    And bid the sickness cease;
And when your goal is nearest
    The end for others sought,
Watch Sloth and heathen Folly
    Bring all your hope to nought.

                    —Rudyard Kipling, on the occasion of
                    America taking possession of the
                    Philippines

Wherever you go, there you are.
                    —Buckaroo Banzai

Acknowledgments

· ·

"The Innocents Abroad, Updated" originally appeared, in some-what different form, in the *International Herald Tribune* 100th Anniversary Edition. "A Ramble Through Lebanon" was commissioned (and magnanimously paid for) by *Vanity Fair* but appeared in the Washington, D.C., *City Paper.* "Through Darkest America" was first published in *Harper's*; "Weekend Getaway," in *Playboy*; "Third World Driving Hints and Tips," in *Automobile*; and "Intellectual Wilderness, Ho" and "What Does the Future Hold In Store for Our Friends in Faraway Lands?," in *The American Spectator.* The author would like to thank these publications for permission to reprint this material. All the other pieces in the book were underwritten by *Rolling Stone* magazine. The author owes an immense debt of gratitude (and quite a bit of money advanced for expenses) to Editor and Publisher Jann Wenner.

Jann convinced me to occupy the International Affairs Desk at *Rolling Stone*; he never complained (well, hardly ever) about the

Holidays In Hell

· ·

cost of my travels, and he persisted in publishing my work despite irate mail (much of it on recycled paper decorated in unicorn motifs) from his more liberal readers. Thank you, Jann, and the piece about terrorist activity on South Pacific nude beaches is in the mail. Really.

I am also greatly beholden to *Rolling Stone* Senior Editor Robert Vare, who rendered the confused absurdity in my manuscripts lucidly absurd, and to *Rolling Stone* Managing Editor Bob Wallace, whose unerring news sense kept me from making a number of silly mistakes such as going off to cover the Spanish Civil War which, as Bob pointed out, is over.

I would also like to thank Joseph Fitchett at the *International Herald Tribune*, Wayne Lawson at *Vanity Fair*, Jack Shafer at the *City Paper*, John Rezek at *Playboy*, David E. Davis and Jean Lindamood at *Automobile* and Wladyslaw Pleszczynski and Andrew Ferguson at *The American Spectator*, all of whom conspired to improve my prose. I hope they succeeded. And I would like to thank Morgan Entrekin—publisher, editor and friend—without whom this book would be a largish stack of yellowing, badly smudged typing paper.

There is one more group of people I need to thank here: the print and broadcast reporters, the editors, producers, camera crews and photographers of the international press corps, especially those who make a career of covering dangerous and disgusting places. These "shithole specialists" were always welcoming when I traipsed through their bailiwicks. They gave me information, advice, background briefings and an awful lot of free drinks. They let me tag along on stories and hang out in news bureaus. And more than once they saved my ass from jail and worse. I owe most of the facts in this book to them. (The truths are theirs, the errors, mine.) In fact, I owe them the whole book. What I tell readers in my stories is nothing but what members of the press tell each other around the bar at 10:00 P.M. Thank you Chris Isham, George Moll, Charles Glass, Derwin Johnson, Tony Suau, Betsey West, Kazim Eddire, Robert Fisk, Chris Harper, Jane Hartney, Ray Homer, David Jaffee, Steve Cocklin, Anne Cocklin, Salim Aridi, Andy Cottum, Dorota Kowalska, John Giannini, Nathan Benn, Robin Moyer, Greg Davis, Steve Gardner, Tom

viii

P. J. O'Rourke

Haley, Jim Nachtwey, Glen Gavin, Darrell Barton, Jerry Gonzalez, Anna Cerrud, Tom Brown, Mike Drudge, Kristina Luz, Clayton Jones, Scott Williams, Mark Littke, Kathleen Barnes, Allen Tannenbaum, James Fenton, Bill Rettiker, Chris Morris, Jeanne Hallacy, Keith Miller, Al Varga, Christine Chavez, Mike Boettcher, Qassem Ali, Nayef Hashlamoun, John Reardon, Tim Llwellyn and a hundred others I know I'm forgetting or whose names are illegible in my scribbled notes. May bad news follow you around.

Contents

. . . .

Holidays In Hell
....

HOLIDAYS IN HELL

Introduction

. . . .

I've been working as a foreign correspondent for the past few years, although "working" isn't the right word and "foreign correspondent" is too dignified a title. What I've really been is a Trouble Tourist—going to see insurrections, stupidities, political crises, civil disturbances and other human folly because . . . because it's fun.

Like most people who don't own Bermuda shorts, I'm bored by ordinary travel. See the Beautiful Grand Canyon. Okay, I see it. Okay, it's beautiful. Now what? And I have no use for vacation paradises. Take the little true love along to kick back and work on the relationship. She gets her tits sunburned. I wreck the rental car. We've got our teeth in each other's throats before you can say "lost luggage." Nor do attractions attract me. If I had a chance to visit another planet, I wouldn't want to go to Six Flags Over Mars or ride through the artificial ammonia lake in a silicone-bottomed boat at Venusian Cypress Gardens. I'd want to see the planet's principal features—what makes it tick. Well, the planet I've got a chance to visit is Earth, and Earth's principal features are chaos and war. I think I'd be a fool to spend years here and never have a look.

I also became a foreign correspondent because I was tired of making bad jokes. I spent most of the Seventies as an editor at *The National Lampoon*, and I spent the early Eighties writing comedy scripts for movies and comic articles for magazines. All the while, the world outside seemed a much worse joke than anything I could conjure. "The secret source of humor itself is not joy but sorrow," said Mark Twain. I wanted to get at that awful source of mirth and make very, very bad jokes.

I thought maybe I could use the techniques of humor to report on real news events. Or, at least, I thought I could use that phrase to convince editors and publishers to pay my way to Lebanon, El Salvador and so forth. Actually, I was just curious. I wanted to know where trouble came from and why the world was such a lousy place. I wasn't curious about natural disasters—earthquakes, mudslides, floods and droughts. These are nothing but the losing side of the Grand Canyon coin toss. Okay, it's sad. Now what? I was curious about the trouble man causes himself and which he could presumably quit causing himself at the drop of a hat, or, anyway, a gun. I wanted to know why life, which ought to be an only moderately miserable thing, is such a frightful, disgusting, horrid thing for so many people in so many places.

Because I was curious and wanted a few facts, there are no important people in this book—no interviews with Heads Of State or Major Figures On The International Scene. These people didn't get where they are by being dumb enough to tell reporters the truth. And, although I admit to most faults, I don't have the Network Anchor-Creature self-conceit that lets some people believe Mikhail Gorbachev will suddenly take them aside and say, "Strictly between you and me, on Wednesday we invade Finland." This book is written from the worm's viewpoint, and the things I've asked my fellow blind, spineless members of the phylum *Annelida* are things like, "What's for dinner?" and "Please don't kill me"—the stuff of mankind's real-life interviews.

There are also no earnest messages in this book. Half the

world's suffering is caused by earnest messages contained in grand theories bearing no relation to reality—Marxism and No-Fault Auto Insurance, to name two. Earnestness is just stupidity sent to college. I'm not sure this book contains *any* serious content. No matter how serious the events I've witnessed, I've never noticed that being serious about them did anything to improve the fate of the people involved. Some writers, the young and the dim ones, think being near something important makes them important so they should act and sound important which will, somehow, make their audience important, too. Then, as soon as everybody is filled with a sufficient sense of importance, Something Will Be Done. It's not the truth. Thirty years of acting and sounding important about the Holocaust did nothing to prevent Cambodia.

Furthermore, there are no answers in this book. Even simple questions do not, with logical necessity, lead to them. I can sum up everything I've learned about trouble in a few words, and I will:

Civilization is an enormous improvement on the lack thereof. No reasonable person who has had a look at the East Bloc (or an issue of the *Nation*) can countenance the barbarities of the Left. And every dorm bull-session anarchist should spend an hour in Beirut. So-called Western Civilization, as practiced in half of Europe, some of Asia and a few parts of North America, is better than anything else available. Western Civilization not only provides a bit of life, a pinch of liberty and the occasional pursuance of a happiness, it's also the only thing that's ever tried to. Our civilization is the first in history to show even the slightest concern for average, undistinguished, none-too-commendable people like us.

We are fools when we fail to defend civilization. The ancient Romans might as well have said, "Oh, the Germanic tribes have valid nationalistic and cultural aspirations. Let's pull the legions off the Rhine, submit our differences to a multilateral peace conference chaired by the Pathan Empire and start a Vandal Studies program at the Academy in Athens."

To extend civilization, even with guns, isn't the worst thing in the world. War will exist as long as there's a food chain. No amount of mushy essaying on the *Boston Globe* editorial page and no number of noisy, ill-kempt women sitting in at Greenham Common will change this. Better that we study to conduct war as decently as possible and as little as necessary. The trouble in Lebanon, South Africa, Haiti and the occupied territories of Palestine should, simply, be stopped by the military intervention of civilized nations. This won't stop trouble, of course. Trouble is fun. It will always be more fun to carry a gun around in the hills and sleep with ideology-addled college girls than to spend life behind a water buffalo or rotting in a slum.

Finally, people are all exactly alike. There's no such thing as a race and barely such a thing as an ethnic group. If we were dogs, we'd be the same breed. George Bush and an Australian aborigine have fewer differences than a lhasa apso and a toy fox terrier. A Japanese raised in Riyadh would be an Arab. A Zulu raised in New Rochelle would be an orthodonist. I wish I could say I found this out by spending arctic nights on ice floes with Inuit elders and by sitting with tribal medicine men over fires made of human bones in Madagascar. But, actually, I found it out by sleeping around. People are all the same, though their circumstances differ terribly. Trouble doesn't come from Slopes, Kikes, Niggers, Spics or White Capitalist Pigs; it comes from the heart.

The Innocents Abroad, Updated

On Saturday, June 8, 1867, the steamship *Quaker City* left New York harbor. On board was a group of Americans making the world's first package tour. Also on board was Mark Twain making the world's first fun of package tourism.

In its day *The Innocents Abroad* itinerary was considered exhaustive. It included Paris, Marseilles, the Rock of Gibraltar, Lake Como, some Alps, the Czar, the pyramids and the Holy Land plus the glory that was Greece, the grandeur that was Rome and the pile of volcanic ash that was Pompeii.

When these prototypical tourists went home they could count themselves traveled. They had shivered with thoughts of lions in the Colosseum, "done" the Louvre, ogled Mont Blanc, stumbled through the ruins of the Parthenon by moonlight and pondered that eternal riddle—where'd its nose go?—of the Sphinx. They had seen the world.

But what if Mark Twain had to come back from the dead and escort 1980's tourists on a 1980's tour? Would it be the same? No.

Holidays In Hell
· ·

I'm afraid Mr. Twain would find there are worse things than innocents abroad in the world today.

In 1988 every country with a middle class to export has gotten
into the traveling act. We Yanks, with our hula shirts and funny
Kodaks, are no longer in the fore. The earth's travel destinations
are jam-full of littering Venezuelans, peevish Swiss, smelly Nor-
wegian backpackers yodeling in restaurant booths, Saudi Arabian
businessmen getting their dresses caught in revolving doors and
Bengali remittance men in their twenty-fifth year of graduate school
pestering fat blonde Belgian *au pair* girls.

At least we American tourists understand English when it's
spoken loudly and clearly enough. Australians don't. Once you've
been on a plane full of drunken Australians doing wallaby imita-
tions up and down the aisles, you'll never make fun of Americans
visiting the Wailing Wall in short shorts again.

The Japanese don't wear short shorts (a good thing, considering their legs), but they do wear three-piece suits in the full range
of tenement-hall paint colors, with fit to match. The trouser cuffs
drag like bridal trains; the jacket collars have an ox yoke drape;
and the vests leave six inches of polyester shirt snapping in the
breeze. If the Japanese want to be taken seriously as world financial powers, they'd better quit using the same tailor as variety-show
chimps.

The Japanese also travel in packs at a jog trot and get up at six
A.M. and sing their company song under your hotel window. They
are extraordinary shoplifters. They eschew the usual clothes and
trinkets, but automobile plants, steel mills and electronics factories seem to be missing from everywhere they go. And Japs take
snapshots of everything, not just everything famous but *everything*.
Back in Tokyo there must be a billion color slides of street corners,
turnpike off-ramps, pedestrian crosswalks, phone booths, fire
hydrants, manhole covers and overhead electrical wires. What are
the Japanese doing with these pictures? It's probably a question we
should have asked before Pearl Harbor.

Worse than the Japanese, at least worse looking, are the
Germans, especially at pool-side. The larger the German body, the
smaller the German bathing suit and the louder the German voice
issuing German demands and German orders to everybody who

doesn't speak German. For this, and several other reasons, Germany is known as "the land where Israelis learned their manners."

And Germans in a pool cabana (or even Israelis at a discotheque) are nothing compared with French on a tropical shore. A middle-aged, heterosexual, college-educated male wearing a Mickey Mouse T-shirt and a string-bikini bottom and carrying a purse—what else could it be but a vacationing Frenchman? No tropical shore is too stupid for the French. They turn up on the coasts of Angola, Eritrea, Bangladesh and Sri Lanka. For one day they glory in *l'atmosphère très primitive* then spend two weeks in an ear-splitting snit because the natives won't make a *steak frite* out of the family water buffalo.

Also present in Angola, Eritrea and God-Knows-Where are the new breed of yuppie "experience travelers." You'll be pinned down by mortar fire in the middle of a genocide atrocity in the Sudan, and right through it all come six law partners and their wives, in Banana Republic bush jackets, taking an inflatable raft trip down the White Nile and having an "experience."

Mortar fire is to be preferred, of course, to British sports fans. Has anyone checked the passenger list on *The Spirit of Free Enterprise?* Were there any Liverpool United supporters on board? That channel ferry may have been tipped over for fun. (Fortunately the Brits have to be back at their place of unemployment on Monday so they never get further than Spain.)

Then there are the involuntary tourists. Back in 1867, what with the suppression of the slave trade and all, they probably thought they'd conquered the involuntary tourism problem. Alas, no. Witness the African exchange students—miserable, cold, shivering, grumpy and selling cheap wrist watches from the top of cardboard boxes worldwide. (Moscow's Patrice Lumumba University has a particularly disgruntled bunch.) And the Pakistani family with twelve children who've been camped out in every airport on the globe since 1970—will somebody please do something for these people? Their toddler has got my copy of the *Asian Wall Street Journal*, and I won't be responsible if he tries to stuff it down the barrel of the El Al security guard's Uzi again.

Where will Mr. Clemens take these folks? What is the 1980's equivalent of the Grand Tour? What are the travel "musts" of today?

7

Holidays In Hell
· ·

All the famous old monuments are still there, of course, but they're surrounded by scaffolds and green nets and signs saying, "Il pardonne la restoration bitte please." I don't know two people who've ever seen the same famous old monument. I've seen Big Ben. A friend of mine has seen half of the Sistine Chapel ceiling. No one has seen Notre Dame Cathedral for years. It's probably been sold to a shopping mall developer in Phoenix.

We've all, however, seen Dr. Meuller's Sex Shop in the Frankfurt airport. Dr. Meuller's has cozy booths where, for one deutsche mark a minute, we modern tourists can watch things hardly thought of in 1867. And there's nothing on the outside of the booths to indicate whether you're in there viewing basically healthy Swedish nude volleyball films or videos of naked Dobermans cavorting in food. Dr. Meuller's is also a reliable way to meet your boss, old Sunday School teacher or ex-wife's new husband, one of whom is always walking by when you emerge.

Dr. Meuller's is definitely a "must" of modern travel, as is the Frankfurt airport itself. If Christ came back tomorrow, He'd have to change planes in Frankfurt. Modern air travel means less time spent in transit. That time is now spent in transit lounges.

What else? There are "local points of interest" available until the real monuments are restored. These are small piles of stones about which someone will tell you extravagant lies for five dollars. ("And here, please, the Tomb of the Infant Jesus.") And there are the great mini-bars of Europe—three paper cartons of anise-flavored soda pop, two bottles of beer with suspended vegetable matter, a triangular candy bar made of chocolate-covered edelweiss and a pack of Marlboros manufactured locally under license. (*N.B.*: Open that split of Mumm's ½-star in there, and $200 goes on your hotel bill faster than you can say "service non compris.")

In place of celebrated palaces, our era has celebrated parking spots, most of them in Rome. Romans will back a Fiat into the middle of your linguine al pesto if you're sitting too close to the restaurant window.

Instead of cathedrals, mosques and ancient temples, we have duty-free shops—at their best in Kuwait. I never knew there was so much stuff I didn't want. I assumed I wanted most stuff. But that was before I saw a $110,000 crêpe de chine Givenchy chador and a

8

solid-gold camel saddle with twelve Rolex watches embedded in the seat.

The "sermons in stone" these days are all sung with cement. Cement is the granite, the marble, the porphyry of our time. Someday, no doubt, there will be "Elgin Cements" in the British Museum. Meanwhile, we tour the Warsaw Pact countries—cement everywhere, including, at the official level, quite a bit of cement in their heads.

Every modern tourist has seen *Mannix* dubbed in forty languages and the amazing watch adjustments of Newfoundland, Malaysia and Nepal (where time zones are, yes, half an hour off), and France in August when you can travel through the entire country without encountering a single pesky Frenchman or being bothered with anything that's open for business—though, somehow, the fresh dog crap is still a foot deep on the streets of Paris.

Astonishing toilets for humans are also a staple of up-to-date foreign adventure. Anyone who thinks international culture has become bland and uniform hasn't been to the bathroom, especially not in Yugoslavia where it's a hole in the floor with a scary old lady with a mop standing next to it. And, for astonishing toilet paper, there's India where there isn't any.

No present-day traveler, even an extra-odoriferous Central European one, can say he's done it all if he hasn't been on a smell tour of Asia. Maybe what seems pungent to the locals only becomes alarming when sniffed through a giant Western proboscis, but there are some odors in China that make a visit to Bhopal seem like a picnic downwind from the Arpege factory. Hark to the cry of the tourist in the East: "Is it dead or is it dinner?"

Nothing beats the Orient for grand vistas, however, particularly of go-go girls. True, they can't Boogaloo and have no interest in learning. But Thai exotic dancers are the one people left who prefer American-made to Japanese. And they come and sit on your lap between sets, something the girls at the Crazy Horse never do. Now, where'd my wallet go?

Many contemporary tourist attractions are not located in one special place the way tourist attractions used to be. Now they pop up everywhere—that villainous cab driver with the all-consonant last name, for instance. He's waiting outside hotels from Sun City to the Seward Peninsula. He can't speak five languages and can't understand another ten. Hey! Hey! Hey, you! This isn't the way to the Frankfurt airport! Nein! Non! Nyet! Ixnay!

American embassies, too, are all over the map and always breathtaking. In the middle of London, on beautiful Grosvenor Square, there's one that looks like a bronzed Oldsmobile dashboard. And rising from the slums of Manila is another that resembles the Margarine of the Future Pavilion at the 1959 Brussels World Fair. I assume this is all the work of one architect, and I assume he's on drugs. Each American embassy comes with two permanent features—a giant anti-American demonstration and a giant line for American visas. Most demonstrators spend half their time burning Old Glory and the other half waiting for green cards.

Other ubiquitous spectacles of our time include various panics—AIDS, PLO terror and owning U.S. dollars predominate at the moment—and postcards of the Pope kissing the ground. There's little ground left unkissed by this pontiff, though he might think twice about kissing anything in some of the places he visits. (Stay away from Haiti, San Francisco and Mykonos, J.P., please.)

Then there's the squalor. This hasn't changed since 1867, but tourists once tried to avoid it. Now they seek it out. Modern tourists have to see the squalor so they can tell everyone back home how it changed their perspective on life. Describing squalor, if done with sufficient indignation, makes friends and relatives morally obligated to listen to your boring vacation stories. (Squalor is conveniently available, at reasonable prices, in Latin America.)

No, the Grand Tour is no longer a stately procession of like-minded individuals through half a dozen of the world's major principalities. And it's probably just as well if Mark Twain doesn't come back from the dead. He'd have to lead a huge slew of multinational lunatics through hundreds of horrible countries with disgusting border formalities. And 1980's customs agents are the only thing worse than 1980's tourists. Damn it, give that back! You know perfectly well that it's legal to bring clean socks into Tanzania. Ow! Ouch! Where are you taking me!?

Of course you don't have to go to Africa to get that kind of treatment. You can have your possessions stolen right on the

Piccadilly Line if you want. In fact, in 1987, you can experience most of the indignities and discomforts of travel in your own hometown, wherever you live. Americans flock in seething masses to any dim-wit local attraction—tall ships making a landing, short actors making a move, Andrew Wyeth making a nude Helga fracas—just as if they were actually going somewhere. The briefest commuter flight is filled with businessmen dragging mountainous garment bags and whole computers on board. They are worst pests than mainland Chinese taking Frigidaires home on the plane. And no modern business gal goes to lunch without a steamer trunk-size tote full of shoe changes, Sony Walkman tapes and tennis rackets. When she makes her way down a restaurant aisle, she'll crack the back of your head with this exactly the same way a Mexican will with a crate of chickens on a Yucatán bus ride.

The tourism ethic seems to have spread like one of the new sexual diseases. It now infects every aspect of daily life. People carry backpacks to work and out on dates. People dress like tourists at the office, the theater and church. People are as rude to their fellow countrymen as ever they are to foreigners.

Maybe the right thing to do is stay home in a comfy armchair and read about travel as it should be—in Samuel Clemens's *Huckleberry Finn*.

A Ramble Through Lebanon

OCTOBER 1984

I visited Lebanon in the fall of '84, which turned out to be pretty much the last time an American could travel in that country with only a risk (rather than a certainty) of being kidnapped. I was just taking a vacation. Somehow I had convinced Vanity Fair *magazine to let me do a piece on the holiday pleasures of Beirut and its environs. What follows is, with a few parenthetical addenda, the article I wrote for* Vanity Fair, *an article that they—wisely, I think— decided was much too weird to publish.*

"Bassboat." "Bizport." "Passboot." "Pisspot." It's the one English word every Lebanese understands and no Lebanese can say. The first, deepest and most enduring impression from a visit to Lebanon is an endless series of faces, with gun barrels, poking through the car window and mispronouncing your travel documents.

Some of these faces belong to the Lebanese Army, some to the Christian Phalange, some to angry Shiites or blustering Druse or grumpy Syrian draftees or Scarsdale-looking Israeli reservists. And

12

who knows what the rest of them belong to. Everybody with a gun has a checkpoint in Lebanon. And in Lebanon you'd be crazy not to have a gun. Though, I assure you, all the crazy people have guns, too.

You fumble for passes and credentials thinking, "Is this Progressive Socialist or Syrian Socialist National Party territory? Will the Amal militia kill me if I give them a Lebanese Army press card? And what's Arabic, anyway, for '*Me? American?* Don't make me laugh'?"

The gun barrels all have the bluing worn off the ends as though from being rubbed against people's noses. The interesting thing about staring down a gun barrel is how small the hole is where the bullet comes out, yet what a big difference it would make in your social schedule. Not that people shoot you very often, but the way they flip those weapons around and bang them on the pavement and poke them in the dirt and scratch their ears with the muzzle sights . . . Gun safety merit badges must go begging in the Lebanese Boy Scouts.

On the other hand, Lebanon is notably free of tour groups and Nikon-toting Japanese. The beaches, though shell-pocked and occasionally mined, are not crowded. Ruins of historical interest abound, in fact, block most streets. Hotel rooms are plentiful. No reservation is necessary at even the most popular restaurant (though it is advisable to ask around and find out if the place is likely to be bombed later). And what could be more unvarnished and authentic than a native culture armed to the teeth and bent on murder, pillage and rape?

One minor difficulty with travel to Lebanon is you can't. There's no such thing as a tourist visa. Unless you're a journalist, diplomat or arms salesman, they won't let you in. And if you believe that, you'll never understand the Orient. Type a letter saying you're an American economist studying stabilization of the Lebanese pound or something. (Sound currency is one thing all factions agree on. The Central Bank is the best guarded and least shelled building in Beirut.) I had a letter saying I was studying the tourism industry in Lebanon.

"The *tourism* industry?" said the pretty young woman at the Lebanese Consulate.

"Yes," I said.
"Tourism?"
I nodded.
She shrugged. "Well, be sure to go see my village of Beit Mery. It's very beautiful. If you make it."

Middle East Airlines is the principal carrier to Beirut. They fly from London, Paris, Frankfurt and Rome—sometimes. When the airport's being shelled, you can take a boat from Larnaca, Cyprus.

There are a number of Beirut hotels still operating. The best is the Commodore in West Beirut's El Hamra district. This is the headquarters for the international press corps. There are plenty of rooms available during lulls in the fighting. If combat is intense, telex Beirut 20595 for reservations. The Commodore's basement is an excellent bomb shelter. The staff is cheerful, efficient and will try to get you back if you're kidnapped.

There's a parrot in the bar at the Commodore that does an imitation of an in-coming howitzer shell and also whistles the Marseillaise. Only once in ten years of civil war has this bar been shot up by any of the pro-temperance Shiite militias. Even then the management was forewarned so only some Pepsi bottles and maybe a stray BBC stringer were damaged. Get a room away from the pool. It's harder to hit that side of the building with artillery. Rates are about fifty dollars per night. They'll convert your bar bill to laundry charges if you're on an expense account.

Beirut, at a glance, lacks charm. The garbage has not been picked up since 1975. The ocean is thick with raw sewage, and trash dots the surf. Do not drink the water. Leeches have been known to pop out the tap. Electricity is intermittent.

It is a noisy town. Most shops have portable gasoline generators set out on the sidewalk. The racket from these combines with incessant horn-honking, scattered gunfire, loud Arab music from pushcart cassette vendors, much yelling among the natives and occasional car bombs. Israeli jets also come in from the sea most afternoons, breaking the sound barrier on their way to targets in the Bekáa Valley. A dense brown haze from dump fires and car exhaust covers the city. Air pollution probably approaches a million parts per million. This, however, dulls the sense of smell.

P. J. O'Rourke
· ·

There are taxis always available outside the Commodore. I
asked one of the drivers, Najib, to show me the sights. I wanted to
see the National Museum, the Great Mosque, the Place des Martyrs, the Bois de Pins, the Corniche and Hotel Row. Perhaps Najib
misunderstood or maybe he had his own ideas about sight-seeing.
He took me to the Green Line. The Green Line's four crossings
were occupied by the Lebanese Army—the Moslem Sixth Brigade
on one side, the Christian Fifth Brigade on the other. Though under
unified command, their guns were pointed at each other. This
probably augurs ill for political stability in the region.

The wise traveler will pack shirts or blouses with ample breast
pockets. Reaching inside a jacket for your passport looks too much
like going for the draw and puts armed men out of continence.

At the Port Crossing, on the street where all the best
whorehouses were, the destruction is perfectly theatrical. Just
enough remains of the old buildings to give an impression of
erstwhile grandeur. Mortars, howitzers and rocket-propelled grenades have not left a superfluous brush stroke on the scrim. Turn
the corner into the old marketplace, the Souk, however, and the set
is a Hollywood back lot. Small arms and sniper fire have left
perfectly detailed havoc. Every square inch is painstakingly bullet-
nibbled. Rubble spills artfully out of doorways. Roofs and cornices
have been deftly crenulated by explosion. Everything is ready for
Ernest Borgnine, John Cassavetes and Lee Marvin in a remake of
The Dirty Dozen, except the Lebanese can't figure out how to
remove the land mines.

We went back and forth across the Green Line six times, then
drove into Beirut's south suburbs. This area was once filled with
apartment buildings housing the Moslem middle class. The buildings were destroyed by Israeli air strikes during the invasion of
1982. Modern construction techniques and modern war planes
create a different kind of ruin. Balconies, windows and curtain
walls disintegrate completely. Reinforced concrete floors fold like
Venetian-blind slats and hang by their steel rebars from the buildings' utility cores. Or they land in a giant card-house tumble. Shiite
squatter families are living in the triangles and trapezoids formed
by the fallen slabs. There's a terrible lack of unreality to this part of
the city.

Outside the areas controlled by the Lebanese Army the checkpoints are more numerous, less organized and manned by teenagers in jeans, T-shirts and Adidas running shoes. They carry Russian instead of U.S. weapons. Some belong to the Shiite Amal militia, others to the even more radical Hezbullah. All have strong feelings about America. Fortunately, they can't read. One even held my Arabic press credentials upside down, picture and all, and tipped his head like a parakeet to see if I matched my inverted photo. At the most dangerous-looking checkpoints, Najib said something that made the guards laugh and wave us through.

"Najib," I said, "what are you telling them?"

He said, "I tell them you travel for pleasure."

Finally, we got to a place where we could go no further. Down the street the Sunni Moslem Mourabitoun militia was having it out with the Shiite Amal militia—part of the long-standing Sunni/Shiite dispute about whether Muhammad's uncle Abbas or Muhammad's son-in-law Ali should have succeeded the Prophet and, also, about who gets the take from the south-side gambling joints.

West Beirut can also be toured on foot. You'll find the city is full of surprises—a sacking of the Saudi embassy because of long lines for visas to Mecca, for instance, or shelling of the lower town by an unidentified gunboat or car bombs several times a day. Renaults are the favored vehicles. Avoid double-parked Le Cars. Do not, however, expect the population to be moping around glassy-eyed. There's lots of jewelry and make-up and the silliest Italian designer jeans on earth. The streets are jammed. Everyone's very busy, though not exactly working. They're rushing from one place to another in order to sit around drinking hundreds of tiny cups of Turkish coffee and chat at the top of their lungs. The entire economy is fueled, as far as I could see, by everyone selling cartons of smuggled Marlboros to each other.

It turns out I didn't miss much on Najib's style of guided tour. The Bois de Pins, planted in the 1600s by Emir Fakhr ed Din to protect Beirut from encroaching sand dunes, had all its foliage blown off by Israeli jets and looks like a phone-pole farm. The Place des Martyrs, so-called because eleven nationalists were hanged there by the Turks in 1915, is right on the Green line and now all that much more aptly named. Most of the buildings on the Corniche have literally been face-lifted. The old American Embassy is here, in the same state as U.S. Middle East policy. The British Embassy down the street is completely draped in anti-bomb nets imported from Belfast. Hotel Row was ravaged at the beginning of the civil war in 1975. The high-rise Holiday Inn is a delight to the eye. Who, when traveling around the earth faced with endless Holiday Inns, has not fantasized blowing one to flinders? The National Museum is bricked up and surrounded with tanks— no nagging sense of cultural obligation to tour this historical treasure trove. I couldn't find the Great Mosque at all.

A surprising lot of Beirut stands, however. A building with a missing story here, a lot with a missing building there, shattered this next to untouched that—all the usual ironies of war except with great restaurants.

The Summerland Hotel, on the beach in the ruined south suburbs, has good hamburgers. The wealthy Moslems, including Shiites, go here. All Shiites are not stern zealots. Some have string bikinis. And, like an American ethnic group with origins nearby, they wear their jewelry in the pool. (It was at the Summerland where the Amal militia feted its American captives during the 1985 TWA hostage crisis.)

Downtown on the Corniche you can lunch at the St. Georges Hotel, once Beirut's best. The hotel building is now a burned shell, but the pool club is still open. You can go waterskiing here, even during the worst fighting.

I asked the bartender at the pool club, "Don't the waterskiers worry about sniper fire?"

"Oh, no, no, no," he said, "the snipers are mostly armed with automatic weapons—these are not very accurate."

Down the quay, pristine among the ruins, Chez Temporal serves excellent food. A short but careful walk through a heavily armed Druse neighborhood brings you to Le Grenier, once a jet-set mob scene, now a quiet hideaway with splendid native dishes. Next door there's first-rate Italian fare at Quo Vadis. Be sure to tip the man who insists, at gunpoint, on guarding your car.

Spaghetteria is a favorite with the foreign press. The Italian specials are good, and there's a spectacular view of military patrols and nighttime skirmishing along the beachfront. Sit near the window if you feel lucky.

Addresses are unnecessary. Taxi drivers know the way and

when it's safe to go there. Service at all these establishments is good, more than good. You may find ten or a dozen waiters hovering at your side. If trouble breaks out, the management will have one or two employees escort you home. When ordering, avoid most native wines, particularly the whites. Mousar '75, however, is an excellent red. Do not let the waiters serve you Cypriot brandy after the meal. It's vile.

The Commodore also has restaurants. These are recommended during fighting. The Commodore always manages to get food delivered no matter what the situation outdoors.

Nightlife begins late in Beirut. Cocktail hour at the Commodore is eight P.M., when U.S. editors and network executives are safely at lunch (there's a seven-hour time difference). The Commodore is strictly neutral territory with only one rule. No guns at the bar. All sorts of raffish characters hang about, expatriates from Palestine, Libya and Iran, officers in mufti from both sides of the Lebanese Army, and combatants of other stripes. I overheard one black Vietnam veteran loudly describe to two British girls how he teaches orthodox Moslem women to fight with knives. And there are diplomats, spooks and dealers in gold, arms and other things. At least that's what they seem to be. No one exactly announces his occupation—except the journalists, of course.

I met one young lady from Atlanta who worked on a CNN camera crew. She was twenty-six, cute, slightly plump and looked like she should have been head of the Georgia State pep squad. I sat next to her at the Commodore bar and watched her drink twenty-five gin and tonics in a row. She never got drunk, never slurred a word, but along about G&T number twenty-two out came the stories about dismembered babies and dead bodies flying all over the place and the Red Cross picking up hands and feet and heads from bomb blasts and putting them all in a trash dumpster. "So I asked the Red Cross people," she said, in the same sweet Dixie accent, "like, what's this? Save 'em, collect 'em, trade 'em with your friends?"

Everyone in Beirut can hold his or her liquor. If you get queasy, Muhammad, the Commodore bartender, has a remedy rivaling Jeeves's in P.G. Wodehouse's novels. It will steady your stomach so you can drink more. You'll want to. No one in this part of the world is without a horror story, and, at the Commodore bar, you'll hear most of them.

Dinner, if anyone remembers to have it, is at ten or so. People go out in groups. It's not a good idea to be alone and blonde after dark. Kidnapping is the one great innovation of the Lebanese civil war. And Reuters correspondent, Johnathan Wright, had disappeared thus on his way to the Bekáa Valley a few days before I arrived.

If nabbed, make as much noise as possible. Do not get in anyone's car. If forced in, attack the driver. At least this is what I'm told.

Be circumspect when driving at night. Other cars should be given a wide berth. Flick headlights off and on to indicate friendly approach. Turn on the dome light when arriving at checkpoints. Militiamen will fire a couple of bursts in your direction if they want you to slow down.

Clubs, such as the Backstreet near the Australian Embassy, keep going as late as you can stand it. There's some dancing, much drinking and, if you yell at the management, they'll keep the Arab music off the tape deck. Cocaine is available at about fifty dollars a gram and is no worse than what you get in New York.

Beirut nightlife is not elaborate, but it is amusing. When danger waits the tables and death is the busboy, it adds zest to the simple pleasures of life. There's poignant satisfaction in every puff of a cigarette or sip of a martini. The jokes are funnier, the drinks are stronger, the bonds of affection more powerfully felt than they'll ever be at Club Med.

East Beirut is said to also have good restaurants and nightclubs. But the visitor staying on the West side probably won't see them. No one likes to cross the Green Line at night. And, frankly, the East isn't popular with the West-side crowd. All the window glass is taped, and the storefronts are sandbagged over there. It gives the place a gloomy look. No one would think of doing this in the West. It would be an insult to the tradition of Oriental fatalism, and nobody would be able to see all the cartons of smuggled Marlboros stacked in the window. Anyway, the East-side Christians are too smug, too pseudo-French and haven't been shelled enough to turn them into party reptiles.

* * *

To travel to the rest of Lebanon you just hail a taxi. The country is only one hundred and twenty miles long and forty miles wide, and no Lebanese cab driver has to call home to ask his wife if he can take off for a couple days. Settle the price first. This won't be easy. It's not the way of the Levant to come to the point. I asked Akbar, one of the Commodore's taximen, how much he'd charge to take me through the Israeli lines and into South Lebanon.

"I have been in this business twenty-seven years," he said.

"Yes," I said, "but how much is it going to cost me?"

"I will tell you later."

"Give me a rough idea."

"Would you like a coffee?"

"What's your hourly rate?"

"Across the street—fine rugs at the best price. I will get you a discount."

"What do you charge by the mile?"

"I have a cousin in Detroit."

"Akbar," I shouted, "what's it going to cost?!"

"If you do not like my price, I tell you what," Akbar gestured grandly, "you do not hire me anymore again."

Make sure your driver knows English well enough to translate. Lebanese English is often a triumph of memorization over understanding. "I come from the village of Baabdat," the driver will say in quite an acceptable accent, "it is very beautiful there in the mountains."

"Right," you'll say, "but you'd better pull over, that guy behind the sandbags is leveling an anti-tank gun at us."

"You do?" the driver will say, "Is that in Texas? I have a nephew in Houston."

Wherever you go, it's important to leave early in the morning. Those who think the war is dangerous have not seen the traffic in

Beirut. It's a city of a million people with three stoplights and these aren't working. There are some traffic cops, but they are on no account to be minded as they tend to wave you into the path of dump trucks going sixty miles an hour. All driving is at top speed, much of it on the sidewalks since most parking is done in the middle of the streets. The only firm rule is: Armored personnel carriers have the right of way.

Once outside Beirut there are, of course, other difficulties. The only land route into the Israeli-occupied South goes through the Chouf mountains to a crossing point in the town of Bater, which is separated from Beirut by forty miles of armed Druse. You can also take a boat to Sidon from the Phalange-controlled docks in East Beirut if you're a Christian. I am, but there seemed to be some difficulty anyway. First they said they would have to ask Israeli permission because I was a journalist. Next they told me they didn't speak English. Then they quit speaking French.

On the way to Bater my driver took me past "Green Beach," the former U.S. Marine emplacement and very interesting to students of military history. It's as defensible a position as the bottom of the air shaft in the Plaza Hotel. There's hardly a spot in Lebanon from which you can't fire a gun and hit it. Don't get out of the car. The beach is now an Amal military base under heavy guard because it's next to the orthodox Shiite women's bathing area. They wear ankle-length chadors in the water, which may explain the lack of a world-class Shiite women's swim team.

In the Chouf mountains, the land is green and exquisite, cut through with precipitous gorges. Even the steepest slopes have been terraced and planted with fruit trees, vineyards, olive groves and gun emplacements. The road is narrow with no railings or shoulders, and traffic is slow because the Druse are usually moving artillery around preparing to blast the Phalangists on the coast. Be sure to keep a mental note of such things. It's considered good manners to convey information about military movements to the next faction down the road. This takes the place of celebrity gossip in Lebanese small talk.

The Druse militiamen were good-natured. "Do you speak Arabic?" asked one. I shook my head, and he said something to another soldier who poked face and gun into the car and shouted,

"He just said he wants to fuck your mother!" At least, I assume this was good-natured.

The Druse villages are built in the Ottoman style, graceful, foursquare sandstone buildings with balconies, arched windows and fifteen-foot ceilings. The low-pitched hip roofs are covered in red tile. Tidy gardens surround each house. Peasants in white skull caps and baggy-crotched jodhpurs ride donkeys along the road. Herds of goats meander in the streets. It's all quite timeless except for the video-cassette rental stores, unisex hair salons and Mercedes-Benz sedans all over the place.

The Bater crossing was another matter. A couple hundred Lebanese, mostly old people, women and children, were jammed into line behind barbed wire, waiting for the crossing to open. Several hundred more squatted in the dirt or milled about disconsolate. These, apparently, did not have their papers in order. Some had been there for days. A few tents had been provided but no toilets. There was no running water and no food other than what people had brought with them. Soldiers from the Israeli-hired South Lebanon Army were yelling, pointing guns and threatening everyone. The sun was hot. A few of the women and all of the babies were crying. The smell was horrendous.

There seemed to be no way to tell when the crossing would open. My driver, Akbar, didn't have any ideas. I was not about to get in line behind the barbed wire. It looked too much like Bergen-Belsen. No one in sight, as far as I could tell, was in charge of anything but pistol waving.

On top of an embankment about a hundred yards on the other side of the crossing was a machine gun nest with the star of David flying over it. I took my passport out and, holding it shoulder high, walked through the barbed wire and tank traps. I fixed the South Lebanon Army guards with a stare I hoped would remind them of Grenada. *"American,"* I said. They backed away, and I headed as coolly as I could for the muzzle of the Israeli .50-caliber machine gun now being pointed at my chest.

Israelis are not well-liked in West Beirut. During 1982 the Israelis besieged the Moslem part of town. There was no electricity and little food or water. The shelling and air strikes sometimes went on for twelve hours at a stretch. Beirut's journalists call the Israelis

P. J. O'Rourke

. . . .

"Schlomos" and consider them war criminals and also real squares.

Personally, I was glad to confront the only armed maniacs in the Middle East who aren't allowed to shoot U.S. citizens. I hoped they remembered.

"That's *my* helmet you're wearing," I was thinking. "Those are *my* boots, and *I* paid for that gun so you can just go point it at someone else." Not that I said this aloud. The hole a .50-caliber bullet comes out of is *not* small. It looks as if you could put your whole foot in there.

The Israelis motioned for me to come up, and I climbed the embankment. They held the machine gun on me until it became clear I was not a peroxided Iranian. "You must speak to the captain," they said.

He proved to be a boy of twenty-five. "Do you speak English?" I said.

"Gee, sure," said the captain. The Lebanese kept a respectful distance until they saw him talking to me. Then they descended in a horde waving unlikely-looking slips of paper and shouting the interminable explanations of the east. The captain's escort chased them away with shoves and curses. The women, children and old folks pressed back with no apparent fear. Finally, they pushed the officer and me under a guard tower. "Welcome to Lebanon" is the phrase everyone uses whenever anything untoward or chaotic breaks loose.

"Welcome to Lebanon," said the Israeli captain. He read my credentials and smiled. "*Tourism?*"

"Yes," I said, "I'm the only tourist in Lebanon."

The captain laughed. "Oh no, you're not. I'm a reservist, you know, and this is my vacation, too."

The Israelis wouldn't, however, allow my car through. I told Akbar to meet me there in two days and then hiked across no-man's-land to a line of taxis on the other side.

There were three stages in crossing the Israeli lines. Once through the checkpoint at Bater, I had to go by taxi to an interrogation center a few miles up the road. From the interrogation center I took a bus eight or ten miles to another checkpoint in Jezzine.

At the interrogation stop I was searched and questioned by Shin Bet, the Israeli F.B.I. An enlisted man apologized for the

23

Inconvenience. Less auspicious-looking travelers were being led off to be grilled in windowless huts.

In Jezzine I was questioned again by the South Lebanon Army, an interesting process since we had no language in common.

I hired another taxi to take me the fifteen miles from Jezzine to Sidon. It took five hours to get through the Bater–Jezzine crossing and a total of eight hours to make it from Beirut to Sidon. Before the war it was an hour drive on the coast road.

Sidon and Tyre, the two coastal cities of southern Lebanon, were once the principal towns of ancient Phoenicia and spawned a mercantile empire from Turkey to Spain. Important archaeological work has been done in both places, exposing six millennia of human misbehavior. Lebanon has been overrun in turn by Canaanites, Egyptians, Assyrians, Babylonians, Persians, Greeks, Romans, Arabs, Crusaders, Arabs again, Turks, French, more Arabs, Israelis and occasional U.S. Marines. Perhaps by means of the past one can begin to comprehend the present. Or learn which way to run from the future.

I hired a Palestinian Christian driver named Simon and had him take me twenty-five miles down the lush coast littoral to Tyre. We passed through ten or a dozen Israeli guard posts. These are heaps of sandbags with anxious eyes and many gun barrels sticking over the top. They look down upon a series of "Khomeini gates," cement barriers that jut into the road like meshing-gear teeth and force vehicles to zig-zag slowly between them in single file. If you stall in the middle of these, you die.

The roadsides all over Lebanon are piled with trash, the coast road especially so. Beaches and parks are even worse. There's something about a civil war that brings out the litterbug in people.

Tyre is an awful mess of dirty modern architecture, offal and the detritus of battle. The Elissa Beach Club hotel, on the south shore of the Tyre peninsula, may be one of the few oceanside hotels anyplace where none of the rooms face the sea. But it's clean, the hot water is not actually cold and the food's passable. Also, there's nowhere else to stay.

Simon went home for the night, and I was left on the hotel's roof terrace about a thousand miles from the nearest example of the Four Freedoms. "I have a cousin in Cincinnati" was the only

P. J. O'Rourke
. . . .

English anyone could speak. I watched the sun go down behind the ruins of some previous attempt to bring the rule of law to these climes.

I'd hoped at least for a good night's sleep. There'd been quite a few bombs going off in Beirut. I'd heard five the night before, starting with one at midnight in a bar a few blocks from the Commodore and winding up with a spectacular attempt on the life of the minister of education at six A.M. This took windows out for three blocks around and shook the furniture in my room. The minister survived but my repose did not. But this night, it turned out, was the beginning of the Hajj, the Moslem holiday marking the return of the Mecca pilgrims, and the urchins next door celebrated with a six-hour firecracker fight in the street. Then at two A.M. there was a truly horrendous explosion.

No use looking around the next day to see what's been blasted. Everything has been already.

Later I read in the Beirut newspapers that while I was in the south there were four sniping attacks on Israeli patrols, the South Lebanon Army had stormed a section of Sidon, there was a riot at a Palestinian refugee camp near Jezzine, and the coast road was heavily shelled. I noticed none of this. On the other hand, no explosion in Tyre was reported. This illustrates the difficulty, in Lebanon, of knowing what's happening, even to yourself.

In the morning I visited the principal archaeological digs. These are all decorated with small blue and white signs saying the ruins are national treasures protected by the convention of the Hague of 12 May 1954, and in case of armed conflict notify UNESCO. I suppose I should have phoned.

The oldest and most extensive excavation, near the ancient port, has revealed Phoenician house foundations, a Hellenistic theater, a long, colonnaded walk from Roman times and parts of a Crusader wall. Some pretense is made of keeping these in order. They are guarded by one desultory fellow in a fez. After I'd wandered beyond the palings for an hour, he whistled at me to get out. Nearby a newer dig has uncovered a Roman temple now being used as a garbage dump.

Half a mile or so inland is a much larger site, which I couldn't find mentioned in any guidebooks. Not that there are many

25

Lebanon guidebooks. I couldn't find any in U.S. bookstores. And the Hachette guide I purchased in Beirut was twenty years old. Other than this I was relying on a 1876 Baedeker I found in a New England thrift shop. It was not without useful advice:

> The transaction of business in the East always involves an immense waste of time, and as Orientals attach no value whatsoever to their time, the European will often find his patience sorely tried.

> Many travelers rejoice in displaying a stock of revolvers and other arms, which add greatly to their importance in the eyes of the natives, but are not often brought into actual use.

The larger excavation contains what looks to be an aqueduct, another theater and a vast Roman necropolis. Simon had come back to get me at the hotel, and I had him drive me into the middle of these ruins. Garbage was being dumped here, too, and burned automobile seats, Pepsi cans and lots of spent ordnance was mingled on the ground with ancient pot shards and mosaic tile chips. Simon picked up an amphora handle. "How old you think?" I told him about two thousand years. He nodded, "Two thousand-years-old garbage."

Antiquity hunters have been at work in Tyre. All the Roman tombs are broken open, and many of the fracture marks in the marble are fresh. I peeked inside one grave, and there was a muddle of antique bones. It was, by sheer chance, the only dead body I saw in Lebanon.

I'd been given the name of a Lebanese-American, Billy Hadad, who has a farm on the coast near Sidon. We drove around looking for him. It's hard to know what your driver is doing when he talks to the natives. He'll pull up somewhere and make a preliminary oration, which draws five or six people to the car window. Then each of them speaks in turn. There will be a period of gesturing, some laughter, much arm clasping and handshaking, and a long speech by the eldest or most prominent bystander. Then your driver will deliver an impassioned soliloquy. This will be answered at length by each member of the audience and anybody else who happens by. Another flurry of arm grabbing, shoulder slapping and handshakes follows, then a series of protracted and emotional good-byes.

"What did you ask them?" you'll say to your driver.

"Do they know of your friend?"

"What did they tell you?"

"No."

Eventually, we were directed to an old fortresslike farmhouse near the shore. There on the terrace was a big American preppie kid in chino pants and a button-down shirt. He looked at me and said, "Awesome. Man, I haven't heard English in months!"

The farm near Sidon has been owned by the Hadads since the time of the Ottoman Turks. Its two hundred and thirty acres are irrigated by springs and planted in avocados, bananas and other fruit. The house dates from 600 A.D., with Arab and Turkish additions. It stands on a rock outcrop above a pool in use since Phoenician days. Centuries-old Ficus trees grow over the walls, and flowers bloom all around it.

Billy's father was Druse, his mother from Oregon. They met at college in California. In the middle of the civil war Mr. Hadad was killed in, of all things, a skiing accident on Mt. Lebanon. Mrs. Hadad took the younger children back to America, and Billy, just graduated from a Connecticut boarding school, came out to Lebanon to manage the property. He has five families, some thirty-five people, working for him.

We had lunch with one of his tenants and sat around a low table under a loggia indulging in Arab table manners. These are the best in the world or, anyway, the most fun. For the midday meal there are a dozen large bowls of things—salad; hot peppers; yogurt; a chick-pea paste called hummus; kubbeh, which is a kind of meatball; and things I have no idea the names for. You get a flat loaf of pita bread and make flaps to grab the food. The bread is your napkin, also your plate. We had too much Arak, the regional version of absinthe, and drank endless tiny cups of drug-strength coffee. You can smoke in the middle of the meal, and no one considers it impolite.

The tenant brought out his guns. It's like an Englishwoman showing you her roses. There was a Soviet AK-47, a Spanish Astra 9mm automatic pistol, a Smith and Wesson .38 revolver, an old British military rifle and a very nice Beretta over-and-under shotgun. This is a modest collection. More militant people have mortars and the like. Serious gunmen favor the rocket-propelled grenade, or RPG, which is something like a bazooka. It's inaccurate and tremendously noisy, a perfect Lebanese weapon.

After lunch we went for a swim. This far south of Beirut the ocean is clean. From out in the water distant rumblings could be heard. I thought it was artillery in the Chouf. "Dynamite fishing," said Billy. (Dynamite is one bait fish always rise to.)

There was a wedding party in a nearby village that night. Lebanese wedding parties are held on the eve of the marriage. Thus the groom is given an excuse for looking green at the altar. A hundred or more chairs had been placed in a circle behind the bride's house. A few light bulbs were strung in the grapevines and a huge table had been laid with food, Scotch and Arak. Parties in Lebanon start slow. Everyone sits primly in the chairs, neither eating nor drinking, and talking only in low voices. Or they would usually. In this case the men and boys must all discuss politics with the American. Every one of them has cousins in Texas.

"Just tell them what you think," said Billy. I couldn't very well do that. After a week in Lebanon what I thought would hardly make fit conversation at a wedding feast.

This was a Christian village. "If the Moslems take over," said a young man (Billy translating), "They'll close the bars during Ramadan. But we won't make them drink at Christmas if they really don't want to." A lather of self-justification followed. Justifying the self is the principal form of exercise in Lebanon. The principal form of exercise for a visitor in Lebanon is justifying American foreign policy. The Marine incursion was the question of the hour. Moslems wanted to know why the Marines were sent here. Christians wanted to know why they left. And Druse wanted to know why, during the Marines' brief stay, they felt compelled to shell the crap out of the Chouf.

My answer to everyone was that President Reagan wasn't sure why he sent the Marines to Lebanon. However, he was determined to keep them here until he figured it out, but then he forgot.

Nobody held it against me personally. The Lebanese never hold anything against anyone personally. And it's not considered rude to root for the home team. There were a number of Moslem guests at the party. The villagers had nothing but affection for the Druse Billy Hadad, who towered over most of them. One teenager, summoning all the English at his command, told me, "Billy, il es . . . le homme vert, tu connais, 'Credible Hulk!'" Billy said the only real trouble he's had with his neighbors and tenants was when he tried to convince them that professional wrestling is fake. It's the most popular program on Lebanese TV.

About ten o'clock there was a change in the festivities. Acting on some signal I couldn't perceive everyone suddenly began to drink and shout. A little later the bridegroom was carried in on the shoulders of his friends accompanied by drums, flutes and the eerie ululation Arab women use to mark every emotional occasion. Awful tapes were put on a large Rasta box. There was bad Arab music, worse French rock and roll, and Israeli disco music, which is the most abominable-sounding thing I've ever heard in my life. A sister of the bride got in the middle of the circled chairs and did quite a shocking traditional dance.

There was something of the freshman mixer to the party. The young men and women held to opposite sides of the crowd, eyeing each other furtively and being shoved out to dance only after prolonged giggling and conspiracy among their fellows.

"I haven't been laid since I was in Beirut last June," said Billy. "Out in the country it's marriage or death."

Good-fellowship in the Middle East can be a bit unnerving. You'd best get used to being gripped, hugged and even nuzzled. I was taken aback the first time I saw two fully armed militiamen walking down the street holding hands. Large amounts of Arak aid in acclimitization. The sense of affection and solidarity is comforting, actually, when you realize how many of the men throwing their arms around you have pistols in the waistbands of their pants. A Mercedesful of gunmen kept watch on the road.

Eventually I was thrust onto the dance floor and matched with a hefty girl who had me do Arab dances. This was, justly, thought hilarious. But my discotheque dancing made an impression. I gather the locals are not familiar with the Watusi, the Jerk and the Mashed Potatoes.

The whole celebration was being videotaped, and every now and then one of the revelers would use the Sony's quartz-halogen light to dry the skin on a snareless Arab drum.

Sometime in the early morning Billy and I returned to his farm. There was protracted questioning from his housekeeper on the floor above. She wanted to make sure we were us before she threw down the door keys. We locked ourselves in with five dead-bolts.

I never did get to see the historical points of interest in Sidon.

The overland crossing going north was a horror. The Israelis run Betar and the midpoint interrogation center, and conditions there are ugly but organized. However, the clumsy and violent South Lebanon Army has control of the Jezzine checkpoint.

There were about a thousand angry and panicked people in the small town square when I arrived. Most of them were poor Shiites, and all of them seemed to have screaming children and every earthly possession with them. One group of two or three hundred were fighting with fists to get on a bus. Soldiers ran through the crowd screaming and firing Uzis in the air. It was only ten in the morning but already 90 degrees. I looked for Israeli officers. There were none. I sent Simon into the crowd. He returned in a few minutes.

"No ways but bus across," he said.

"How do I get on it?"

"You can not."

I paid him off and sent him home. I was sick with the dysentery every foreigner in Lebanon suffers. My head ached from the wedding party Arak. There was, it appeared, a man with a gun selling bus tickets. But every time he tried to sell one a crowd of three hundred would rush him like a rugby scrum. The man fired his pistol directly over the people's heads. Bullets smacked into nearby masonry. The crowd quailed and ran backward, trampling each other. Then they gathered themselves and rushed the ticket seller again. He grew purple with shouting, reloaded, fired again.

The crowd moved away and back like surf. Then with one great surge they chased him on top of a truck.

Most of these people had been camping at Jezzine, if that's the word for sleeping in the streets for days with your children and no food. They were desperate and fully insane. The crowd began running against itself, into walls, up the sides of buildings.

I was at a loss. I might be at Jezzine still if my arm hadn't been grabbed by someone who said, "I ken you're new here." It was a magnificent Scotswoman, tall, thin and ramrod straight. With her was a gentle-looking Lebanese girl. The woman was Leslie Phillips, head of the nursing school at a medical center near Sidon. She was on her way to get textbooks in Beirut. The girl was named Amal, the same as the militia. It means "hope." She was headed to America for college.

Miss Phillips placed us in a protected corner and said, "I'm going to speak to the man with the gun. I always go straight for the man with the gun. It's the only way you get anywhere in this country." She vanished into the melee. The crowd went into a frenzy again and made right for Amal and me. I suppose I would have been filled with pity if I'd been in a second-story window. As it was I was filled with desire to kick people and I gave in to it.

Miss Phillips was gone for two hours. She emerged from the donnybrook perfectly composed and holding three bus tickets. I asked her what all the shooting was about. "Oh," she said, "that's just Lebanese for 'please queue up.'" An ancient horrible Mexican-looking bus pulled into the crowd smacking people and punting them aside. Amal was carrying a co-ed's full complement of baggage in two immense suitcases. I handed my kit bag to Miss Phillips, grabbed these and made for the bus. Or tried to. Three steps put me at the bottom of a clawing, screeching pile-up, a pyramid of human frenzy. I heard Miss Phillips's voice behind me. "Don't be shy," she said, "it's not rude to give a wee shove to the Lebanese." I took a breath, tightened my grip on the suitcases and began lashing with Samsonite bludgeons at the crowd of women, old men and children. If you ask me, it *was* pretty rude, but it was that or winter in South Lebanon. I fought my way to the side of the bus. There was a man on top loading luggage and kicking would-be roof rack stowaways in the head, knocking them back on top of the crowd. I hoisted one of Amal's fifty-pound suitcases onto my head, waved a fistful of Lebanese money at the loader, kept hold of Amal with my other hand and fended off the mob with both feet. This doesn't sound physiologically possible, but it was an extreme situation.

I got both suitcases on top at last. Then we had to scrimmage our way to the bus door in a flying wedge, Miss Phillips leading the way. Just as we were getting aboard, a worse brawl yet broke loose in the throng. One of the South Lebanon Army guards leapt into the middle of it and began beating people in the face with the butt of his pistol. The crowd exploded. Miss Phillips was heaved inside. I was squashed against the bus door and lost hold of Amal, who was sucked into the maw of the Lebanese. Miss Phillips reached out the bus window and tapped the pistol-whipping soldier on the arm. "Pardon me, lad," she said, "but those two are with me."

The soldier left off his beating for a moment, pushed me into the bus and fished Amal out of the crowd. I pulled her inside, and the soldier went back to hitting people. Everyone in the crowd was yelling. I asked Amal what they said. "They're all claiming to be someone's cousin," she sighed.

About two hundred people were packed inside the bus, which was built to carry fifty. More kept wiggling in through the windows. It was well over 100 degrees in there. Every now and then a soldier would get in and climb across the top of people to beat one of the illegal passengers. There was more shooting outside. I found myself in a full body press with a Shiite girl. She was rather nicely built but over the top from claustrophobia and shrieking like a ruptured cow. "What's Arabic for 'calm down'?" I yelled.

"As far as I can tell," said Miss Phillips, "there's no such word."

We did eventually get under way, the bus backing over people then swaying horribly in blinding dust on the half-lane-wide mountain road. We were only stopped, unloaded, searched, interrogated and held at gunpoint several times.

Fortunately, the Lebanese are a clean people, even the very poor ones. It wasn't like being packed into a bus on a sweltering day with a bunch of French or anything.

Akbar was waiting at Bater. I found out later he'd also come up from the city the day before and waited all afternoon in case I got thrown out or evacuated or tried to get back to Beirut on foot.

Travel to the North is less arduous. George Moll, the video editor at ABC-TV's Beirut bureau, and I went on a trip to the Bsherri Cedars. Traffic on the coast road north of the city is stalled by checkpoints. Amazing what a few guys standing around with guns can do to create gridlock. "I ♡ Lebanon" bumper stickers are popular with the motorists. "Kill them all—Let God sort them out" T-shirts are popular with the militias.

It's important to remember, when dealing with these militias, that the gunmen are mostly just kids and they're getting a big kick out of the whole thing. I suppose this is only natural when young people lack proper recreational facilities and well-supervised activities to keep them out of mischief. They need sympathy and understanding. Or a sixteen-inch shell from the battleship New Jersey.

I wanted to visit the gorge of the Nahr el Kelb, the River of the Dog, a strategic point on the Lebanese coast just north of Beirut where for more than three thousand years invading armies have carved stelae commemorating their passage. A tunnel for the coast highway now cuts through the gorge wall, and the carvings are reached via a ramp above the traffic. The cuneiform characters of Nebuchadnezzar II, the stela of the Pharaoh Ramses, the Assyrian bas reliefs, a Latin inscription from the Emperor Marcus Aurelius, Greek carvings from the Selcucid empire—they've all been completely effaced by air pollution.

Don't go to the famous Jeita Grottoes at the source of the Dog River, either. These have been turned into a military training base. Although what kind of military training goes on among a bunch of stalactites lit by colored spotlamps, I can't tell you.

A few miles north of Nahr el Kleb is the Casino de Liban on Juniye Bay. This was pre-war Lebanon's attempt at Monte Carlo and used to have elaborate floor shows featuring plump blondes who were out of work in Europe. You can still gamble there, though just being in this part of the world is a gamble enough for most people. The blondes are gone.

On up the coast road, twenty-four miles from Beirut, is
Byblos. Since the Christians were run out of the Beirut airport, the
Phalange has taken to landing planes on the highway here. Expect
another traffic jam. Byblos was considered by the ancients to be the
oldest city in the world. In fact, it has been an established metrop-
olis for at least six thousand years. Main Street, however, looks
most like the oldest part of Fort Lauderdale.

By the seaport, however, is an Arab fortification atop a Fran-
kish castle constructed with chunks of Roman temples which had
been built over a Phoenician town that was established on the
foundations of a Neolithic village—quite a pile of historic van-
dalism.

The war has not touched Byblos except to keep anyone from
coming here. We found one consumptive tour guide playing soli-
taire in a shack by the entrance to the ruins. He took us through the
deserted remains spieling, with pauses only to cough, a litany of
emperors, catastrophes and dimensions.

The Lebanese are chock-full of knowledge about their past.
Those who *do* learn history apparently get to repeat it of their own
free will. The whole business filled me with inchoate emotions and
a desire for lunch.

The Byblos Fishing Club at the base of the Crusader seawall
has wonderful food and no other customers. They don't speak
English anymore so I went back to the kitchen and picked out what
I wanted. Seafood got with dynamite fishing is very tender, it
seems. On the wall of the Fishing Club are dusty photos of better
days—Ray Milland, Ann-Margret, David Niven, Jean-Paul Bel-
mondo. "Now *this*," said George, "is archaeology."

There's a very good hotel in Byblos, the Byblos-Sur-Mer,
whose owner hadn't seen anyone in so long he bought us drinks
when we stopped to use the pay phone.

You can proceed to Tripoli on the coast road, but shouldn't.
The Arab Democratic Party, which supports Islamic unification, is
having a big fight there with the Islamic Unification Party, which is
in favor of Arab democracy. And the Syrians are shooting at both of
them.

We turned east toward the mountains at the Syrian lines near
Batrun. There's a medieval Arab castle here that's worth seeing. It
sits in the middle of a cement plant.

34

Once into Syrian-controlled territory the checkpoint scrutiny becomes severe. Ahmed, our driver, began making long explanations to the glowering soldiers. He wouldn't quite confess what he was saying, but I have an idea it went something like: "I have the brother of an important American strongman here and the president of England's cousin. They are traveling in secret as journalists so they may see the justice and resolve of the great Syrian army in its struggle against Zionist oppressors everywhere. Soon they will return to their homeland and tell rich men there to drop a bomb on Tel Aviv."

The Syrian army has dozens of silly hats, mostly berets in yellow, orange and shocking pink, but also tiny pillbox chapeaux, peaked officer's caps with half a foot of gold braid up the front and lumpy Russian helmets three sizes too large. The paratroopers wear shiny gold jumpsuits, and crack commando units have skin-tight fatigues in a camouflage pattern of violet, peach, flesh tone and vermilion on a background of vivid purple. This must give excellent protective coloration in, say, a room full of Palm Beach divorcees in Lily Pulitzer dresses.

The rest of the scenery is also spectacular—Californian, but as though the Sierras had been moved down to Santa Barbara. The mountains of Lebanon rise ten thousand feet only twenty miles from the sea. You can ski in the morning and swim in the afternoon. Actually, of course, it's raining on the beach that time of year, and the skiing is mediocre at best. But it's the kind of thing that made for great Lebanese travel-brochure writing in the old days.

We drove to Bsherri on the lip of the dramatic Qadisha Valley, 650 feet deep and only a half-mile wide. This is the heartland of the Maronites, seventh century A.D. Christian schismatics who sought refuge among these dangerous hairpin turns lacking guard rails and speed limits.

Bsherri was the home of Kahlil Gibran and also where Danny Thomas's family comes from. Thus, the two great cultural figures of modern Lebanon, though in many ways opposites (Danny Thomas does not write poetry. Kahlil Gibran never did "spit-takes."), are linked. Or so I was told. I wouldn't spoil that piece of information with research.

We visited Gibran's house above the town. It's probably the world's only example of the California bungalow style carved out of living rock. Interesting but damp. The place is decorated with a hundred or so of Gibran's artworks. He was a dreadful painter—the gentle insouciance of Rodin and the technical abilities of Blake, all done in muddy earth tones. Gibran's coffin is bricked into the wall of his bedroom if that says anything about the man.

While we were asking directions in Bsherri, a young man named Antoine attached himself to us. He got us into the Gibran house, which was supposedly closed for repairs, then took us home for a Lebanese sit-around with his mother, aunts, sisters, cousins, etc. Hospitality is a must in the Middle East whether anyone wants to have it or not. Pomegranate juice is served, lots of cigarettes are smoked and tiny cups of coffee are drunk while everyone smiles and stares because you can't speak Arabic and they can't speak English, and Lebanese are the only people in the world who pronounce French worse than Americans.

Antoine's house was extraordinary. Like Gibran's it was carved into the side of a hill. The main room was windowless, floored with layers of Persian carpets and hung wall and ceiling with ornate cloths. There were stuffed falcons, brass things, photographs and religious statuettes all over the place and a dozen Mafia-Mediterranean-style dining room chairs. Antoine let us know he thought Kahlil Gibran's house was underdecorated. Antoine's mother told us that she'd lost five sons in the war so far, though that may have been the usual polite exaggeration of the Levantine.

Ahmed, though Moslem, was a great hit with Antoine's family. He brought them up-to-date on Beirut politics and then told Syrian checkpoint stories. Syrian checkpoint stories are the Polish jokes of Lebanon.

A Syrian soldier stops a Volkswagen Beetle and demands that the driver open the trunk. The driver begins to open the luggage compartment at the front of the car. "No!" says the Syrian, "I said the *trunk*."

"This *is* the trunk," says the driver.

"I am not a donkey," says the Syrian, pointing to the back of the car. "Open the trunk!" So the driver does as he's told, exposing the VW's engine. "Aha!" says the Syrian, "You have stolen a motor. Furthermore, you have just done it because it's still running."

Another of Ahmed's stories—and he swears this one is true—
is about a checkpoint on a hill where the Syrian soldier wanted to
inspect a car trunk. "I can't get out," said the driver, "I have no
emergency brake, and I must keep my foot on the brake pedal or
the car will roll away."

"Don't worry," said the Syrian, "I will sit in the car and hold
the brake pedal." So they changed places. "Now open the trunk,"
said the Syrian. The driver opened it. "All right," yelled the Syrian
from inside the car, "is there any contraband in there?"

What the Syrians are looking for in your trunk, by the way, is
Playboy magazines. Be sure to carry some.

We sat and smoked more cigarettes. Lebanon is not the place
to go if you're trying to give that up. Everyone over the age of six
chain-smokes. Long-term health effects are not, these days, a
major concern, and it's the worst sort of rudeness not to offer
cigarettes at every turn. George fell in love with Carmen, Antoine's
sister, a beauty of about fifteen. George could talk of nothing else
for the rest of the trip but getting married and becoming Maronite.
Maybe the feeling was mutual. Antoine took me aside later and
asked me if George was a Christian. I assured him most blond,
blue-eyed Americans over six feet tall are not Druse. He then
nicked me, instead of George, for the two hundred Lebanese
pounds it allegedly cost to get in the Gibran house.

We went on up into the mountains to the Cedars, one of only
three small groves of these trees left. Once the country was forested
with them, a hundred feet high at full growth and forty feet in
circumference. It was from these the tall masts of the Phoenician
galleys were made and the roof beams of Solomon's temple and so
forth. The trees in the Bsherri grove look like they need flea
collars, and the grounds are a mess.

We found a good hotel, the La Mairie, about ten miles west of
Bsherri in Ehdene. Ehdene is notable for the country's best-
looking martyr pictures. There are martyr pictures everywhere in
Lebanon. The Phalangists put up photographs of the ox-faced
Bashir Gemayel, who got elected president in '82 and blown to bits
within the month. The Shiites plaster walls with the face of some
dumpy Ayatollah who went MIA in Libya. The Druse have Kamal
Jumblatt, who looked dead even before the hitmen ventilated his

limo. Ehdene, however, is the headquarters of the Giants militia, led by the very photogenic Franjieh family. In 1978 the Phalangists attacked the Franjieh home and killed a handsome son, his pretty wife, and their little daughter too. If you have to look at pictures of dead people all day, they might as well be cute.

From Ehden, with light traffic and no mood swings at the checkpoints, it's only two hours back to Beirut.

The remaining great thing to see in Lebanon is Baalbek, site of three immense Roman temples, among the largest in the ancient world. Baalbek, however, is in the Bekáa Valley, where Israeli and Syrian forces are faced off and where Israel has been making periodic airstrikes on Syrian missile emplacements. Take sturdy and practical clothing.

Baalbek itself is controlled by an extremely radical pro-Khomeini Shiite group called Islamic Amal. The leader of Islamic Amal is Hussein Mussawi. He has close ties to Iran, and many people believe he personally ordered the suicide attacks on the American Embassy and the U.S. Marine base at Green Beach.

The Islamic Amal people are so far out there that they think *Syria* is a puppet of international Zionism. When I first arrived in Beirut, the Syrian army had Baalbek surrounded with tanks and was shelling downtown.

I went to Baalbek with ABC's chief Beirut correspondent, Charles Glass, and two drivers, one Syrian and one Lebanese Shiite. (Glass was later kidnapped by radical Shiites, possibly this same Islamic Amal; after two months in captivity, he made a harrowing escape.) The ride over the crest of the Lebanese range is breathtaking. The arid reaches of the Anti-Lebanese mountains rise in the distance. Below is the flat, green trough of the Bekáa, where Syrian and Israeli lines are lost in verdant splendor. The thin neck of the fertile crescent is spread out before you, cradle of the civilization that has made air strikes possible. It's overwhelming.

At the foot of the descent is the large Christian town of Zahle, a Phalange outpost surrounded by Moslems. The Syrians shell this sometimes, too. Zahle has a good hotel, the Kadri, and an arcade of outdoor restaurants built along a stream in the Wadi Arayesh, or "Valley of Vines."

The road north to Baalbek runs up the middle of the Bekáa. Marijuana fields stretch for miles on either side. This is the source of Lebanon's renowned hashish. Don't try to export any yourself, however. The airport customs officials won't search you when you arrive, but they're very thorough when you leave. Taking hashish out of the country without payoffs is one of the few crimes they still prosecute in Lebanon.

Bedouins from the Syrian desert camp beside the hemp fields. They're not very romantic up close. Their tents are made from old grain sacks, and everything around them stinks of goat.

The ruins of the Roman temples at the Baalbek are, words fail me, big. The amount of mashed thumbs and noses full of stone dust that went into chiseling these is too awesome to contemplate. The largest, the Temple of Jupiter, is 310 feet long, 175 feet wide, and was originally enclosed by fifty-four Corinthian pillars, each sixty-six feet high and seven and a half feet thick. Only six are left standing now. The temple complex was three centuries in building and never finished. The Christian Emperor Theodosius ordered the work stopped in hope of suppressing paganism and bringing a halt to a very lively-sounding cult of temple prostitution.

Once again we found a lonely tour gide who took us around, spouting names and numbers and pointing out things that are extra odd or large.

The ruins are policed by the Syrians, who are doing a better job than the Israelis at Tyre. The captain in charge came up and introduced himself. His English consisted of "Hello." "Hello," he said and shook hands. "Hello," he said and waved goodbye.

Outside the ruins, Baalbek is a tense and spooky place. All the Christians, Sunnis and Druse have fled. Giant posters of Khomeini are hanging everywhere. There are few women on the streets, and they are carefully scarved and dressed down to the feet. The men gave us hard looks and fingered their weapons. The streets were dirty and grim. Syrian soldiers stayed bunched together. The tanks are still dug in around the city. You cannot get a drink or listen to Western music or dance or gamble, and you'd better not whistle the "Star Spangled Banner."

The tour guide led us directly from the temples to a souvenir store. There was something about risking my life to visit a pest hole full of armed lunatics and then going shopping that appealed to me. The store looked like it hadn't been visited since the Crusades, except all the ancient artifacts were new, made this month and buried in the yard for a week.

The nonsense you hear about bargaining in the Orient is, like most nonsense about the Orient, perfectly true. I had not been in the shop three seconds before the owner was quoting prices that would do justice to a Pentagon parts supplier and flopping greasy, ill-made rugs in every direction—like somebody house-training a puppy with the Sunday *New York Times*. There's a charming banter that goes with all this. I mean, I suppose there is. Some of the verbal flourishes of the Levant are lost in a minimal English vocabulary. "Good, huh? Real good, huh? Good rug! Very good!"

"He has a cousin in St. Louis," added the tour guide, helpfully.

It seemed I had to hold up both ends in this legendary duel of wit in the Bazaar. "Tell him," I said to the guide, "his goods are of the greatest magnificence and pleasure flows into my eyes at their splendor. Yes, and I am astonished at the justice of his prices. And yet I must abase myself into the dust at the humbleness of my means. I, a poor traveler, come many miles over great distances . . ." And so forth. Out came bogus Egyptian dog-head statues, phony Roman coins, counterfeit Phoenician do-dads, and more and worse and bigger rugs. After an hour and a half I felt I had to pay for my fun. I settled on a small bronze "Babylonian" cow with some decidedly un-Babylonian rasp marks on the casting. I bargained the shopkeeper down from $200 to $30. Good work if the cow hadn't been worth $0.

Charles Glass has spent years in the Middle East and was completely bored by this, however. He said we should go meet Hussein Mussawi.

Our Shiite driver was sent to negotiate. After the customary amount of temporizing and dawdle, Hussein consented to see us. We were taken to a shabby and partly destroyed section of town, where we were surrounded by nervous young gunmen. Though whether they were nervous about us or nervous that they might get a sudden invite to make like a human Fourth of July, I don't know. We were marched into a tiny and dirty office and told to sit down.

We waited. Then we were marched to a larger office furnished Arab-style with couches around the sides of the room. Khomeini pictures abounded. We were served tea, and Charles and I, though not our Moslem drivers, were very thoroughly searched. Charles's tape recorder was taken apart with special care. Our guards were pleasant, but small talk did not seem the order of the day. We waited some more. Finally, another group of armed young men came and took us through a warren of narrow filthy alleys to a modest and well-protected house. We were put into a small study lined with Arabic books and decorated with more pictures of Khomeini. There were two young men who spoke English waiting for us. They asked in an affable way what was going on with U.S. foreign policy. "After all," said one, "this part of the world has a Moslem majority. Is your government crazy or what?"

Half an hour later Hussein came in and shook hands with everyone. He's a thin man of middle size, about forty-five. He was dressed in a sort of semi-military leisure suit and was very calm and dignified in his bearing but had, I swear it, a twinkle in his eye.

Hussein ordered a gunman to bring us coffee and cigarettes. The young man who spoke English less well acted as translator. "Were you responsible for the bombing of the Marine base?" asked Charles. I nearly lit my nose instead of the Marlboro. Hussein answered with equanimity, pointing out that any number of people, including the American Democratic Party, stood to benefit from the attack on the Marines.

"How long will this peace last in Lebanon?" asked Charles.

"This is not peace."

"When will there be peace?"

"When there is Islamic justice everywhere," came the answer.

"Everywhere?" asked Charles. "Will there be a place for Christians and Jews under Islamic justice?"

"Islam allows a place for everyone," said Hussein. The translator paused and added on his own, "Except, you know, Zionists and imperialists and other types."

41

"The Zionists will have to be driven out?"

"Yes."

"That may take a long time," said Charles.

Hussein fixed him with a smile. "Long for you. Short for us."

Hussein expounded upon the destiny of Islam and a believing man's place therein. The translator got himself tangled up with "Allah's great wishes . . . I mean, large would-be's . . . That is . . ."
"The will of God," I suggested.
Hussein turned to me and spoke in English. "Do you understand Arabic?"
"No," I said, "I just recognized the concept."
He said something to the translator, who said to me, "He wants to know if you believe in God."
I didn't think I should quibble. "Of course," I said. Hussein nodded. There was intensity in his look and no little human concern. He continued on subjects theological.
"To get back down to earth for a moment . . ." said Charles.
Hussein laughed. "Oh," said the translator, "all this is *very much* down to earth."
Charles continued to ask questions. I continued to ponder Hussein. He was practically the first Lebanese I'd met who didn't tell me he had a cousin in Oklahoma City. Although, as it turns out, his brother is a petroleum engineer who used to work in Dallas.
Charles asked Hussein about Johnathan Wright, the missing Reuters correspondent. "I hadn't heard about this," was the reply. "Also he wasn't headed this way."
Hussein told Charles he should study the Koran.
At length we took our leave. As we were being escorted back to our car I noticed a woman on a nearby roof wearing a chador and hanging out lacy black lingerie on the clothes line.
Less than a week after our visit, the U.S. embassy annex in East Beirut got blown up. I hope it wasn't anything we said.
The hotel at Baalbek is the Palmyra, built in the 1870s. It's a massive Ottoman structure furnished with antique carpets and

heavy mahogany Victorian furniture. The leather-bound guest register bears the signatures of Louis Napoleon, the Duc D'Orleans, the Empress of Abyssinia and Kaiser Wilhelm II. There's an air of twilight and deliquescence to the place. Only the owner and a couple old servants are left. No room had been occupied for months, and only an occasional Syrian military officer comes to dinner.

Charles and I sat alone that night in the vast dining room. Pilgrims were still returning from Mecca, and celebratory gunshots sounded outside. "Happy fire" it's called. The electricity guttered in the bulbs and cast the long tables and tall ceiling into gloom. The forces of darkness and barbarism seemed to gather around. It was as though we were the last two white men in Asia. We sat up past midnight drinking the bottle of Arak a grizzled waiter had smuggled to us, talking politics and literature and citing apt quotations:

> *Turning and turning in the widening gyre*
> *The falcon cannot hear the falconer;*
> *Things fall apart; the center cannot hold;*
> *Mere anarchy is loosed upon the world,*
> *The blood-dimmed tide is loosed, and . . .*

. . . and you just can't find travel like this anymore.

Seoul Brothers

. . . .

When the kid in the front row at the rally bit off the tip of his little finger and wrote, KIM DAE JUNG, in blood on his fancy white ski jacket—I think that was the first time I ever really felt like a foreign correspondent. I mean, here was something really fucking *foreign*.

It wasn't even an act of desperate protest. Opposition candidate Kim Dae Jung hadn't lost the Korean presidential election yet. KDJ was just giving a small pep talk to a group of well-wishers— half a million of them. They spread in every direction out over the horizon, packed flank to flank and butt to loin, all standing at attention in a freezing Seoul drizzle with serious, purposeful expressions on their mugs.

When a Korean political candidate does a little stumping, a little flesh pressing, a little baby kissing, he puts on a sour face, mounts a platform and stares at the crowd. He's surrounded by Samoan-size bodyguards, his *chap-sae*, or goons, (literally "trapped birds"). A couple of the goons hold an inch-thick Plexi-

44

glas shield in front of the candidate's face. The shield has handles bolted on both ends like a see-through tea tray. The crowd shouts the candidate's name for half an hour, then the candidate yells at the crowd. Korean sounds like ack-ack fire, every syllable has a primary accent: *YO-YO CAMP STOVE HAM HOCK DIP STICK DUCK SOUP HAT RACK PING-PONG LIP SYNC!!!!* If the candidate pauses, the crowd responds in unison with a rhymed slogan or with a precise fifteen seconds of waving little paper Korean flags. There's no frenzy in this, no mob hysteria, and it's not a drill or an exercise.

I'd never seen spontaneous regimentation before. And I don't hope to see it again. I was standing on the platform, a couple of goons away from "The DJ," as the foreign reporters call Kim Dae Jung. And I was looking at this multitude, and I was thinking, "Oh, no, they really *do* all look alike,"—the same Blackglama hair, the same high-boned pie-plate face, the same tea-stain complexion, the same sharp-focused look in 1 million identical anthracite eyes. They are a strange northern people who came to this mountain peninsula an ice age ago and have kept their bloodlines intact through a thousand invasions. Their language is unrelated to Chinese or Japanese, closer, in fact, to Finnish and Hungarian. They don't like anyone who isn't Korean, and they don't like each other all that much, either. They're hardheaded, hard-drinking, tough little bastards, "the Irish of Asia."

There was a very un-Irish order to that crowd, however, an order beyond my comprehension—like nuclear fission. There is order to everything in Korea. They call it *kibun*, which means, to the extent it can be translated, "harmonious understanding." Everything in Korea is orderly, except when it isn't—like nuclear fission.

The speech ended, and every single person in that audience pushed forward to be with Kim Dae Jung. I looked down from the platform and saw the kid in the front row wiggle out of his white parka. He was a normal-looking kid (but in Korea everybody is normal looking). He had a sign reading, in garbled English, MR. KIM DJ ONLY BECOME THE 1ST PRESIDENT OF THE WORLD, on one side and the same, I guess, in Korean on the other. Then, with a can-do smile, he nipped the digit and began his calligraphy.

Holidays In Hell
. . . .

The DJ, in a goon envelope, descended to meet his chanting admirers. I tried, without goons, to follow him. I was cross-body-blocked and stiff-armed and went down in a second. I was a one-man zone defense against a football team of 500,000. Squat, rock-hard Korean bodies surrounded me in three dimensions. I was squeezed and heaved and, most of all, overwhelmed by the amazing stink of *kimchi*, the garlic and hot-pepper sauerkraut that's breakfast, lunch and dinner in Korea. Its odor rises from this nation of 40 million in a miasma of eyeglass-fogging *kimchi* breath, throat-searing *kimchi* burps and terrible, pants-splitting *kimchi* farts.

I came to the surface of the crowd and went under again like a toddler in big surf. I was squashed and tumbled. My foot came out of my shoe. My pocket was picked. Finally, I was expelled from the mass with one collective shove and kick.

This is what Koreans are like when they're happy.

And the Koreans were very happy with their first presidential election in sixteen years. They voted like the dickens—an 89.2 percent turnout. But I couldn't get any of them to tell me why. What was this election supposed to be about?

Practically everybody running for president was named Kim. There was Kim Dae Jung, the opposition front-runner, Kim Young Sam, ("Kim: The Sequel"), also the opposition front-runner, and Kim Jong Pil ("Kim: The Early Years"), the opposition straggler. Plus there was the non-Kim candidate, Roh Tae Woo (pronounced "No Tay Ooh" and called "Just Say No" by the foreign press corps). Roh was handpicked by the military dictatorship that's been running South Korea since 1971.

Everybody knew Roh was going to win because Kim the DJ and Kim the Sequel had promised to unite antigovernment opposition behind one candidate, but then they forgot and spent most of the campaign bickering with each other. And Roh was going to win anyway because he had the constituency that votes with M-16s. (When *these* boys make their voices heard in the marketplace of ideas, you'd better listen up.) So the election wasn't about winning.

And the election wasn't about political-party allegiance, either. The distinctively named parties—Peace and Democracy,

46

P. J. O'Rourke
. . . .

Democratic Justice, Reunification Democratic, and New Democratic Republican—all fielded candidates. If I were a hard-working
journalist with a keen eye for detail, I'd sift through my notes now
and tell you what Kim belonged to which. But that would be a waste
of everybody's time. A Korean political party exists solely to boost
the fortunes of its founding candidate and has the average life span
of a trout-stream mayfly hatch.

Campaign promises? Kims 1-2-3 promised to promote freedom of expression, work for reunification of North and South, fight
corruption, improve the country's god-awful human-rights record,
raise living standards, and lower taxes. But then that fascist pig
Roh Tae Woo went out and promised to do the same and lots more of
it. Nobody, Kim or un-Kim, said too much about Korea's near
absence of social-security programs, the $140-a-month minimum
wage, the seventy-two hour work week or the fact that it's illegal to
have an independent labor union. Kim Dae Jung is supposed to be
the big liberal in the bunch. When interviewed by a Canadian
business magazine, the DJ, that feisty champion of the common
man, was quoted as saying, "Of course we want to advocate some
social welfare, but we do not want to be excessive. . . . If trade
unions advocate extreme or radical demands, the law must prohibit
this." So the election wasn't about campaign promises.

Why was everybody voting so hard? The only answer I could
get from Koreans was "democracy."

"What's this election all about?" I asked.

"Democracy," they answered.

"But what *is* democracy?" I said.

"Good."

"Yes, of course, but why exactly?"

"Is more democratic that way!"

Well, this is heartening to those of us who prefer a democratic
system. But I still don't know what they're talking about. "Korea
must have democracy," my Korean friends told me. "Democracy is
very good for Korea." "Korean people want very much democracy."

47

I guess democracy is something that if you're going to be really up-to-date, you just can't do without—like a compact-disc player. (Actual South Korean experience with democracy, by the way, consists of one thirteen-month period between the April 1960 overthrow of strongman Syngman Rhee and the May 1961 military coup by General Park Chung Hee.)

On election day I cruised Seoul with an old friend from the democracy fad in the Philippines, photographer John Giannini. It was supposed to be a national holiday, but the Koreans went to work just the same, the way they do six days a week, starting before dawn and stopping who knows when. Rush hour doesn't even begin until seven P.M.

Traffic in Seoul is a 50 mph gridlock with nobody getting anywhere and everybody driving like hell. The sidewalks are endless rugby scrums. Elbowing your way through a crowd is Korean for "excuse me." The city is as gray as a parking garage and cleaner than a living room. People stoop and pick up any piece of litter they see. You can spend twenty minutes in an agony of embarrassment trying to figure out what to do with a cigarette butt. And they yell at you if you cross against the light. Everything is made of concrete and glass and seems unrelentingly modern, at first glance. But many buildings have no central heating, and the smell of kerosene stoves pours out every shop door, mixing with *kimchi* fumes, car smoke, sewer funk and the stink of industry. It's a tough, homely stench, the way America's ethnic factory towns must have smelled seventy-five years ago.

Giannini and I tried to find the slums of Seoul, but the best we could do was a cramped, rough-hewn neighborhood with spotless, bicycle-wide streets. Every resident was working—hauling, stacking, hawking, welding, making things in sheds no larger than doghouses. Come back in a few years, and each shed will be another Hyundai Corporation. We felt like big, pale drones in the hive of the worker bees.

The voting was just what every journalist dreads, quiet and well organized. There were no Salvadoran shoot-'em-ups, no Haitian baton-twirler machete attacks, no puddles of Chicagoan sleaze running out from under the voting booths. People were standing patiently in line, holding their signature seals, their *chops*, at the ready. Poll watchers from each candidate's party sat to one side, rigid on a row of straight-backed chairs. A reporter who could make an interesting paragraph out of this would get that special Pulitzer they give out for keeping readers awake during discussions of civic virtue. Kim Dae Jung and Kim Young Sam said there was massive vote fraud. But if there was, it was serious, orderly *Korean* massive vote fraud.

Giannini and I did see one fellow getting roughed up by a crowd outside a polling place. We shoved people, in the Korean manner, until we found someone who spoke English. He told us the fellow being kicked and punched was a suspected government agent. The police came, punched and kicked the fellow some more, and hauled him off. It was certainly the first time I'd ever seen police arrest somebody on suspicion of being a government agent. But that's Korea.

We went out in the country to find people voting in authentic traditional funny clothes. But this, too, was a bore. So we gave up and went to a restaurant—a few floor mats and a kerosene heater in a tent beside the Han River.

The Han is as wide as the Hudson, and its valley is as beautiful as a Hudson River–school painting—but more serious, with a gray wash over it. The Koreans are serious about fun, too, thank God. They're perfectly capable of a three-hour lunch, and so are Giannini and I. We ordered dozens of bowls of pickles, garlics, red peppers and hot sauces and dozens of plates of spiced fish and vegetables and great big bottles of OB beer and mixed it all with *kimchi* so strong it would have sent a Mexican screaming from the room with tongue in flames. By the time we drove, weaving, back to Seoul, you could have used our breath to clean your oven.

After the votes were counted, the Koreans were *not* very happy with their first presidential election in sixteen years. Most citizens responded in the Korean way, by going to work in the morning. But some student-radical types decided they'd found a big vote fraud in a ward, or *gu*, office in the industrial district of Kuro, in southern Seoul.

As usual, I couldn't figure out what was going on. Korea has

an infinite capacity to make you feel dumb. This is a whole nation
of people who did their homework on Friday night. Even when they
don't know what they're doing, they're doing so damn much of it
that they're still going to get an A.

Anyway, the student radicals discovered a locked ballot box
under a stack of bread and milk in a truck leaving the Kuro *gu*
compound. Local officials gave some lame excuse about how the
ballot box had to go to a special vote-counting place, and how the
bread and milk truck just happened to be headed that way, and how
they'd covered the ballot box to keep the votes from getting
cold. . . . The students were having none of it. They invaded the
five-story Kuro *gu* building, took the local officials hostage and
called for one of those massive violent student demonstrations for
which Korea is justly famous.

The way famous, massive, violent Korean student demonstrations work is that the students get a sound truck, turn the volume
up to Mötley Crüe and take turns screaming at themselves. Violent
student demonstrators sit around cross-legged in an appreciative
half circle and, between screams, holler *"Dok chae tado! Dok chae
tado! Dok chae tado!"* which means "Smash the dictatorship." The
chant is punctuated with unnerving, black-shirtish synchronized
karate chops.

This can go on for days, and at Kuro it did.

Meanwhile, extra-violent student demonstrators were breaking paving stones into handy projectiles, filling *soju* rice-wine-
bottle kerosene bombs, building desk-and-filing-cabinet barricades in the Kuro *gu* doorways and pulling apart some nearby
scaffolding to make quarterstaves out of iron pipe. A line of
command had been created, and all defense preparations were
taking place behind a row of stick-wielding young malcontents.

Lack of press freedom in Korea is one of the big student
gripes. But the students don't like actual reporters any better than
the government does, at least not American reporters. The radicals—in counterfeit New Balance shoes, Levi's knockoffs and
unlicensed Madonna T-shirts—are much given to denouncing
American dominance of Korean culture. It took a lot of arguing to
get past these ding-dongs. One pair, a dog-faced, grousing fat girl
in glasses and a weedy, mouthy, fever-eyed boy, were almost as

obnoxious as my girlfriend and I were twenty years ago at the march on the Pentagon. However, they had some oddly Korean priorities. "Don't you step on bushes!" shouted the fat girl as I made my way into the building that they were tearing to shreds.

Inside, firebombs were parked neatly in crates, stones were gathered in tidy piles, more lengths of pipe were laid in evenly spaced rows to booby-trap the stairs, and additional barricades were being carefully constructed on the landings.

Looking down from the roof, I saw little groups of students break away from the chanting and form themselves into squads, squatting in formation. They *dok chae tado*ed for a while then quick-marched to the front lines around the Kuro *gu* compound, where each was given an assigned position and his own firebomb to sit patiently beside. Demonstrators continued to arrive, bringing boxes of food, fruit juice and cigarettes.

You had to admire the students' industry and organization, if not their common sense. The Kuro *gu* building faced a spike-fenced courtyard with only one narrow gate to the street. There was no way out the back of the place except through the upper-story windows or off the roof. And right next door, completely over-shadowing the scene, was a huge police station. Four thousand policemen gathered there that evening, in their distinctive Darth Vader outfits—black gas masks, Nazi helmets and stiff olive-drab pants and jackets stuffed with protective padding.

The government assault came on Friday morning, two days after the election. It was well under way by the time I arrived at eight A.M. You go to cover a Korean riot story looking more like a Martian than a Woodward or a Bernstein. You wear heavy clothes for protection from the cold and rocks, good running shoes, a hard hat or motorcycle helmet marked PRESS in English and Korean, and the best gas mask you can find on the black market. (It's illegal for civilians to buy them in Korea.)

Korean riot police use the pepper gas developed during the Vietnam War, which is fast becoming a favorite with busy dictators everywhere. I'd been hit with the stuff before, in Panama, but the Koreans lay it on in lavish doses, until the air is a vanilla milkshake of minuscule caustic particles. Pepper gas can raise blisters on exposed skin. Any contact with a mucous membrane produces the same sensation as probing a canker sore with a hot sewing needle. The tiniest amount in your eyes and your eyelids lock shut in blind agony. Breathing it is like inhaling fish bones, and the curl-up-and-die cough quickly turns to vomiting. Pepper gas is probably the only thing on earth more powerful than *kimchi*.

There was street fighting going on all around Kuro *gu*, in an orderly way, of course. First the Darth Vader cops form a line with shields interlocked. Then the students run up and throw firebombs at them. The police respond with a volley of tear-gas rifle grenades. The students throw stones. The police fire tear gas again and then charge.

The police hardly ever catch a student. That would disturb the *kibun* of the set-piece battle. Instead, there's a squad of volunteers from the police ranks called "grabbers." The grabbers dress in down-filled L.L. Bean–type parkas, jeans, Nikes and white motorcycle helmets. They carry hippie-tourist-style canvas shoulder bags filled with tear-gas grenades, and swing long batons that look like hiking staffs. Their jackets are all in pleasant shades of beige and baby blue, color coordinated by squadrons. With gas masks in place, the grabbers look like a bunch of mentally unbalanced freelance writers for *Outside* magazine.

The grabbers huddle behind the riot police. As soon as the students break ranks, the grabbers spring out and do their grabbing, beating the shit out of anyone they lay hands on. The beaten students are then led away. Student demonstrators are not often formally arrested in Korea. They are just "led away." What happens to them next is, I hear, even less fun than getting caught in a Kim Dae Jung rally.

Being out in no-man's-land between the students and the police isn't much fun either. Rifle grenades were flying through the air, and stones were racketing on the top of my hard hat; plus there was this creepy xxx video rubber-fetish thing all over my face. No gas mask is fully effective against the pepper-gas clouds, and mine looked as if it dated back to the Crimean War. Inside it, I was coughing and weeping and thoroughly panicked, and outside it, barely visible through the scratched and fogged-over eyepieces, was the world's only mayhem with choreography. I had stumbled onstage in midperformance of some over-enthusiastic Asian production of *West Side Story.*

Back at Kuro *gu* itself, the police had retaken the courtyard and first four stories of the building, but the students were still holding the top floor and roof.

The students don't wear gas masks. They put on those little Dr. Dan and Nurse Nancy cotton face things, and they smear toothpaste on their skin, but otherwise they riot unprotected. The police in the courtyard were firing salvos of gas grenades, twenty at a time, into the fifth-floor windows and onto the roof. The gas bursts looked like albino fireworks. The police also have armored cars with gun turrets that shoot small tear-gas cannisters at hundreds of rounds a minute. Two of these had been set in flanking positions and were raking the rooftop. That the students could even stand in this maelstrom was a testament to Koreanness. But they were not only standing; they were fighting like sons of bitches.

The barricades in the stairwells had been set on fire, and columns of ash were rising above the building. I could see blurred hand-to-hand action inside as windows shattered and pipes and batons flashed. The students were raining everything they could lift on the police. The "Irish confetti" was dancing off upraised shields and bouncing and ricocheting all around in the courtyard. Two fire trucks had been brought through the gate, and their extension ladders were thrust as near to the roof as even a Korean would dare.

A couple of overbrave firemen went scurrying topside in a smoke of stones. The adrenaline-zanied kids fended off water blasts with their protest placards and with ordinary umbrellas, the fabric tearing from the spokes in seconds. A stray gas grenade slammed into one of the extension ladders, inspiring vivid gestures from the fireman to his colleagues below.

The top of the otherwise modern cement Kuro *gu* office was fringed, Burger King fashion, with a mansard roof of traditional tiles. When the students ran out of stones and bottles, they began pulling loose these fat parentheses of baked clay and sailing them out over the courtyard. Weighing ten pounds apiece and coming from fifty feet in the air, they had the impact of small mortar shells. If you kept your eye on the trajectories, you could move out of the way in time. But to stop watching the sky for even ten seconds was curtains. I saw six or seven cops carried away, heads lolling and blood running out from under their helmets. I turned a shoulder to the building to write that in my notebook, and half a tile flew past me so close I felt the wind through the fly of my 501s. If I'd been standing one inch to the south, I'd be writing this in soprano.

About 8:45 the police cleared the top floor and the grabbers—or "white-skull police," as the students call them—appeared at the windows waving victoriously. But the cops below were slow on the uptake, and the grabbers got hit with another round of gas.

The students on the roof kept at it. One wild young fool spent the entire battle balanced on the roof tiles, dancing back and forth, chased by streams of water from the fire hoses and ducking the gas grenades fired at his head. Every time a grenade missed he'd bow grandly to the police. It's not enough that these guys are better than we are at making cars, ships, TVs, stereos, cameras, computers, steel and binoculars; now they're building a better Berkeley and Kent State.

The final assault came about nine A.M. There was one double door to the roof, and only four grabbers could get through it at a time. Photographer Tony Suau, with whom I'd covered the Aquino-Marcos election mess, was standing right behind the first wave. He said the grabbers were obviously scared. And the first four who charged out were flung back inside, bruised and bleeding. But the grabbers persisted, four by four, until they secured the doorway. Then a hundred of them pushed outside.

From the ground it was a Punch-and-Judy show. The down-bulked grabbers in their helmets and masks were visible only from the chest up behind the parapets. They were thrashing maniacally with their long batons. You could tell when they got a student down—suddenly a stick would be moving in a single arc with burlesque speed: *wack-a-wack-a-wack-a-wack-a-wack*. I saw the bowing kid pulled from his perch and given the Mrs. Punch treatment.

One section of the roof was raised half a story above the other. A dozen determined students held out here, throwing folding chairs, bricks and roof tiles. For a few last seconds their silhouettes were etched in heroic silliness against the sky.

The paved Kuro *gu* courtyard had been turned into a gravel

patch by the battle. Inside the building the air was a mud of smoke and gas. Fires were still burning in some corners, and water from the fire hoses ran in rivulets down the stairs. The police were making the students carry out their wounded. Several were unconscious, and one girl, wrapped in a blanket, had a hand's breadth of skull laid open and a bad, bloodless look to her face.

The students were swollen and red from the gas. They stumbled around, dazed and stupid. The cops were gathering them in Kuro *gu*'s larger rooms, making them prostrate themselves, obeisant like Moslems in prayer but more tightly hunched—children trying to make themselves disappear. These balled-up figures were packed into perfect squares of one hundred. The grabbers strolled over every now and then and gave the kids a few kicks for good measure.

The building had been fought over inch by inch. Every stick of furniture was destroyed, every breakable thing was broken. This was Korea, however—the bathrooms were still spotless.

About one hundred hostages, including several children, were released. They looked thoroughly sick. Nobody seemed interested in them. (According to the next day's official report, twenty-four policemen and forty students were seriously injured. One thousand and five students and student-allied radicals were "led away.")

The captured students were made to "elephant walk" down the stairs and into the courtyard, bodies bowed double, one hand on the waistband of the student ahead. Kicks and swats hurried them along. I noticed the dog-faced girl stumbling by, with glasses missing and a big shiner.

Then the mommy riot began. A dozen middle-aged women arrived at the police lines. They shoved their plump bodies against the riot shields and screeched, "You murderers!" and "Where is my son?!" and "I hate this country!" Then they fell into brief faints, tore their hair, wept, screeched some more and went into other histrionics—enough for a French actress on a farewell tour. This is better than my mother would have behaved. She would have been there yelling, "Keep the bum!"

That night, the journalists who'd covered the Kuro *gu* riot— having showered and dumped our gas-soaked clothing in hotel hallways—had a long, well-lubricated dinner. Between the blowing of gas-scalded noses and the wiping of gas-curried eyes, we discussed Korean democracy. As I recall, the discussion went something like this:

"What the fuck?"

"Beats the shit out of me."

"Yo, waitress, more whiskey."

When the dinner was over, I went with two photographers, Greg Davis and Tom Haley, for a little constitutional up the hill to Myongdong Cathedral, a few blocks from the restaurant. About a hundred students with the usual rock piles and firebombs were sitting-in up there for no reason anyone was very clear about.

The students had blocked the street on the hilltop in front of the church and weren't going to let us through. "Democracy! Free press!" said Davis, as we flashed our credentials.

"No free press!" shouted student number 30. They'd all given themselves numbers, which they wore pinned to their chests.

"No democracy?" said Davis.

"No democracy!" shouted 30.

Then, out of the gloom, appeared a pair of American preppies, he in tweeds and a necktie, she in a demure loden coat. "Hi!" the boy said brightly. "We're from the International Human Rights Law Group. We're here to observe Korean democracy."

"Ask number 30 about that," said Davis.

Down at the bottom of the hill, riot police were forming up, shield to shield, grenade launchers loaded.

"Yeah, you little fuck," I said to number 30. "What do you think about getting democratically hammered, about half a minute from now?"

The members of the International Human Rights Law Group gasped to hear someone speaking to a genuine Korean like that, right in the middle of Korea's first presidential elections in sixteen years. But then they caught a look at the advancing police. The law group took off like surprised mice.

Haley, Davis and I were too slow. We could hear the grenades being fired, half a dozen of them, *KA-CHUNK/CHUNK/CHUNK/ CHUNK/CHUNK/CHUNK.* "Incoming!!!" yelled Haley, the last thing he'd be able to say for half an hour. The grenades burst just above our heads.

We ran screaming down an alley, slamming into walls and garbage cans, coughing and gagging, a scum of tears running down our sightless faces. After two hundred yards we collapsed, bent over in pained hacking and gasps. A group of Korean men, earnestly merry with drink, were coming up the other way. They stopped in front of our little spectacle. The lead fellow bowed and said, "You Americans yes what do you think about Korean democracy?"

"Awwwwk ugch ugch ugch," said Haley.

But the Koreans were not making a joke. "What do you think about Korean democracy?" said their leader, gravely.

"Tastes terrible!" said Davis.

They hustled us into a storefront cafe and bought us a great many large bottles of OB beer. We sat there sneezing and weeping and coughing. They sat there asking, "What do you think about Korean democracy?"

That turned out to be all the English they knew.

Panama Banal

Panama has the damndest anti-government protestors. They're all dressed up in neckties or linen dirndl skirts and driving around in BMWs and Jeep Wagoneers, honking horns and waving white hankies out the windows. Opposition HQ is that infamous center of treachery and sedition worldwide, the Chamber of Commerce building. A National Civilian Crusade has been formed from more than a hundred trade associations and charity-ball-type organizations. Everybody is full of moral indignation, also civic boosterism. *Cruzada Civilista Nacional* demonstrations take place before luncheon and at the cocktail hour along Calle 50, Panama City's main artery for the shop-till-you-drop set. It's like watching your mom and dad riot at the mall.

White is the opposition color, appropriately enough. Less affluent Panamanians, who tend to have more black and Indian blood, call the opposition *rabe blancos*, "white butts." The *rabes* who've soiled their handkerchiefs wave white business stationery

58

and pages torn from Month-At-A-Glance calendars. Office towers are festooned with white adding-machine tape streamers; white three-by-five index cards flutter from the windows; and white confetti is made with document shredders. (This is only the second known use—after Fawn Hall's—of the shredding machine in the fight for democracy.) Protest signs are done with computer graphics and slogans displayed on word processor printouts.

In the better residential neighborhoods the noon and six P.M. demos are marked by children, housewives and kitchen help banging on pots and pans. At least one enterprising member of the opposition is selling a pot-banging cassette so dinner won't be late. There are no sweaty marches or boring sit-ins. When the opposition wants to stage a mass rally it calls for a "White Caravan," and everyone drives through town with the air conditioning on. If people can't make it, they send the maid.

This is genius, to use littering, noise-making and traffic jams as political protest in a Latin country. Think how quickly we would have been out of Vietnam if golf, commuting and watching *Mayberry R.F.D.* had been anti-war in the United States.

A full-blown Civilian Crusade shindig musters eight to ten thousand people. But a government-sponsored whoop-up can draw as many or more. The pro-government types, who more or less support military strongman General Manuel Antonio Noriega, are fatter, have worse teeth and wear more polyester. Their Panamanian flag–draped *caravanas patrioticas* are filled with Japanese economy cars. It's not really rich versus poor. It's more like the Elks versus the Rotary Club. The dentists and bank tellers are mad at the meter maids and postal clerks.

I couldn't always tell them apart. On my first day covering the Panama shenanigans I saw a phalanx of riot police, or "Dobermans," as they affectionately call themselves. Nearby was a group of neatly dressed businesslike folk holding bundles of leaflets. I rushed up to them and said, "Is this the anti-government demonstration?"

"We *are* the government," replied one, in a huff. They were members of the national legislature.

The government cheats a bit with its anti-demonstration demonstrations, handing out gas money and giving public employees the day off then taking roll call at the rally. During a week of ceremonies marking the anniversary of the 1981 death of national hero General Omar Torrijos, the government staged a wonderfully named "Carnival of National Dignity." There were a half-dozen salsa and merengue bands and free beer and firecrackers for everyone.

Not all of the pro-government sentiment is manufactured, however. When gringo reporters are spotted, loyalist crowd members yell complaints that they aren't getting their share of U.S. press coverage. "You must print pictures of this," several people shouted at me (although I wasn't carrying a camera). And one large and beery lady, more full of political spirit than political savvy, leaned halfway out of her car window and shrieked, "This proves Panama does not want communism!" Seeing that the basic conflict in Panama pits right-wing businessmen against a right-wing military, I guess it doesn't.

Sometimes a white caravan and a pro-government caravan get going at the same time, circling around the city like students from rival high schools before a big football game. The pro-government bunch are more willing to mix it up. They're the kids from Central High downtown. The opposition—suburban souls whose real strength is in the tennis team—tend to yell clever things and skedaddle.

I saw one pro-government caravan led by a stake-bed truck full of drunks come across a snazzy black Toyota Supra with a white flag hanging from the window. The drunks let loose at the Supra with slingshots. The Supra driver tried to make a U-turn, but, before he could get his car around, four or five of the drunks leapt off the truck and smashed his windshield with a rock the size of a Thanksgiving turkey. The Supra made a rubber-peeling escape. A volley of stones followed him, and so did I in my rental car. I wanted a pithy quote. I was sticking my head out the window, flashing my lights and screaming, *Prensa internacional! Prensa internacional!*" But the guy was doing eighty miles an hour through side streets, and the last thing I saw was his white flag being tossed onto a lawn.

The college students are demonstrating, too. They claim to be opposed to the government and the opposition and the United

P. J. O'Rourke
· ·

States too. The schools have been closed so there aren't that many
students around, only about two hundred at the demonstration I
saw. Still, they put on the best show. The students chanted,
"Noriega fucks whores" and blocked a four-lane highway in front of
the University of Panama with piles of flaming garbage. One no-
neck in a highway-department truck ran the blockade, and the
students, who had been hoarding rocks and chunks of cement,
scored thirty direct hits on his truck. Hundreds of locals deserted
offices and factories to gather on pedestrian overpasses and watch
the fun.

When three platoons of soldiers arrived, the students hightailed it like a clutter of cats back inside the university gates. They
have a great system in Latin America: The college campuses are
recognized sanctuaries, and soldiers and police aren't supposed to
set foot on the grounds. (Of course, every now and then the
authorities get overexcited and break the rules and kill people, but
usually the tradition is respected.)

After a brief regrouping, the students ran up to the chain-link
fence that surrounds the campus and threw rocks and bottles. Then
the soldiers ran up to their side of the fence and blasted at the
students with shotguns. It was red-necks hunting quail through the
hedge at the bird preserve. Most of the shotgun shells were low-
power loads filled with size 7½ shot—tiny stuff that wouldn't kill
you unless it went right up your nose. (Though I did pick up a
couple of "high brass" shells that held enough powder to take off a
hand or a face.) The soldiers also threw pepper-gas cannisters and
fired pepper-gas rifle grenades into the campus, sometimes making
the mistake of low trajectory, which let the students grab the
grenades before they exploded and toss them back.

There was a lot of quarterback talent on both sides. The
students were sending two- and three-pound projectiles on eighty-
yard TD bombs. And there was one tall black corporal who made
John Elway look like a sissy throwing rice at a wedding. The
students set fire to a car, though not a very good one. My guess is it
belonged to a professor who liked to give surprise quizzes.

During a lull in the action I managed to slip into the school
with an NBC camera crew. The campus was fogged with gas.
Students brought us buckets of vinegar. Apparently, vinegar is the

only specific against the pepper fumes, but it's a toss which hurts worse when you get it in your eyes. An entire medical dispensary had been set up in a lecture hall, complete with volunteer nurses and space for a press conference. We talked to a dozen or so injured students. One kid had at least fifteen pellets in his back and side. He was very crabby.

We had some trouble getting back out again, until the military finally decided that very few rioting students are forty years old, fat, carrying fifty pounds of video equipment and frantically hollering, *"Prensa internacional!"*

A few minutes later a commotion of pro-student pot-banging broke out in a high-rise across the highway from the university. The soldiers happily turned their shotguns on the apartment building. A man in a bathing suit was standing on one of the balconies. He yelled at me, in English, "They're shooting at the fucking building!"

I yelled back, "For chrissake get inside." Panamanians are not particularly brave people. Even Roberto Duran wound up holding his tummy and going *"No más. No más."* And one of the soldiers had lettered this bellicose statement on his helmet cover: "RAMBO—terror of civilians." But no Panamanian can resist an opportunity for self-dramatization.

The fellow in the bathing suit didn't budge. "Tell Reagan we got a great fucking democracy going here," he shouted.

What, you may well wonder, is all this about? I mean, here we've got a country that two-thirds of America thinks is a hat. (Actually, the hats are made in Ecuador.) And, damn it, we can't be expected to stay up to speed on every one of these Third World pissing contests. Crazy greasers—they've always got bees in their panty hose about something. We gave them their silly canal back. Now what's the matter?

Well, fat, pock-faced General Manuel "Pineapple Head" Noriega is nobody's candidate for the Medal of Freedom. Panama is a military dictatorship covered by a thin scum of constitutional formalities. And the Pineapple reigns over the Panamanian Defense Force, which includes the army, police and several kinds of plainclothes thugs. There is virtually no such thing as conflict of

P. J. O'Rourke
· ·

interest under Panamanian law. Senior military officers and their relatives sit on the boards of nearly every corporation and control most government contracts. According to U.S. Embassy sources, Noriega has several large houses in Panama and property in the south of France. At his daughter's wedding, guests were served pink champagne with pictures of the bride and groom on the labels and Baccarat-crystal party favors. If Ugly Mug is living within his modest army salary, he's a better money manager than I am.

There are other, juicier allegations. Noriega and ilk probably pulled the 1985 torture murder of a government critic named Dr. Hugo Spadafora. Panama is a country more greedy than evil. Snuffing your bad-mouthers is not considered the small social gaffe it is in most of Latin America. You're supposed to send them off in exile to "the Valley of the Fallen"—Miami Beach. The U.S. Justice Department is also investigating Noriega's use of Panama as a huge drug money Laundromat. Furthermore, defected Cuban intelligence big-shot Major Florentino Aspillaga says Noriega has been raking in dough selling U.S. high-tech items to Castro.

The opposition has a point. They would prefer nice, stable democratic corruption like we have in the United States. But, unfortunately for the cause of kick-out-the-wheel-chocks partisan journalism, the pro-government people also have a point. Panama used to be run by the normal south-of-the-Rio-Grande kitty litter box of brain-dead hacienda owners and United Fruit business squad. Then, in 1968, General Omar Torrijos led an army-backed coup.

Torrijos was a half-baked socialist and a blow-hard, but he was lovable and good-looking. He took a predictable, feisty underdog stance toward the U.S. and the local rich shitepokes, swearing he would fight all of them in a guerrilla war if he had to, which he knew he didn't. Panamanians, who have absolutely no immunity to theatrics, went nuts over Omar. Actually, he was sort of an all-right guy. He had genuine feeling for the poor, started some only moderately useless social programs and maintained a modest style of life, keeping no more than two or three mistresses on the side. Torrijos also managed, after decades of negotiations, to wrest a new canal treaty from the United States. Admittedly, he wrested it from Jimmy Carter, so it isn't like he played against the varsity, but it gave the

Panamanians a patriotic thrill to get the middle of their country back. And under Torrijos (though, to a certain extent, despite him) Panama prospered. It became a middle-class country with one of the highest per capita incomes in Latin America. Thousands of jobs were added to the government payroll. People came up in the world.

"Even the men who killed Torrijos loved him," a taxi driver told me. (Taxi drivers all over the world, by the way, are under Newspaper Guild contract to give easy quotes to foreign correspondents.) In fact, nobody killed Torrijos. He died of his macho penchant for flying in bad weather. But such is the romance in the Panamanian soul that nothing will do except he be a martyr.

When Torrijos bought the rancho, Noriega, his chief of staff, was the natural heir. Watching him try to act like Omar is like watching Ted Kennedy try to act like Jack. Members of Noriega's own government admit he's a pig. But a lot of people are scared the *rabe blancos* will bring back the bad old days of venal oligarchy. (This is unlikely because most of the opposition belongs to the new middle class, but that's politics for you.) Also, what's the big deal about corruption? This is *Panama*, for godsake. The whole country is a put-up job, sleazed into existence by Teddy Roosevelt so he'd have someplace to put the Big Ditch. One pro-Noriega legislator told me, in a fit of candor about peculation, "We are just doing the same thing the others were from 1903."

The Panamanian government types are also mad about the U.S. Senate resolution of June 26, 1987, in which the Panamanians were advised their democracy had B.O. and they'd better send Noriega to the showers with a family-size bar of Dial. Part of the resolution was in language identical to an opposition manifesto. And how would we like it if the French Chamber of Deputies voted for a Democratic Party policy statement telling everybody in America to listen up when Mario Cuomo speaks? Then the United States trotted out the State Department's human-rights bureau, that feeble Carter Administration leftover, and sent one of its goody-two-shoes "human-rights investigators" to pester the natives. How about a Saudi Arabian human-rights investigator arriving uninvited in D.C.? "By Muhammad, you are not cutting off enough hands of thieves! You are not throwing off of minarets enough adultresses!

You are not branding your slaves on their bottoms!" We'd appreciate that.

So, although the opposition has a point, the government has a point, too, and the college students. . . . Well, the college students *don't* have a point. They're just mouthing the standard Third World college student take-out order: two anti-colonialisms, an anti-capitalism with cheese and a small Che on the side. The students are full of shit. That, however, puts them in perfect harmony with the nation of Panama. The whole country is full of shit. Or—since they're very nice people—let's say "the Panamanians have a poetic conception of the truth."

The opposition movement was set off by anti-Noriega accusations from Colonel Roberto Díaz Herrera, who was forced to resign as the Defense Forces' second in command—not exactly an unbiased source. Díaz claimed, among other things, that Noriega and the ex-chief of the U.S. Southern Command, the hopelessly respectable General Wallace Nutting, planted a bomb on Torrijos's plane after—get this—luring it off-course by changing satellite navigational signals. Díaz Herrera also underwent some kind of religious conversion, then barricaded himself in his walled suburban mansion with the teachings of his spiritual guru and a gang of armed supporters. He was all but receiving Radio Venus on his bridgework when the government finally stormed his house and hauled him off.

Various "eyewitnesses" to the attack on Díaz's house told me there were five dead bodies on the lawn, told me there were eight dead bodies on the lawn, told me Díaz's only son was killed, told me Díaz himself was killed, etc. Díaz has several sons, none of whom were killed; nor was Díaz. Indeed, the ninety-minute fire fight at the Díaz home didn't kill or seriously injure anyone, a very Panamanian touch. Another witness told me Sandinista troops participated in the battle dressed as Dobermans.

Assorted tales from the government camp were just as silly. The government press office circulated subliterate books and pamphlets claiming that the pre-coup president, Arnulfo Arias, murdered Jews and that the Jewish Eisenmann family, which owns the principal opposition newspaper, is running an international cocaine ring.

Holidays In Hell

This is *radio bemba,* "lip radio," and it is—after money, cars and Japanese stereo equipment—the ruling passion of Panama. During one hour in a discotheque, I heard the following nonsense:

1. Noriega has picked every Miss Panama since he took over and deflowers each of them.
2. The last Miss Panama had to be married off to one of Noriega's colonels at the insistence of Noriega's jealous wife.
3. Mrs. Noriega killed her husband's mistress when the mistress was six months pregnant.
4. A pregnant woman was shot by the Dobermans when they mistook the diaper she was hanging on a clothesline for a white opposition flag.
5. Werewolves are loose in the Panamanian countryside.

Of course, an important part of *radio bemba* is blaming absolutely everything on the United States. The opposition tells you the U.S. isn't supporting them because Noriega is a tool of the CIA (usually right after they've told you Noriega is in the pay of Danny Ortega). The government tells you the opposition is controlled by the U.S. embassy DCM, John F. Maistro, because he used to be in Manila where he overthrew Marcos. And the college students tell you all sorts of things very loudly in Spanish while shaking empty pepper-gas cannisters under your nose. In this case the students *do* have a point. TRIPLE CHASER GRENADE/FEDERAL LABORATORIES/ SALTSBURG, PENN. read the cannister labels. I don't know about you, but it makes me sleep better at night knowing the U.S. Defense Department keeps our allies supplied with these. Why, if Panama should ever have to come to our aid in a war against Russia, the Panamanians could just fill the air with pepper gas and make the Soviet air force pilots sneeze like the dickens.

Three thousand words here and it seems I still haven't answered the question, "What's happening in Panama?" Darn these Apple IIs anyway. Where's the BRIEF INSIGHTFUL SUMMARY key on this thing?

The *rabe blancos* are acting like wimps. When the government moved on Díaz Herrera and simultaneously closed all the opposition newspapers, opposition leaders responded by hiding. Pro-Noriega salsa bands took over the streets. On July 26, after nearly two months of *agita*, somebody finally got killed—a quiet, well-bahaved business-administration student named Eduardo Enrique Carrera. Eduardo and some friends apparently yelled, "Down with the Pineapple," at a police cruiser, and the police shot him. Not a single major opposition leader showed at the funeral.

As for the *rabe blanco* demonstrations, I was talking to a senior official in the Panamanian Foreign Ministry, a black guy whose grandparents came from Jamaica. He just laughed. "Man, I went to the toughest high school in Panama City," he said. "*We* knew how to *riot*. Oh, these people should check the confetti in Beirut."

On the other side, the government hacks are acting like morons. They're swamped with debt but spending millions on pep rallies and early bonuses for public employees. Reuters correspondent Tom Brown, the only U.S. reporter based full-time in Panama, was expelled for reporting a Civilian Crusade general strike as 85 percent effective. "You have twenty-four hours to leave the country voluntarily," Brown was told. And on June 30 the government launched what might be the lamest ever "spontaneous" attack on an American embassy. Five thousand government workers were required to participate in the demonstration in order to receive their paychecks. These not-very-enthusiastic anti-imperialists were bused to the embassy compound where cheerleaders led them in dispirited chants while thirty hoodlums threw rocks at the building. Washington presented a bill for $106,000 in damages to the Panamanian government, which promptly apologized and paid up.

Meanwhile, the economy of Panama goes to hell. It's not like they make or grow anything. The whole country is based on international banking and a canal the United States can take back any time it wants with one troop of Boy Scouts. Right now the contents of Panama's banks are on a greenback-salmon run to Luxembourg, the Bahamas and the Cayman Islands.

Noriega's getting to be more trouble than he's worth to the other corrupt military officers. He'll probably "retire" in favor of some more acceptable general. Or maybe he'll hang on. The opposition might even win, and its hundred factions will squabble merrily until the next coup. People knowledgeable in Panamanian political affairs ask themselves, "Who gives a shit?"

The night before I left, I watched an NBC producer who'd been in the country for two months sit on the floor of his hotel room drunk, swaying and keening to himself over and over again, ". . . the rumors, the honking, the confetti, the tear gas, the rumors, the honking, the confetti, the tear gas . . ." Panama can drive you around the bend. Believe me, I know. I went back to my room and put on my best Central Intelligence Agency seersucker jacket and rep tie. Then I went down to the hotel bar to leave the Panamanians with a little of their own *radio bemba,* a sort of going-away present.

"*Buenos noches,* Ramón," I said, speaking to the unctuous bartender in a stentorian American voice. "Looks like those rich *rabe blancos* are too scared to get their own hands dirty."

"*Sí, comó no,*" Ramón agreed.

"You know, I was up at Southern Command today," I said, looking around as though we might be overheard. "I hear the *rabes* are hiring some out-of-work death-squad guys from Argentina." I leaned over and whispered loudly to Ramón, "And they're getting help from the Mossad, MI5 and the KGB." Then I downed my drink and smiled, knowing the news would be all over Panama by morning.

Third World Driving Hints and Tips

. . . .

During the past couple years I've had to do my share of driving in the Third World—in Mexico, Lebanon, the Philippines, Cyprus, El Salvador, Africa and Italy. (Italy is not technically part of the Third World, but no one has told the Italians.) I don't pretend to be an expert, but I have been making notes. Maybe these notes will be useful to readers who are planning to do something really stupid with their Hertz #1 Club cards.

ROAD HAZARDS

. . . .

What would be a road hazard anyplace else, in the Third World is probably the road. There are two techniques for coping with this. One is to drive very fast so your wheels "get on top" of the ruts and your car sails over the ditches and gullies. Predictably, this will result in disaster. The other technique is to drive very slow. This will also result in disaster. No matter how slowly you drive into a ten-foot hole, you're still going to get hurt. You'll find the locals themselves can't make up their minds. Either they drive at 2 mph—which they do every time there's absolutely no way to get around them. Or else they drive at 100 mph—which they do coming right at you when you finally get a chance to pass the guy going 2 mph.

BASIC INFORMATION

It's important to have your facts straight before you begin piloting a car around an underdeveloped country. For instance, which side of the road do they drive on? This is easy. They drive on your side. That is, you can depend on it, any oncoming traffic will be on your side of the road. Also, how do you translate kilometers into miles? Most people don't know this, but one kilometer = ten miles, exactly. True, a kilometer is only 62 percent of a mile, but, if something is one hundred kilometers away, read that as one thousand miles because the roads are 620 percent worse than anything you've ever seen. And when you see a 50-kph speed limit, you might as well figure that means 500 *mph* because nobody cares. The Third World does not have Broderick Crawford and the Highway Patrol. Outside the cities, it doesn't have many police at all. Law enforcement is in the hands of the army. And soldiers, if they feel like it, will shoot you no matter what speed you're going.

TRAFFIC SIGNS AND SIGNALS

Most developing nations use international traffic symbols. Americans may find themselves perplexed by road signs that look like Boy Scout merit badges and by such things as an iguana silhouette with a red diagonal bar across it. Don't worry, the natives don't know what they mean, either. The natives do, however, have an elaborate set of signals used to convey information to the traffic around them. For example, if you're trying to pass someone and he blinks his left turn signal, it means go ahead. Either that or it means a large truck is coming around the bend, and you'll get killed if you try. You'll find out in a moment.

Signaling is further complicated by festive decorations found on many vehicles. It can be hard to tell a hazard flasher from a string of Christmas-tree lights wrapped around the bumper, and brake lights can easily be confused with the dozen red Jesus statuettes and the ten stuffed animals with blinking eyes on the package shelf.

DANGEROUS CURVES

Dangerous curves are marked, at least in Christian lands, by white wooden crosses positioned to make the curves even more dangerous. These crosses are memorials to people who've died in traffic accidents, and they give a rough statistical indication of how much trouble you're likely to have at that spot in the road. Thus, when you come through a curve in a full-power slide and are suddenly confronted with a veritable forest of crucifixes, you know you're dead.

LEARNING TO DRIVE
LIKE A NATIVE

It's important to understand that in the Third World most driving is done with the horn, or "Egyptian Brake Pedal," as it is known. There is a precise and complicated etiquette of horn use. Honk your horn only under the following circumstances:

1. When anything blocks the road.
2. When anything doesn't.
3. When anything might.
4. At red lights.
5. At green lights.
6. At all other times.

ROADBLOCKS

One thing you can count on in Third World countries is trouble. There's always some uprising, coup or Marxist insurrection going on, and this means military roadblocks. There are two kinds of military roadblocks, the kind where you slow down so they can look you over, and the kind where you come to a full stop so they can steal your luggage. The important thing is that you must *never* stop at the slow-down kind of roadblock. If you stop, they'll think you're a terrorist about to attack them, and they'll shoot you. And you must *always* stop at the full-stop kind of roadblock. If you just slow down, they'll think you're a terrorist about to attack them, and they'll shoot you. How do you tell the difference between the two kinds of roadblocks? Here's the fun part: You can't!

(The terrorists, of course, have roadblocks of their own. They always make you stop. Sometimes with land mines.)

ANIMALS IN THE RIGHT OF WAY

As a rule of thumb, you should slow down for donkeys, speed up for goats and stop for cows. Donkeys will get out of your way eventually, and so will pedestrians. But never actually stop for either of them or they'll take advantage, especially the pedestrians. If you stop in the middle of a crowd of Third World pedestrians, you'll be there buying Chiclets and bogus antiquities for days.

Drive like hell through the goats. It's almost impossible to hit a goat. On the other hand, it's almost impossible *not* to hit a cow. Cows are immune to horn-honking, shouting, swats with sticks and taps on the hind quarters with the bumper. The only thing you can do to make a cow move is swerve to avoid it, which will make the cow move in front of you with lightning speed.

Actually, the most dangerous animals are the chickens. In the United States, when you see a ball roll into the street, you hit your brakes because you know the next thing you'll see is a kid chasing

72

it. In the Third World, it's not balls the kids are chasing, but chickens. Are they practicing punt returns with a leghorn? Dribbling it? Playing stick-hen? I don't know. But Third Worlders are remarkably fond of their chickens and, also, their children (population problems not withstanding). If you hit one or both, they may survive. But you will not.

ACCIDENTS

Never look where you're going—you'll only scare yourself. Nonetheless, try to avoid collisions. There are bound to be more people in that bus, truck or even on that Moped than there are in your car. At best you'll be screamed deaf. And if the police do happen to be around, standard procedure is to throw everyone in jail regardless of fault. This is done to forestall blood feuds, which are a popular hobby in many of these places. Remember the American consul is very busy fretting about that Marxist insurrection, and it may be months before he comes to visit.

If you do have an accident, the only thing to do is go on the offensive. Throw big wads of American money at everyone, and hope for the best.

SAFETY TIPS

One nice thing about the Third World, you don't have to fasten your safety belt. (Or stop smoking. Or cut down on saturated fats.) It takes a lot off your mind when average life expectancy is forty-five minutes.

What Do They Do for Fun
in Warsaw?

· ·

Usually, a plane ride gives me some distance on questions of dogma, the way a martini or a lungful of hashish does. We don't call it "high" for nothing; that was slang three centuries before the Wright brothers. Whatever those microbes down there think is no concern of mine—unless I fly into the Soviet Block. Something's wrong when harebrained ideas can be spotted from Olympian heights. On the outskirts of Warsaw, the whole countryside is scarred with the gravel pits and gray dust plumes of cement factories. Commies love concrete.

Commies love concrete, but they don't know how to make it. Concrete is a mixture of cement, gravel and straw? No? Gravel, water and wood pulp? Water, potatoes and lard? The concrete runway at Warsaw's Miedzynarodowy airport is coming to pieces. From bumpy landing until bumpy take-off, you spend your time in Poland looking at bad concrete. Everything is made of it—streets, buildings, floors, walls, ceilings, roofs, window frames, lamp posts, statues, benches, plus some of the food, I think. The concrete that hasn't cracked or flaked has crumbled completely. Generations of age and decay seem to be taking place before your eyes.

Yet all of this is new. The Poles rebelled against Nazi occupation in 1945, and the Germans, in their German way, dynamited Warsaw house by house. Some stumps of churches and museums survived, but nothing major in the central city is older than Candice Bergen. And the place is dirty with a special kind of Marxist dirt. I've seen it before in Moscow, Rostov and East Berlin. It doesn't reek like the compost heap squalor of Mexico City. It isn't flung all over the place like the exuberant trash of New York. There's no litter. There isn't much to litter *with*. It's an orderly and uniform kind of dirt, a film of dry grit and slough on everything and an atmosphere lachrymose with diesel stink and lignite-coal smoke.

I got into an airport taxi, and the driver came right to the point, "Do you want to change dollars?" The Polish zloty is an animal tranquilizer on the international currency market. Even the official exchange rate is enormous, 163zl to $1. Dinner at the best restaurant in Warsaw costs only 3000zl, a street car ride is 3zl. "I'll give you 500 to 1" said the driver.

"How much is the fare?" I asked.

"Business is business," he said, "the cab ride is free." I handed him ten twenties, made myself rich and tried to go shopping.

The Polish Communists have done their dim-bulb best to recapture something of the pre-war Warsaw style. That is to say, not *every* building looks like a parking garage. And the Russian-type "Stalin's wedding cake" architecture is absent except for the huge Palace of Culture and Science, a "gift from the Soviet people," which everyone execrates. But there was only so much they could do with bad materials and worse sense. And they seem to have built the city from broad-shouldered, quick-breeding New Masses who never showed up. Meanwhile, a sparse stand-in population rattles around—tired looking, tending to middle age, not completely clean. There's too much room on the sidewalks and in the vast public squares. The farty little East German Wartburg cars and dinky Polish-built Fiats are at sea on the huge boulevards. Warsaw is empty. But not silent—too many trucks and buses are missing their mufflers, and the ill-machined wheels of the street cars squeal on the badly laid rails. The place sounds and smells more like a lonely freight yard than a capital city.

I found the three main department stores, "Wars," "Sawa" and "Junior," next to each other on Marszalkowska Street, the main drag. They had a little neon on their signs, which was a relief. Lack of advertising leaves a weird hole in the urban landscape. You think, "What could be uglier than billboards?" But have you ever looked behind them? In Communist countries you don't get to see the giant pictures of the cars, boats and pretty faces that fill people's dreams. You just see the people and where they live.

Each department store had the look of a small-town five-and-dime a few months after the new mall opened out on the highway. Except they don't have malls here or many highways either. The merchandise in all three was identical. Pants, coats, blouses and jackets were badly stitched and lumpy and cut like Barbie and Ken clothes blown up to life-size. Everything was made of imitation polyester, if there is such a thing. Muddy purples and cheap sky blues predominated—the kind of colors you see when antinuclear activists try to dress up. The mannequins had hems falling down and collar points awry and lint in their synthetic hair. The housewares section was filled with nasty little glass *tchotchkes* and disposable-looking aluminum skillets and pans. The toys were fat, pad-faced dolls and sagging truck-shaped doodads made from plastic Americans wouldn't use for the bags the toys came in. The only interesting things I saw were the appliances, and the only interesting thing about them was that I couldn't tell the stoves from the washing machines or the washing machines from the refrigerators.

There's a joke in Poland about shopping, as there's a joke about everything. A woman sends her husband to buy meat for dinner. He stands in line for six hours at the butcher shop, and then the butcher comes outside and says there's no more meat. The man explodes. He shouts, "I am a worker! I am a veteran! All my life I have fought and toiled for socialism! Now you tell me there's no more meat. This system is stupid! It's crazy! It stinks!"

A big fellow in a trench coat comes out of the crowd and puts his arm around the man's shoulder. "Comrade, comrade," says the fellow in the trench coat, "control yourself. Do not go on so. You know what would have happened in the old days if you had talked like this." And the fellow in the trench coat pantomimes with a finger at his temple. "So, please, comrade, calm down."

The man goes home empty-handed. His wife says, "What's the matter? Are they out of meat?

"Worse than that," says the man, "they're out of bullets."

I crossed Marszalkowska Street to a row of small private shops rented from the government. The first shop had a single shirt in the display case. The second had five hair ribbons and a ladies hat from the Jack and Jackie White House era. But in front of the third shop twenty or thirty people were gathered gawking at something in the window. I elbowed into the crowd and pushed my way to the front. They were looking at plumbing fixtures.

I had 100,000 zlotys in my pocket, more than some Poles make in six months. I finally bought a hot dog. I suppose it was no worse than an American hot dog. Horrible things go into hot dogs. But in this hot dog you could taste them all.

When I was applying for my Polish visa, I didn't know what to tell the people at the consulate. I couldn't very well say I was doing a story on "Does Thirty Years of Involuntary Marxism Make Folks Nuts or What?" The press officer wanted to see a copy of *Rolling Stone*, the publication I work for, so I told him I was doing a piece on Polish rock and roll. There actually is such a thing, if anybody cares. Poles themselves would rather listen to The Clash and Bob Dylan.

But this fib got me press credentials so I could go to news conferences in Warsaw and listen to the Polish government do the "Modifier Bop." It takes a lot of adjectives and adverbs to give the Marxist side of the news. The official Polish press agency is called, no joke, Pap. Here's an excerpt from one of their releases:

> Wojciech Jaruzelski and Gustav Husak stated concordantly that Poland and Czechoslovakia attach essential importance to the further deepening of the relations of friendship and cooperation between the two countries, based on the princi-

Holidays In Hell

ples of Marxist-Leninism and socialist internationalism, the
consolidation of fraternal ties with the USSR, cooperation
within the political-defensive alliance of the Warsaw
Treaty . . .

You get the idea.

At the first press conference I attended, government
spokesman Jerzy Urban was refuting some statement on long-term
effects of Chernobyl fallout. "False, erroneous news," said Urban,
"due to a general psychosis which is being established in the
West."

An American reporter asked him, rather gleefully, "How's the
blanket collection going?" Poland had volunteered to donate five
thousand sleeping bags to New York City's homeless. But so far
only five hundred sleeping bags had been found in the country and
only one had been donated by a private individual. The American
reporter wanted to know if there wasn't something strange about
donations to the homeless from a country where so many people
want to leave home. Everyone in the room, including Jerzy Urban,
tittered.

The person next to me whispered, "A classified ad ran in the
Warsaw papers, 'Will exchange two-bedroom apartment in Warsaw
for sleeping bag in New York.'"

The American reporter quoted Lech Walesa as saying, "If the
borders of Poland are ever opened, will the last person out please
turn off the lights and close the windows."

Urban laughed at that, too, and said Walesa could leave
anytime he liked and "didn't have to bother with lights or windows."

Then Urban went back to straining credulity on the fallout
topic. "When you say you can't confirm something," asked a BBC
reporter, "does this mean it's completely untrue?"

"Is this your first time at a press conference?" said Urban.

What ails Poland is, as the Poles say, "fatal but not serious."
When I went to Interpress, the government agency that provides
services to (and presumably keeps tabs on) foreign reporters, my
"minder" immediately told this week's General Jaruzelski knee-
slapper. The general is on a Polish TV quiz show. He has to answer

78

four questions to win a prize. The host asks the first question, "What happened in Poland in 1956?"

Jaruzelski says, "There were riots and strikes resulting from the justifiable anger of the working class."

"Correct," says the host. "What happened in Poland in 1970?"

"There were riots and strikes," says Jaruzelski, "resulting from the justifiable anger of the working class."

"Correct," says the host. "What happened in Poland in 1980?"

"There were riots and strikes resulting from the justifiable anger of the working class."

"Correct. And now for the fourth and final question. What will happen in Poland in 1987?"

Jaruzelski thinks for a long time and finally says, "I don't know but I'll take a shot at it . . ."

"CORRECT!!!"

Telling the Poles I was writing about rock and roll turned out to be an inspired lie. It let me get official help to go have fun. It gave me not only an excuse but a mandate to be out prowling around at night, checking the dance halls and juke joints and trying to find the wild get-down side of communism. A nation's fun will tell you more about that nation than anything except its jails. And, if I got into enough fun, maybe I'd get into jail too.

Interpress hired a translator for me, who I'll call Zofia, a tall and pretty, bespectacled and intense girl—half head librarian and half fashion model. She spoke five languages. "Will you want to interview many prominent figures in the field of popular music?" she asked, looking bored.

I said, "Zofia, there's only one way to cover this story. We have to get inside it. We have to experience it in the social context. We have to capture the gestalt, get the big picture. We've got to go out and drink too much and boogie."

"Your magazine *pays* you for this?" she said.

"Of course they do. I'm behind the Iron Curtain. This is dangerous. No agency of the U.S. government can help me now. I might be grabbed for a spy at any minute. Held incommunicado. Interrogated. Days without sleep. Drugs. Electric shock. A story like this is bound to put me in touch with antisocial elements, people opposed to the government."

Zofia began to giggle, "*Everyone* in Poland is opposed to the government."

Zofia rounded up two friends, Mark and Tom, both Americans. Tom was a graduate student, studying Slavic languages in Warsaw. Mark was a college professor bumming around Europe on vacation. We drove off in Tom's car and were promptly stopped by the police, who stop you all the time in Poland for no particular reason, like your mother did when you were a kid and trying to get out the back door.

"Do you know why the police have dogs?" said Tom in English as he smiled pleasantly at the cop. "Somebody has to do the brain work." "Do you know why police cars have white stripes on the side?" Tom continued, "To help policemen find the door handles." Tom turned to me, "Before Solidarity was crushed in 1981, these were all Russian jokes." The puzzled copper wanted to look in the trunk. Maybe we had the other 4,500 sleeping bags in there or some plumbing fixtures. "A man goes into a bar," Tom told him, "and tells the bartender, 'I just heard a new policeman joke.' A man who's sitting three stools away says, 'Wait a minute, I'll have you know *I'm* a policeman!' 'That's all right,' says the first man, 'I'll speak very slowly and clearly.'"

"Let's start with nightclubs," I said as soon as the cop had given up on us. Zofia raised an eyebrow.

"There's one called Kamieniolomy, 'The Quarry,'" said Tom. The decor was budget Mafia. Because of the name, I guess, the walls were covered with Permastone house siding. There were little strips of disco lights around the dance floor, but they just flashed off and on; they didn't move around the room or change colors or anything.

A bored combo—one singer, one guitar player and a guy on the electric organ doing the rhythm, bass and drum parts—played a Ramada Inn lounge arrangement of "I Got You, Babe," lyrics in memorized English:

> *Ugh gut you to told me height*
> *Bucket jute tuchus god night*

P. J. O'Rourke
. . . .

A fat lady came out and sang "Feelings," also in English. A dance team gave a disco exhibition more reminiscent of *Saturday Night Live* than *Saturday Night Fever*. There was a mild strip act, the stripper winding up in the kind of two-piece bathing suit worn by Baptist ministers' wives, but with sequins. The fat lady came back and sang "My Way." A very pretty girl in a harem outfit did a dance with a python. The disco team returned in Twenties costume and did a Forties tap routine. The fat lady came back a third time and sang "Hello Dolly." "Maybe they should put the snake in every act," said Mark. And the stripper finished the show doing "Dance of a Couple of Veils" with three large scarves and a blink of total nudity at the end. To grasp the true meaning of socialism, imagine a world where everything is designed by the post office, even the sleaze.

There were some odd ducks in the audience. The women were all milkmaid types with too much hair spray. The men were dark and greasy with Cadillac-fin lapels on their suits and tie knots as big as their ears. "What kind of people go to nightclubs in Poland?" I asked Zofia.

"Whores and Arabs," she said.

"What do Poles really do for fun?"

"Drink," said Zofia.

The next night we went to a student club, Stodola, "The Barn." (They do not have the knack of snappy nomenclature in Poland.) During the winter Stodola is the Student Union for Warsaw Technical University. The dance was held in the gym. The records were American or British with an occasional ABBA cut that cleared the dance floor. This night the kids were mostly high-school age. They had dressed up, doing their best to find T-shirts, at least, in bright, clear free-world colors. Some almost succeeded in looking American in a Michael J. Fox way. The crowd was shy and square acting: The boys danced in groups of boys; the girls danced together in pairs. And the dancing was terrible, stiff and clunky like spilling a can of Tinkertoys. There's a tragic lack of black people behind the Iron Curtain, which explains the dancing. "The only ethnic group we ever had was Jews," said Zofia, "and they only dance in circles."

Several video moniters were suspended above the dance floor

showing Polish and European music videos and American cartoons. Whenever the brilliant hues of Porky Pig came on, the
teenagers would dance in place and gape at the screens.

Stodola captured perfectly the sock-hop ennui of the early
1960s. One whiff of Canoe and I would have time-warped completely and started doing the Pony and the Locomotion. Those
freshman mixers were fun, I remember, sort of. But I also remember how a bland future stretched out before us like an endless
front yard full of crab grass. There would be school and more
school, job and more job, a wife or two and indifferent kids of our
own. Of course, we were crybabies. When a Polish kid says he's
facing a boring and meaningless life, he's not just pulling his dad's
chain at the dinner table.

A few of the boys were sweat-faced and stumbling. "Guess
they got into the vodka," I said to Zofia. "At least you don't have the
drug problem we do in the West."

"They are not drunk," she said, "they are on heroin." Poles,
she explained, were the first to figure out how to extract opiates
from poppy straw, the stubble that's left in the field after the poppy
harvest. Now kids are doing it all over Europe. It's called "the
Polish method."

Outside two cops were manhandling a stoned teen. "Maybe if
we stand here and look well-dressed, they will not beat him," said
Zofia. One cop had the face of a young Barney Fife from hell—
nasty pop eyes, a receding fish chin and big, weak lips. Four or five
of the stoned kid's friends interceded. First they reasoned. Then
they yelled. "The police are scared," said Zofia. "That is why they
travel in pairs. Everyone hates the police." The ugly cop pulled out
his rubber truncheon and waved it. But he didn't do anything.
Finally, the policemen walked away. The ugly cop called the kid a
name. "That policeman is from a very low element," said Zofia.

"You could tell from one word?"

"Yes."

"Zofia, I thought this was a classless society."

"You are kidding."

The third night we went to Remont, Warsaw's only punk club.
The kids didn't look very punky; more like it was a party game
where everybody had to do a quick impression of Patti Smith.

Remont was, however, as smelly as CBGB's or the Mudd Club ever used to be. The manager, Grzegorz Brzozowicz, showed me a videotape about the Polish punk scene done by West German television. The punks all said the usual stuff: "Everything is shit." "Life is shit." "This is shit." But they were matter-of-fact about it. These were foregone conclusions, not statements of rage.

I couldn't, off hand, think of anything to ask Grzegorz. "Does the Polish punk movement have any political significance?" I said and realized I'd put my foot in it. In a Marxist country even a dank and stinky place like Remont needs some kind of official sanction, and Grzegorz must have some kind of official status. He looked miffed.

"I notice a certain regularity in questions from the West," said Grzegorz. "First you're interested in punks. Usually your stories have two objectives, that punks are opposition to authority, breaking the rules that exist here. Also your articles show that there are no polar bears walking the streets." He gave me a condescending smile. "There are moments when our country is very normal."

"Hopelessly normal," I said. "I notice your punks don't go in much for spiked hair and face tattoos."

"They have some inhibitions," said Grzegorz. "Also we don't have the commercial products to do the hair styles."

Grzegorz paused. He didn't want me to get a bad impression, but he didn't want me to think Polish punks were complete wimps, either. "There was a smoke bomb a week ago," he ventured. And then he sighed. "There are contradictions within the Polish punk scene. Remont is the only place they can come to express their rebellion against institutions. But once they get here they enjoy rebelling against the institution of the club. The root problem is boredom."

"That's what made my generation rebel in the sixties in America," I said, trying to be nice. "You know, we were bored with commercialism, bored with materialism . . ."

Grzegorz sighed again. "They're rebelling here from lack of this."

The two bands playing at Remont that night were *Trubuna Brudu* ("Dirt Tribune") and *Garaz w Leeds* ("Garage in Leeds"). *Trubuna Brudu* rhymes with *Trybuna Luda* ("People's Tribune"), the

Communist Party newspaper. *Garaz w Leeds* is a "Cold Wave" band. Cold Wave being, according to Grzegorz, the latest English style, like New Wave but gloomier. Both bands were rotten.

Some of the punks began slam-dancing, or trying to. They were so drunk they kept missing each other. An enormous punk with a knife in his belt and a neck like a thigh began eyeing Zofia, Mark, Tom and me. "One good thing about a socialist system," I said to Zofia, "is the low crime rate."

"There are neighborhoods in Warsaw that I will not even go to," said Zofia.

"At night?"

"In the daytime."

"Is this one of them?"

"Now it is."

A large fight broke out as we left.

Remont is as hip as it gets in Poland. "That's enough of that," I said. "Let's do something normal. Let's see what ordinary people do in the evening—you know, just by way of contrast."

Zofia looked dubious. Tom shrugged. But Mark was all for it. He had one of those over-earnest guidebooks to Europe's nooks and crannies. "There's a wild boar restaurant," he said, flipping through the guide's back pages. "It's supposed to have local color." Zofia looked very dubious.

We found the restaurant, at the corner of two dark streets. It was called Dzik, which means "wild boar." A political argument was raging as we came in. Two elderly and very inebriated men were shouting nose to nose.

FIRST OLD SOUSE: "Reagan's our man!"

SECOND OLD SOUSE: "He's a prick!"

FIRST OLD SOUSE: "Reagan and Gorbachev, they're both pricks!"

SECOND OLD SOUSE: "Not Reagan! Reagan's our man!"

Zofia translated and said, being serious, I think, "There is a wide range of political opinion in Poland, fundamentally it is pro-American."

"The only pro-American country in Europe," said Tom, "except for maybe Czechoslovakia and Hungary."

We sat down and ordered vodka. An ancient bag lady clumped in and began screaming at a woman at the table next to ours. I asked Zofia to translate this, also. "It is very vivid language," she said.

"Remarkable colloquialisms," said Tom, and he pulled out a notebook and began to scribble. The waitresses leaned against the walls, listening intently to the tirade. The cook came out of the kitchen and listened, too.

"The nicest thing she's said so far is that the woman at the table is a whore," said Zofia.

The bag lady stumbled out and stumbled back and started over again. This somehow set off a fight between two men who didn't seem to have anything to do with either of the women. They cuffed and wrestled their way across the room until the head waiter reluctantly pried them apart. But one of the men was too drunk to stand up without the support of the fellow who had been slugging him. He fell onto our table, which flipped into the air catapulting vodka and Mark (who'd been leaning his elbows on the dirty place mat) across the room. Nobody made a move to clean up. We changed seats.

A large and extraordinarily unwashed young man came up and jabbered at us. "He says his name is Zygmunt," said Tom, "and he wants to shake our hands because we are Americans." We each shook the fellow's filthy mitt. Three minutes later he came back and said his name was Zygmunt and he wanted to shake our hands. This continued through dinner. When we left, the fight victim was snoring on the sidewalk. "I usually try to pull them into a doorway," said Tom, "so the police won't get them." But this one was too befouled to touch.

The wild boar, by the way, wasn't bad. Pig meat in any form is pretty good in Poland. Everything else except the beer and vodka is horrid. You could use the beef for tennis balls, the bread for hockey pucks and the mashed potatoes to make library paste. If you swallow any of the gravy, do not induce vomiting. Call a physician immediately. I had mentioned to Tom that we should probably avoid fresh, leafy vegetables because of the recent Chernobyl contamination. He almost choked laughing. "If you *see* a fresh, leafy vegetable, let someone know," he said, "they'll want to announce it on television as a triumph of state planning."

The subject on which I was supposed to be reporting was not, as you may have guessed, very interesting. The only thing that seemed to set Polish rock apart from the rest of Europe's colorless pop music was a certain dark and somber tone. I talked to an American exchange student who'd been kicked out of *Dupa* ("Ass"), a Krakow Cold Wave band, because his guitar playing "wasn't gloomy enough."

But the meetings that Interpress set up with musicians, producers, studio engineers, etc., *were* interesting—morbid and horrible, but interesting. It's amazing what obstacles are thrown in the way of work-a-day existence when the government is bigger than the country it governs and bureaucracy encompasses all animate and most inanimate objects. I talked to music-makers, but, if they'd been brain surgeons, architects or biochemists, only the details of frustration would have been different.

Every song, whether it's to be recorded or performed in concert or even sung in the smallest club, must be submitted to the censor board. "Poland is the only country in the Eastern Bloc that admits to having censorship," a Polish record producer told me, with something akin to pride. The censors look for political meaning and sexual innuendo. They may veto a whole song or bowdlerize it line by line. As a result, lyrics tend to be Dylanesque. But, unlike old Minnesota Mud Throat, Poles have good reason to be cryptic. Zbig Holdys, leader of *Perfect*, which I was told was the best Polish band of the eighties, went too far with his song, "There Is No God."

> There is a tear on the altar
> A little bit smaller than a drop of blood
> There is nothing else on the altar
> Not even a drop of blood

Any content is suspect. The Commies objected even though they're supposed to be atheists.

In Poland a Fender guitar costs between 150,000 and 200,000 zloyts. There are only about five officially sanctioned places to play in the whole country. I visited one of the best sound studios. It had sixteen tracks. To do a proper final mix the tape has to be taken to West Germany. It's impossible to say how many records the most popular groups could sell. There's a shortage of record plastic. But the Poles plug along, keeping up with the trends. The music videos I saw were no worse than MTV's, though many had been shot on 8mm home-movie film. The synthesizer tunes I heard were done on the kind of electric keyboards we used to have at roller rinks, but the results weren't any dippier than the new Prince album. All this jury-rigging was admirable, but it was like watching genius high school sophomores tinkering in the rec room with dad's dictaphone. And the people I talked to were no happier than genius high school sophomores usually are.

I had some drinks with an extraordinary rock critic I'll call Kazimierz. Indeed, I had a great many drinks with him. We sat down with a bottle of vodka at three in the afternoon and drank—Polish style—two-ounce shots taken at a gulp until the bottle was gone. Then somebody stopped by his house with another bottle and we drank that.

Kazimierz is a *vade mecum* of popular music from Johnny Ace to Joy Division. He's a well-known editor and commentator in Poland and a popular disc jockey and journalist. He speaks English, German and Russian. And he lives with his mother in a housing development.

The housing development was a high-rise, but with freight-elevator-style electric lift and steel stairs and doors. The apartment had three tiny rooms. The walls were concrete, of course. It was a sort of basement in the sky. And here was Kazimierz, an educated, hard-working man of forty, with only an eight-by-ten-foot bedroom to call his own. We didn't talk about music for long.

"I was working overseas when martial law came," said Kazimierz. "I was terrified of what might be happening here. It took me six months to get back in the country. And all that time I could get no news about anyone I knew. When I landed at the airport, I saw the ZOMO, the new riot police that had just been constituted. And they were standing at the airport eating ice cream cones. At that moment I knew they were human. I knew there was hope."

And that was all the hope he had to cling to, just that the enemy was human. "This country has not had a hopeful history," I said.

"I'll tell you a Polish joke you may understand now," said Kazimierz. "It explains something about our national survival. One Pole is telling another about his visit to America. He says, 'I went to see a fellow and he fixed us drinks.'

'Yes,' says the second Pole.

'Then do you know what he did?' says the first.

'No,' says the second.

'He put the cap back on the bottle!' "

I asked Kazimierz what had happened to Solidarity. "I haven't heard anyone mention Lech Walesa," I said, "except one American reporter."

"No one cares about that any more. It's old history," said Kazimierz. "Only people from the West think it means anything anymore."

We drank ourselves blind. In the next room Kazimierz's mother sat between narrow slab walls, stolidly watching government TV. My notes are a jumble. I can make almost nothing of them, except at the bottom of one page, in wobbly, painstaking letters I've written: "We have no weapons and no chances. No weapons and no church. We live in a land that's not ours."

On the day before I left I took a long walk with Zofia. "I'd like to see the West," she said.

"Can you leave?"

"If you are of a certain level, it can be arranged. But you need an invitation, a job or a sponsor of some kind. Do you think I could find a job in the West?"

"Zofia, you're fluent in what, Polish, English, German, Spanish and Arabic?"

"Yes. But I am only fair in Russian and Latin."

"And you have how many higher degrees?"

"Nearly three now."

"Zofia, you'd have to carry a pistol to keep from being made president of the World Bank. Would you defect?"

P. J. O'Rourke
. . . .

"No. It would break my parents' hearts. My father fought in the resistance. He is not a Communist but he belongs to the Peasant's Party, that is allied with the government." Zofia shrugged, "Besides, this is my country. I should see it through."

We were walking down Nowy Swiat Street in front of the offices of the Central Committee of the Polish United Workers' Party, which is what the Communists call themselves in Poland. Zofia said, "This will sound strange to you, but when the army took over and martial law was first declared, there was hope somehow. The army has always had prestige—for their bravery against the Germans in 1939 and the Russians in the 1920s and so on. All the reserves were called up, all the young men. When we saw the soldiers at the barricades, they were friends of ours from school—not like the police who come from a different class. General Jaruzelski raised the Polish national flag for the first time next to the Party flag on the Central Committee building." Zofia paused.

"And?" I said.

"And that was all." Zofia gestured to the street, to the lumpy, gray-faced people. "Everything is the same as it was." Then she brightened. "Have you heard about the Russian and American generals? They are arguing about who has the best troops. The Russian general says, 'We feed our troops one thousand calories a day.' The American general says, 'We feed our troops *three thousand* calories a day. 'Nonsense!' says the Russian general, 'no one can eat an entire sack of potatoes in twenty-four hours.'"

On the way back to my hotel I finally got arrested. Four large policemen blew their whistles and surrounded me on the plaza in front of the Palace of Culture and Science. They hustled me into a police van. One paged through my passport, while the other three glowered menacingly. I met their stares with a steady gaze. They weren't going to break me. I sat in the sweltering van with my legs crossed casually, a faint smile on my lips; I was determined to let no emotion show. I fancied they'd rarely dealt with as cool a customer as I. And I'd composed the lead sentence and first two paragraphs of the *New York Times* story about my arrest on trumped-up espionage charges before they got it across that I'd been nabbed for jaywalking. I was fined $2.

* * *

So I didn't become a prisoner of conscience or see any salt
mines or brain washing in Poland—that would have been too
exciting. And I didn't see any Evil Empire—that would have been
too interesting. Communism doesn't really starve or execute that
many people. Mostly it just bores them to death. Life behind the
Iron Curtain is like living with your parents forever—literally, in
many cases. There are a million do's and dont's. It's a hassle getting
the car keys. No, life behind the Iron Curtain is worse than that.
It's Boy Scout Camp—dusty; dilapidated; crummy food; lousy
accommodations; and asshole counselors with whistles. TWEET!
"Count off by threes!" TWEET! TWEET! "Who short-sheeted the
politburo?"TWEET! TWEET! TWEET! "A good Pole is loyal, help-
ful, obedient . . ." It's reveille and the buddy system and liver and
Kool-Aid and capture the flag for all eternity; and Mom and Dad
will never come to get you—they're snoring in the next bunk.

Is it worth risking nuclear war and the annihilation of mankind to avoid living like this? Don't ask anybody who just got back
from Warsaw.

Weekend Getaway: Heritage USA

JANUARY 1987
My friend Dorothy and I spent a weekend at Heritage USA, the born-again Christian resort and amusement park created by television evangelists Jim and Tammy Bakker, who have been so much in the news. Dorothy and I came to scoff—but went away converted.

Unfortunately, we were converted to Satanism. Now we're up half the night going to witch's sabbaths and have to spend our free time reciting the Lord's Prayer backward and scouring the neighborhood for black dogs to sacrifice. Frankly, it's a nuisance, but if it keeps us from going to the Heritage USA part of heaven, it will be worth it.

Just kidding. In fact, we didn't actually come to Heritage USA to scoff. At least I didn't. I came because I was angry. Normally I take a live-and-let-live attitude toward refried Jesus-wheezing TV preachers. They've got their role in life, and I've got mine. Their role is to be sanctimonious panhandlers. My role is to have a good time. They don't pray for cocaine and orgies. I don't go on the tube and ask people to send me $100. But, when a place like Heritage

USA starts advertising fun in the sun and Heritage's founders start
having drug blasts and zany extramarital frolics, I feel they're
stepping on my turf.

Heritage USA is a fair-size chunk of Christendom, 2,300
acres. It's half an hour from the go-go New South Sun Belt town of
Charlotte, North Carolina—just over the border into the poky Old
South Bible Belt county of York, South Carolina. The Heritage
entrance gate appears to be a colonial Williamsburg turnpike toll
plaza. Admission is free, however. Inside the gate you have the
same vaguely depressing pine barrens that you have outside. A
dozen roads meander through the scrub with the sly pur-
poselessness of burglary lookouts.

Not that Heritage USA is an "empty vessel" (Jeremiah 51:34).
By no means. Recreation facilities are "ministered unto you abun-
dantly" (II Peter 1:11). There are playgrounds, kiddie rides, bridle
paths, tennis courts and swimming pools, where I guess you have to
lose faith at least temporarily or you'll just stand around on top of
the water. And there are vacation cottages for rent and condo homes
for sale, plus campgrounds and acres of gravel to park your Winnebago on. You can see the house where Billy Graham grew up and
make *Amityville Horror* jokes about it. A golf course is being laid
out. I'll rush back as soon as it's done, to hear what new kinds of
blasphemy Christian golf leads to:

"The rough ways shall be made smooth"

—*Luke 3:5*

"Thou shalt not lift up any iron."

—*Deuteronomy 7:5*

"This cup is the New Testament in my blood."

—*I Corinthians 11:25*

"I will put my hook in thy nose."

—*II Kings 19:28*

And you can visit the world headquarters of PTL, which is in the
middle of a huge scandal right now, just like a real television
network.

Midst these lesser marvels is an artificial lake with a fifty-two-foot water slide and the world's largest wave-making pool. A little choo-choo train goes all the way around the lake shore. And across from the train station is an enormous hotel, shopping mall, theater, restaurant and indoor inspirational loitering center.

The architects must have been touched by the holy spirit because they were definitely speaking the language of design in tongues when they did this. At one end there's the Heritage Grand Hotel—Georgian on steroids, Monticello mated with a Ramada Inn and finished in Wendy's Old Fashioned Hamburgers gothic. This is attached to a two-hundred-yard stretch of bogus Victorian house fronts, which screen the shopping mall. The house fronts have extruded plastic gingerbread details and are painted in colors unfit for baboon posteriors. Interesting that the same God who inspired the cathedral at Chartres, Westminster Abbey and the Sistine Chapel also inspired this. That Big Guy Upstairs can be a real kidder.

The Christmas decorations were still up at Heritage. From the entrance gate all the way to the water slide, the place was festooned with Yule lights and other pagan symbols of the season—tinseled evergreens, holly wreaths, snowmen, candy canes. But no Santa Claus. His elves were there, stuffing stockings and wrapping presents, but Santa himself was nowhere to be found. When we walked into the hotel lobby, carolers were singing:

> *You'd better not frown,*
> *You'd better not cry,*
> *You'd better not pout,*
> *I'm telling you why.*
> *Jesus Christ is coming real soon.*

And I thought Heritage USA was going to be dumb. But I'd only been there fifteen minutes and I was already confronted by enough serious theological questions to send St. Thomas Aquinas back to Bible college. Did Santa die on the cross? Will he be resurrected at Macy's? Were Christ's disciples really elves? When the second coming happens, will Jesus bring toy trains?

While I puzzled over these mysteries Dorothy went shopping.

She's normally as good at this as any human female. But she was back in minutes with no bags or packages and a dazed, perplexed expression, like a starved Ethiopian given a piece of wax fruit. What could be the matter?

We went into the bookstore and I found out. There on the shelves were personal affirmations of faith by Roy Rogers and Dale Evans, a born-again diet plan, a transcription of the horrible (though rather unimaginative) things you can hear if you play rock and roll records backward, and a weighty tome arguing that every time the New Testament says "wine" it really means "grape juice." But I couldn't find anything you'd actually call a book. The Bibles themselves had names like *A Bible Even You Can Read* and *The Bible in English Just Like Jesus Talked*.

Then we went into the music store. It was the same thing. There were racks of tapes and records by Christian pop groups, Christian folk groups, Christian heavy-metal groups, Christian reggae groups, all of them singing original compositions about the Lord. No album was actually titled *I Found God and Lost My Talent*, but I'm sure that was just an oversight. There was even a "Christian Rap Music" cassette called *Bible Break*:

> *The Bible is the holy book*
> *So let's open it up and take a look*
> *You got Genesis*
> *Exodus*
> *Leviticus*
> *Deuteronomy*

And so on to Revelations with complete lack of rhythm or meter. (I was witnessing a miracle, I was sure, or auditing one anyway: Here was something that sounded worse than genuine rap.)

The toy store was weirder yet. The stuffed toys had names like "Born-Again Bunny" and "Devotion Duck." A child-size panoply of biblical weapons was for sale, including a "shield of righteousness," a "helmet of faith," and a "sword of truth" that looked ideal for a "clobber of little sister." And there were biblical action figures—a Goliath with a bashed skull, David looking fruity in a goat-skin sarong, Samson and Delilah as Arnold Schwarzenegger

and Maria Shriver. "Comes seductively dressed" read the sell copy
on Delilah's bubble pack. Here was a shopper's hell indeed.

I looked at the people crowding the Heritage "Main Street"
mall. They didn't seem to be having much fun. Many of them were
old, none looked very well-off. There was a dullness in their
movements and expressions. Even the little kids looked somber
and thick. In the men's room stall where I went to sneak a cigarette
there were only four bits of graffiti:

> *Do you know were [sic] you wife is at*
> *Jesus is #1*
> 666
> Please don't mark these walls

The last scratched into the paint with a key or pocketknife.

I almost don't have the heart to make fun of these folks. It's
like hunting dairy cows with a high-powered rifle and scope. Then
again, I have to consider what they'd do to me if they caught me
having my idea of a vacation—undressed bimbo in a sleazy Florida
hotel room, bottle of Vaseline Intensive Care lotion, some drugged
wine. . . . In fact, you already know what they did when they
caught Jim Bakker. Heck, they want to hang the likes of Jim and
me. And all I want to do is rib them a little.

I've always figured that if God wanted us to go to church a lot
He'd have given us bigger behinds to sit on and smaller heads to
think with. But God or carbohydrates or something had done that
for these people. They all had huge bottoms, immense bottoms. It
looked like everyone in the place had stuffed a chair cushion down
the back of his leisure slacks. And what leisure slacks! Heal them,
oh Lord, for they are injured in the taste buds. Dorothy and I had
dressed quietly for the occasion. But my button-down shirt and
chinos and her blue blazer and tartan skirt made us stick out like
nude calypso dancers. We were wearing the only natural fibers for
2,300 acres in any direction.

"You know what you've got here?" I said to Dorothy. "This is
white trash behaving itself—the only thing in the world worse than
white trash *not* behaving itself."

"Shhhh!" said Dorothy. "That's mean."

"These people aren't having any fun," I said. "They should join the Klan. They'd be better off. They could hoot and holler and what-not. The Klan doesn't do all that much really bad stuff anymore because there are too many FBI double agents in it. And if these folks joined the Klan, they could smoke and drink again. Plus, they'd get to wear something halfway decent, like an all-cotton bed sheet."

"P.J.!" said Dorothy, "Stop it! Everybody can hear you."

"I'm serious," I said. "All you people, you really ought to. . ." Dorothy slapped a hand over my mouth and pulled me outside.

The next day, Dorothy and I pretended to be married and went house hunting in the Christian condominium sub-development. The homes were mostly free-standing ranch jobs built on slab foundations and supplied with a couple hundred dollars of old-timey exterior trim. Each unit is supposedly built to order, but neither the designs nor the floor plans can be altered. (What God and contractor have joined together let no man put asunder.) Condo prices range from $128,000 to $144,000. I checked the real estate sections in the local papers, and this seemed to be almost a third again the going rate.

The model homes showed no special religious features, no Last Supper–style dining areas, walk-on-the-water beds or total-immersion adult-baptismal pools in the johns. There was also a sad lack of evangelical hard sell. Dorothy and I had hoped for a real estate sales person who spoke in tongues, not that real estate persons don't usually.

Instead, there was a lonely-looking middle-aged lady with a layer of Tammy Bakker–style makeup. "Now, I live by myself here," she said, "but gosh there are so many things going on I never have a moment to feel lonely." She was interrupted by a phone call from Maine. "Excuse me," she said, "this lady is calling from all the way up in Maine."

The caller was, I gathered, very elderly.

"Yes," said the real estate lady on the phone, "you can live right here at Heritage USA. . . . No, Jim and Tammy don't actually live at the Heritage Center. . . . But they live real close by. . . .

P. J. O'Rourke
· ·

No, dear, you shouldn't buy something you haven't even seen. . . .
Well, maybe you can get your minister to drive you down."

We slipped out during the phone call, feeling a little creepy.
Something is drawing forlorn old ladies and poor, morose families
to Heritage USA. Five million of them came in 1985. It can't be
Jesus doing a thing like that. He's a compassionate guy, isn't He?

We took one more walk through the Heritage mall. I was
eavesdropping hard, hoping for some final, telling quote. No luck.

Everybody was on good behavior just like the day before.
There were no screaming toddlers, no running kids, no griping
adults. It was like being in the First Church of Christ Hanging Out
at the Mall. Dorothy heard a jewelry salesman tell his customer, "It
has a life-time guarantee—or until Jesus returns, whichever."

A goody-two-shoes treacle seemed to flow sluggishly through
the place, and I think it was making Dorothy a little crazy. She kept
tugging on my coat sleeve and whispering that we should go behind
a Coke machine or in a mop closet or someplace and "pet." They
must have this problem a lot at Heritage USA because all the Coke
machines were right out in the middle of the rooms and the mop
closets were locked. We tried a stairwell, but it had a floor-to-
ceiling window opening to the hotel lobby.

And that was when it dawned on me. There's only one expla-
nation for Heritage USA. Jim and Tammy were *working for the other
side*. Their own recent behavior seems to make that obvious. And
consider the other evidence: a bookstore without books, a record
shop without music—what else could these be but the vain and
empty works of the devil? And Heritage USA has lots of rules and
ugly architecture just like communist Russia, that den of Satan.
And don't forget that fundamentalism prohibits premarital sex, yet
you can't have a proper Black Mass without using a naked virgin as
an altar. Put two and two together—it's not a pretty picture.
Furthermore, as a result of our visit to Heritage USA, Dorothy and I
had committed every one of the seven deadly sins:

> **Pride**—Looking at our fellow visitors had turned us into awful
> snobs.
> **Wrath**—We wanted to murder the architects.
> **Lust**—If we could have found an open mop closet.

Holidays In Hell

. . . .

Avarice—By proxy (Jim and Tammy Bakker, as founders of Heritage USA, had committed this sin for us.)

Envy—How come Jim and Tammy get to live so high on the hog? Why didn't *we* think of Heritage USA?

Gluttony—For a quick drink.

Sloth—We spent three days in bed recovering from the drunk we went on after we got out of there.

This is no way to have fun. Everybody likes a good laugh, and there's nothing wrong with that. But on this year's vacation steer clear of Heritage USA. For the sake of your immortal soul, stay home and take drugs and have sex the way Jim and Tammy do. (After all, I understand they've been forgiven.)

98

The Post-Marcos Philippines—
Life in the Archipelago After One
Year of Justice, Democracy and
Things Like That
· ·

MARCH 1987

Well, everything's fine in the Philippines now. Smelly old Marcos has been given the gate and earnest, Catholic, good-to-the-bone Cory Aquino is president. Everyone in the country has a fulfilling career. All those cardboard houses down in the Manila slums are being gentrified—track lighting, redwood decks, nickel-plated Victorian plumbing fixtures from Renovator's Supply. The citizens of the Philippines are rich and happy. They won't go Communist or get another corrupt and egomaniacal dictator for at least a week.

I was nine years old when I fell in love with the Philippines. My father had been there during World War II, practically the only place he'd ever been outside Ohio. He was a salesman who had wanted to be an engineer. He'd taken some night courses but, what with the Depression and a family to support, it never happened. Yet for one moment he *was* an engineer, a chief petty officer in the Navy Construction Battalions, the CBs, building docks, warehouses and barracks in the Philippines.

Holidays In Hell

When my father died in 1956, I found his photo albums from the war. To a more sophisticated kid, the Philippines might not have seemed like much. Famous for what, house boys and ugly mahogany water buffalo carvings? But to me, in Toledo, Ohio, the Philippines represented everything I could hope for in the way of romance. The albums were filled with pictures of burned-out Jap tanks, bomb craters and sunk LSTs and also of lustrous beaches, mangrove-edged lagoons and ancient Spanish mission churches. There were pictures of my dad, not the pale, workaday dad I'd known, but a thin, tanned guy in faded khakis with one foot on the bumper of a Jeep and a Lucky jammed in the corner of his mouth. That dad had a smile I don't think you can get in Ohio. And, at the back of one of the albums, folded behind a flap of paper, were pictures of Philippine women—dark, smooth, small, beautiful women who seemed to have misplaced their bathing suits.

It was thirty years before I got to the Philippines, but the islands were no disappointment. I arrived in February 1986, in the midst of the Marcos ouster. I found adventure and excitement; in fact, I saw more action than my father had. (His battalion went through the whole war with only one casualty—a palm tree fell on somebody.) The country was as exotic and the people were as attractive as I'd known they would be. I met a young woman I liked very much, a Filipino journalist named Tina Luz, with anthracite hair and the most beautiful color skin I've ever seen—something between peanut butter and bronze. And the society, culture and politics of the Philippines were unfathomable, desperate, violent and strange, which is a large part of what romance is all about.

I was there for a month and spent the next year trying to wrangle a way back. I invented dozens of journalistic "hooks" for Philippine articles. I told my editors at *Rolling Stone* that each bungled coup attempt was the hottest story since Morton Thiokol used the Challenger to move teacher hazing into the space age. "The Philippines are Democracy with its thumb in the door hinge of history," I'd bluster. "Civilization-as-we-know-it is walking the balance beam in the political gymnastics of death." And other such. Finally, on the first anniversary of the Cory takeover, they gave in.

* * *

P. J. O'Rourke
· ·

I returned to Manila to find myself a hero, sort of. Each of the one thousand plus members of the foreign press who'd been present at the Marcos heave-ho was made a "Hero of the Revolution." There was an austerely dignified award ceremony. By that I mean we had to buy our own drinks—in clear violation of the international journalists' code of truth, fairness and an open bar. But Cory Aquino came to thank us in person for having suddenly discovered, in 1986, that Marcos was a pig. "Joe Rorke from *Rolling* magazine," said the master of ceremonies. I mounted the podium, and General Ramos, the Philippine Army chief of staff, put the medal around my neck as canned applause played on the PA system.

It's a silly-looking medal, showing a hand making the pro-Cory LABAN–coalition "L" sign with a little happy face on the tip of the upraised index finger. But it's the only medal I'm ever going to get, and, hell, I'm proud.

"Freedom Week," as the anniversary of the Cory revolution was called, was choked with self-congratulatory festivities—songwriting contests, public-speaking competitions, a display of children's art about "people power," fireworks, street dances and eleven million Catholic masses. Dignitaries and various fans of social justice arrived from all over the world. Even Peter, Paul and Mary came to play. The Filipinos were pretty sure they were famous. Everybody recognized "Puff the Magic Dragon," anyway, and sang along.

"We were in El Salvador in 1983 and in Nicaragua last year," a fervent Mary Travers said to the puzzled crowd, who didn't see what that had to do with anything. The Cory government was supposed to get *rid* of communists.

On the last day of Freedom Week a million and a half people shoved themselves into the avenue along the front of Camp Carne. Camp Carne is the military base where Defense Minister Enrile and Chief of Staff Ramos had announced the revolt that brought Cory to power. Marcos sent loyalist troops to snuff the coup, and unarmed civilians (though rather less than a million and a half of them) blocked tanks and armored personnel carriers with their bodies.

Camp Carne's gates were opened for the anniversary. Some of the troops inside had already been involved in another revolt—

101

against Cory. And six months later nearly half of them would rise up in more stupid mutiny. But, today, they were all smiles. You could tell it was a special occasion because the soldiers had their shoes on.

A thousand vendors sold mementos of the revolution, all of them yellow, Cory's campaign color, and most of them bearing Mrs. Aquino's likeness. One T-shirt said simply, "I Am A Filipino." But what passes for a size XL in the Philippines splits right down the beer gut when I put it on.

There were lots of speeches. It was hard to tell who was making them or where. But loudspeakers had been nailed to all the phone poles so everyone could hear. Filipinos enjoy a good political diatribe. But in the hopelessly decent Cory administration rhetorical bombast is always trimmed with polite qualifications. "Professionals, students, rich and poor embraced themselves and fought," bellowed the kick-off speaker, "*almost* nonviolently against what we *thought* might be an autocratic government."

The autocrats themselves were by no means gnashing their cosmetic orthodontia. The parking lot at the Manila Polo Club was as full of Range Rovers and BMWs as it had been in Marcos days. The club was holding a "Freedom Cup" match to celebrate the revolution and decide the Philippine polo championship. A priest blessed the ponies with a squirt bottle full of holy water and then prayed at length for Cory and her government. The Hermès-scarfed and Ralph Lauren–shirted crowd (People at polo matches actually *do* wear Polo-brand clothes, at least in the Philippines.) prayed along and applauded vigorously.

Meanwhile, Manila was the same squalid mess it's always been.

Cory Aquino is the most upright, kindly and honorable person running a country today. Given the other people running countries, that's probably safe to say. And there doesn't seem to be anything particularly wrong with the men and women she's got helping her, especially compared with the pack of muck spouts, scissors bills, jacklegs and goons who used to be in charge. But it would be nice if cashews on the top always meant ice cream on the bottom. It would be nice if swell national leaders meant instant peace and plenty.

P. J. O'Rourke
....

There are more than 57 million Filipinos spread across 7,107 islands. Almost every island has a communist or moslem insurrection of some kind. Per capita income is $652 a year. It seems hard to find an army officer who isn't ready to toss a coup d'état. And pages could be filled just listing the country's other problems. It would be amazing if the Cory government even knew where to start.

One of the features of Freedom Week was an inventor's convention. It was a modest affair. Most of the inventions had to do with improved charcoal braziers for home heat and better ways to spread water buffalo dung. But there was one very complicated mechanical device with a hand-lettered sign taped on the front:

MACH-7 SUPER MACHINE
Compact and Portable
90% Local Materials
Durable, All Metal Parts
Very Simple and Practical
Will Create Job Opportunities for the Out-of-School Youth

Here was a paradigm of the Aquino administration—nowhere on that sign did it say what the MACH-7 SUPER MACHINE was supposed to *do*.

I asked Franco, the driver I'd hired for the duration of my stay, if things were better since Cory took over.

"Oh, yes," he said. "There are lots of firecrackers. This was forbidden before."

Some things *had* changed in Manila. There was a new statue of Cory's husband, the martyred Ninoy Aquino, in the Makati business district. Ninoy is portrayed on the steps of an airline ramp, at the moment the assassin's bullets hit him. The original bronze casting had a clear plastic rod, with a dove of peace mounted on top, emerging from Ninoy's left clavicle. This made the hero of the anti-Marcos opposition look like he was getting crapped on by a pigeon. So the rod was removed and the bird attached directly to the shoulder, for a Long John Silver effect. Ninoy now looks like a drunk pirate in a business suit falling down the cellar stairs.

The police were easier to bully, at least if you were a "Hero of the Revolution." Franco had nipped a big "ABC PRESS" placard from the Manila hotel and stuck it in the front window of his car. This was enough to get us waved through most of the nighttime roadblocks set up around Manila, supposedly to keep communist infiltrators from coming to town. But one evening I was on the way back from a party with Tina and Black Star photographer John Giannini. Some grubby-looking over-armed cops motioned us over for a search.

"They think I'm a prostitute," said Tina. "See, the sergeant is unscrewing his flashlight already. That's where he hides his payoffs."

"Rank him out in Tagalog," said Giannini.

"Believe me," said Tina, "it would be much better if I speak English."

Giannini, who is a big guy, got out of the car. "Just what's the problem here?"

"Well," said the policeman, "we are holding these roadblocks of narcotics, illegal guns, robberies and guerrillas."

"We don't have any," said John.

"Well," said the policeman, "when we were seeing two foreign journalists with a Filipina . . ."

"*Three* foreign journalists," said John. "Miss Luz here works for *The Washington Post.*"

Washington Post? Big nervous smiles from all the police. They knew what had happened to the last strong-arm type who ran afoul of the Yankee newshogs—he's ass-canned and stuck off in exile with his fat, crazy wife and her shoe collection. "Please be our guest to go," said the sergeant.

Other things, I didn't have the heart to go see whether they'd changed or not. There's a ski slope–size pile of rotting, burning trash on the north side of town called Smokey Mountain. A thousand people, many of them sick and dying, live in the filth. I never want to go back there. There are some kinds of desolation that leave you impotent in the fucking that's life. I could turn my pockets out for the Smokey Mountain residents, but that wouldn't go far. I could throw up, but I don't see how that would help. I could pester the dump-pickers as I had in '86 and write it up in a colorful way and make a buck off the thing, which is what I guess I'm doing anyway. I asked Giannini, who'd just been to shoot the place for Black Star, if Smokey Mountain had changed since Marcos.

"It's bigger," he said.

"But are the people any better off?"

"Yeah, they've got more garbage."

Of course *I* was happy in Manila. I had Franco standing by with the car. I had a big room at the Manila Hotel, General MacArthur's wartime HQ. No doubt, if I hung around long enough, somebody'd take another whack at insurrection, and I could write about that. Meanwhile, I spent my afternoons by the hotel pool and lolled through sunset cocktails at Tina's house, chaperoned by the maid her father had sent up from the family sugar plantation on Negros Island. Some of the local journalists chartered a boat, and we went sailing on Manila Bay. We drank at the servicemen's bars on Mabini Street and joked with the lackadaisical, semi-naked go-go dancers. We went to parties and dances. There is suffering on earth, I know. And plenty of that suffering is in the Philippines. But, if I can't subtract from the world's sum of misery, do I have to add to it personally? It's one of these questions I mean to take up if I ever get religion.

Unfortunately, the phone messages and telexes from *Rolling Stone* were beginning to pile up. "What are you doing over there?" "What the *hell* are you doing over there?" "What is this story *supposed to be about?*" etc. I had to earn my keep. I had to go explain why the Philippines hadn't immediately turned into Japan or Singapore when Cory took over. And I had to find some nastiness to illustrate the problem. "No bodies, no by-lines," as journalists say.

Up in the hills the communist NPA, the New Peoples Army, was plugging along with its decade-old civil war. That might be a good excuse to stay for another couple of weeks. However, the NPA were press-shy at the moment. They'd had a cease-fire with the Cory government and some peace talks, but, when the communists found out Cory wasn't going to give them a hug and hand them the country, they coped a mope. My fellow reporters were lined up all over Manila waiting on NPA contacts so they could slog through the hills and get an earful of Bolshi gripes. Some had been waiting for more than a month.

I complained to Franco. "If I just keep going to polo games," I said, "and working on my tan and taking Tina out to dinner, sooner or later my editors are going to catch on and I'll be covering the Bon Jovi Iowa tour. I've got to find some trouble to get into."

"You want to talk to NPA?" said Franco. "My Uncle Carlos is NPA, the brother of my wife's mother. I will take you there tomorrow already, to Marlita, in Pampanga province."

"But, Franco," I said, "you're a real *Coryista*."

"Oh, yes."

"Don't you argue with your uncle?"

Franco looked confounded. "We go a couple times in the year to see the family of my wife," he said, as if that explained any possible political contradiction. This wasn't exactly like the American Civil War—where brother fought brother and all that.

So I got up at dawn the next day. The front-page story was headlined, COP CHIEF SLAIN IN AMBUSH.

"The Police Chief of San Luis, Pampanga," read the lead, "was killed in an ambush shortly before noon yesterday by jeepney riding communist rebels . . ." San Luis was the town next to Marlita.

About thirty kilometers from Marlita Franco and I stopped for a cup of coffee. A teenage kid gave me a careful look and then jumped on a motor tricycle and sped up the road. Franco nudged me. "You see, they know you already."

I'm not sure what I was expecting in the uncle—an addled old veteran of the Fifties Communist HUK rebellion I guess—certainly not the fat and amiable politician who greeted us at the door of a cement six-room house, the only sizable home in the village. Franco's Uncle Carlos had been a barrio captain in Marlita for sixteen years. There was a pickup truck in the carport and an immense color television in the living room draped in a sort of chintz slipcover with tassel-fringed curtains pulled back to reveal the screen. Professional wrestling played the whole time we were there. Full liquor bottles were displayed around the room along with the kind of large china dogs won at carnival booths.

"People here like the NPA," said Carlos. "If things are stolen, the NPA will help. Once you need the help, if you are right, the NPA will help you. But if you are wrong . . ." Carlos made a grave face. I'm willing to bet he's recently seen *The Godfather* on that color TV. ". . . they may be the ones to kill you."

"I understand there was a little trouble over in San Luis," I ventured. I didn't know if the police chief bump-off was a touchy subject or what.

"Hah!" said Carlos. "The police chief shot for corruption! The third police chief in Pampanga this year!" Apparently it wasn't a touchy subject.

"He was charging ten pesos to each person for each load of vegetables to go to Manila. People complained to the NPA."

Then Carlos started in on the mayor of Marlita. "The mayor here, if his son has a birthday, he will tell the barrio captain, 'You give me one big pig, one sack of rice.' The barrio captain has to collect it," said Carlos, pointing at himself. "The NPA is always helping people," he added ominously. So, Mr. Mayor, if you happen to read this, I recommend you look for other work.

"How many NPA are around here, anyway?" I said.

"One or two only—by day," said Carlos and winked. "Group by group at night."

As we talked, a number of young men were strolling too casually in and out of the barrio captain's house. I gathered the NPA guerrillas were trying to make up their minds whether to schmooze, shoot me or skedaddle. Mrs. Carlos kept stuffing us with food—sugar rolls, heaps of steaming rice, fresh eggs and beef stew from a can (canned foods, like the full liquor bottles, are rural status symbols) and jugs of iced water, iced tea and Pepsi Cola, all this at ten in the morning. Just before I burst, word came the NPA would chat.

Carlos, Franco and I drove along a levee through the rice paddies to another barrio two kilometers away. It was a group of forty little houses on a rise. Small children, the watchdogs of Philippine villages, could see everything that approached. Dozens of paths spread from the barrio toward Mount Arayat, where the guerrillas hide. Dozens of vapor trails spread in the sky, too, from F-16s. The NPA's Mount Arayat base and the U.S.A.'s Clark Air Force Base are twenty kilometers apart.

Although the Pampanga River runs through Marlita, the rice paddies were parched and fallow. Carlos said it had been a dry winter, too dry for a second rice crop. "What about irrigation?" I asked.

He shrugged. "The irrigation pump is broken."

We drove by it, a little gasoline job the size of a rider-mower engine. They were killing each other over nickel-and-dime corruption in these villages, while the wealth of the entire community could be doubled with one high-school shop-class water-pump fix-it project. Understand that and you can understand the whole Third World. And please phone or write if you do.

Once we were inside the second barrio, a dozen kids showed us where to park. We got out of the car, and an old man motioned for us to follow him. He took us to a little house on stilts, weathered black and half-hidden by a bamboo grove.

But the old man wouldn't just let us inside. First he had to lead us through a vegetable patch beside the house and over a fence into a chicken pen in the backyard, out through a hole in the chicken wire, into a pigsty on the other side of the house, over another fence and back to the front door. I guess this was supposed to confuse us as to our exact whereabouts.

The house had no windows. The light came through the bamboo-slat walls and floor as though we were in a world made entirely of Levolor blinds. Seven NPA fighters were sprawled in two tiny rooms. They were finishing a meager lunch—bread crumbs and a couple of dried fish tails were left on two communal plates. Three guns were visible, one Armalite, which is what the Filipinos call the M-16, and two Korean War vintage Chinese Communist infantry rifles. Half a dozen .223-caliber Armalite bullets were arranged neatly on a table in a corner.

The NPA leader was called Commander Melody, not an unusual moniker by Philippine standards. There are Manila tycoons of sixty who call themselves "Boy," stuffy dowagers known as "Baby" and one of Cory's cabinet ministers has the given name "Joker." Commander Melody was in his forties. He was barefoot and dressed in camouflage pants, a sky-blue T-shirt with the logo of the Benedictine Sisters on it, a jean jacket, and a red, white and blue cotton beach hat. His men were only a little younger and

P. J. O'Rourke

* *

clothed more like teenage New York bicycle messengers than Viet Cong. Part of a large, faded tattoo was visible on Commander Melody's ankle, the kind of tattoo worn by Philippine street gangs. The commander had the skinny, somber intensity of an ex-fuck-up.

"How do you feel about Cory Aquino?" I asked. "Is she better than Marcos?"

"Yes. Marcos—a dictator man," said Commander Melody. "Not democracy. If our own new constitution . . ." He trailed off, wrestling with the English. Commander Melody thought for a moment, then made a pronouncement. "We will now surrender over our guns if we can find a good government that we can keep."

This was strange. The NPA national leadership had just announced a new offensive, to carry revolutionary violence into Manila proper. "Do you feel you can surrender to Cory?" I said.

"Yes."

"How about General Ramos? Do you trust Ramos?"

"Yes."

"You can surrender to him."

"Yes."

I was mixed up. "Well why don't you, just, you know, *surrender?*"

Commander Melody told me a story which, I think, was supposed to explain that. He said he'd been an ordinary citizen, driver of a Manila jeepney bus, a jeep with a long covered bed and two beach seats in back. He'd had an accident and killed three policemen. This seemed pretty careless, even considering the way people drive in Manila. Anyway, he'd been sentenced to ten years in prison and had escaped and headed for the hills.

Commander Melody said the NPA was hungry, poor, almost out of bullets and tired too. "Our guys, always climbing mountain, then to barrio, and toward city." He and his men all shrugged like the whole thing was getting to be a pain in the neck.

"Do you consider yourself communists?" I asked—the old 50,000-Casualty Question, *Ground War in Asia* category. This is the only thing Americans ever really want to know. It's how we

109

decide whether to send in Oliver Stone and his platoon of pals to atrocity everybody.

"We are not looking for that," said Commander Melody with some heat. "We don't need a communist country. We know communist countries are dictatorship countries. We are only fighting for our rights."

"But the ideology of the NPA . . ." I mumbled vaguely. One thing they don't teach you at the Close-Cover-Before-Striking School of Journalism is how to badger people who've got guns.

"There are big differences upon our procedures," mumbled Commander Melody, pretty vaguely himself. I guess he was referring to NPA internal snits and quarrels.

I nodded sympathetically. "What would it take to get you to make peace with the Cory government?"

"If you are not rich, you can't do your own business," he said. "Better if Cory makes a lot of factories for poor people to work in." Much better, I would think, but Commander Melody didn't seem to have any specific suggestions about how that was to be done.

"How could the United States help?" I asked.

Commander Melody's eyes lit up, and his mouth dropped open. "They would *help* our organization??!!" He looked like a kid who'd been told that next year would have Christmas on every weekend. It broke my heart to disabuse him.

"No," I said, "I'm afraid not. They think you're communists."

Commander Melody nodded. He'd known all along it was too good to be true. "We have no justice," he said, "so our justices are guns and bullets." He told me they had just completed a mission. (". . . jeepney riding communist rebels," the newspaper had said, and jeepney driving had been Commander Melody's profession before he took up politics.) And he said they delayed another mission just to talk to me.

I took this as a hint for a donation.

Now, nobody hates a commie worse than me. And Commander Melody's line of hooey aside, the New Peoples Army *is* communist. When they were negotiating with Cory, their demands were straight out of the Mickey Maoist Club bylaws. They are red as a baboon's ass, and that means freeze-and-assume-the-position as far as I'm concerned. I've been to your communist countries. They are crap-your-pants-ugly, dull-as-church, dead-from-the-dick-up places where government is to life what panty hose are to sex.

But then I looked at Commander Melody in his Gilligan's Island hat. He and his ragamuffin bunch were sitting there with the entire population of the barrio acting as their lookouts. They were underarmed and underfed, but, you know, I think they were having a good time too. I'd rather be running around the country at night with a gun than sitting in jail. I could understand why they weren't *too* eager to surrender. What the fuck, I gave them a thousand pesos.

Commander Melody held up an Armalite bullet in one hand and my sheaf of peso notes in the other. "This will buy some answers," he said. If they were going to shoot mayors, they couldn't be all bad. Maybe they'd take a shot at Ed Koch.

It was hard to figure what kind of story I could write about Commander Melody's goofy NPA. But it was a flagrantly beautiful afternoon—much too pretty to spend the whole day indoors playing with guns. I'd worry about what to write later. *"Bahala na,"* as the Filipinos say, which is an untranslatable phrase containing the same germ of philosophy as the Arabic *inshalla* or the Spanish *mañana* or the English *you must have me mixed up with somebody who gives a shit.* Franco and I decided to fuck off and take a drive in the country.

It was Sunday, cockfight day. We stopped in the town of Santa Ana, about half an hour south of Marlita. It seemed like the people there hadn't seen an American in ages. They all waved and shouted "Hi, Joe! Hi, Joe!" just like they'd shouted to my dad, forty years ago.

Cockfighting has always been my idea of a great sport—two armed entrées battling to see who'll be dinner. The Santa Ana cockpit was an open-sided structure with grandstands, the most elaborate building in town except the church. The "pit" itself was raised, dirt-floored, about twice the size of a boxing ring and enclosed with blood-smeared glass panels.

The roosters are allowed to peck each other's behinds to get them in a bad mood. Then the owners carry them around for everyone to see. The bookies are right in the ring with the poultry and follow in the wake of the McNuggets display taking bets. If you bet big, you get to sit down in the front and press your nose against the glass. Would "Joe" bet?—a subject of great interest and levity in the audience. The birds are bred not only to be crabby but to have insane plumage. I won 100 pesos on a chicken that looked exactly like David Lee Roth.

I don't know why the ASPCA gets its boxer shorts in a wad every time our Hispanic cousins have a cockfight in the Bronx. This is a lot less violent than the Super Bowl and who wants an extra-crispy quarterback anyway? Each cock gets one razor-steel spur about half the length of a ball-point pen. This is tied on the back of his claw just below the drumstick. The fights are one or two sneezes long and, as a visual spectacle, resemble watching someone kick a down vest with a pointy-toed boot. Feathers fly, spectators holler and—*voilà*—dead clucker. The fun parts are betting and screaming and, especially, arguing the merits of this or that combat fricassee. I was good at this. Nobody spoke English, but that isn't a handicap if you can do a pantomime of Big Bird.

After the main event, one of the owners let me hold his champion—another source of amusement to all. Apparently there is a cool way and a nerd way of holding a fighting cock, and I was the worst chicken grasper anyone had ever seen.

Franco was hungry again, though we'd eaten enough for six at his uncle's house. I wasn't hungry, but the girl running the roadside food stand was so pretty I was willing to stand there and eat things for days if that would keep the gleam in her enormous brown eyes.

Franco bought a disgusting *batok* which is a fertilized duck egg in which the duckling has been allowed to grow until it's almost ready to hatch, then it's hard-boiled. The result looks like an anti-abortion movie produced by the Duckburg branch of the Right-To-Life organization. You eat its little feathers, beak and bones and all. It's bar food in the Philippines. I had a bite and, believe me, *batok* is not going to replace buffalo wings as the USA's favorite happy-hour snack anytime soon.

Then Franco began poking around in a big stew pot. He asked the girl something in Tagalog, and she said, "Aso."

"Ha, ha, ha, ha, ha. Oh, you should have some of this already," said Franco, jabbing me in the ribs and barely able to contain himself.

However, *aso* happens to be one of the few words I understand in Tagalog. "*You* have some," I said.

"Oh, no, no, no," said Franco, taking another bite of duck down. "I'm from Manila. I am a city man, you know. Ha, ha, ha. *You* have some."

I gathered dog was a strictly rural delicacy. The pretty girl was looking expectant, however. And I'd already underwritten a political assassination that day, indulged in the vice of gambling and committed adultery in my heart.

It's dark meat, in case you were wondering, and on the fatty side. Considering what a hot, wet dog smells like, dog stew has a surprisingly savory odor. To tell the truth, it tastes pretty good, like oxtail. To be perfectly honest, it's delicious. (Anything about this to my golden retriever, and I'll punch your lights out.)

"It's supposed to be very *warming*," said Franco. "Good for love. Ha, ha, ha."

Maybe. But I wasn't going to be allowed to gold-brick in Manila and find out. A whole pile of angry telexes from *Rolling Stone* were stuffed under my hotel-room door. It seemed I'd been in the Philippines for two weeks and hardly anybody was dead. There hadn't even been a coup attempt—practically the only two weeks in the Cory regime without one.

Tina suggested I do a story about vigilantes. A lot of people with guns were running around unsupervised in the Philippines. And not all of them were opposed to the government. Armed anti-communist citizen posses were the latest fad. It seemed the NPA was not as welcome everywhere as it was in Marlita.

The largest of these vigilante groups was called Alsa Masa, which translates as "Masses Arise" or "Giddyup Masses," depending on your translator's sense of humor. Alsa Masa was based in Davao City on the southern island of Mindanao. So I bestirred myself again and flew down there the next day with Kathleen Barnes, an ABC radio reporter.

Mindanao is an historical skunk nest of Moslem, communist and other insurrections. The colonial Spaniards failed to subdue Mindanao, so did the Americans and ditto the Japanese and Ferdinand Marcos.

Vast, impoverished Davao City was the NPA's first urban

target. Until a few months ago they held the place hostage, the only Philippine city they'd ever penetrated in force. But, after the Cory election, the Davao slum-dwellers went fickle on the communists. Now there are about a thousand Alsa Masa gunmen running the city, all of them claiming to be former members in good standing of the NPA.

Kathleen wanted to interview Colonel Calida, "The Cowboy Colonel," commanding officer of the Philippine Constabulary in Davao. The Philippine Constabulary is a national military police force with the same equipment and training, or lack thereof, as the regular armed forces. Colonel Calida, Kathleen said, had been acting as the *ninog*, or godfather, to the Alsa Masa vigilantes, letting them keep some of their NPA arms and giving them a semi-official status patrolling the city's toughest districts.

Camp Leonor, Calida's HQ, occupied about ten square blocks in downtown Davao. It was all peeling paint and sprung screen doors, like the YMCA camps I used to be shipped to in the Fifties. Security was everywhere, much of it asleep. Soldiers on duty wandered around in their undershirts, and groups of civilians loitered on the parade ground. A sign in the hall outside Calida's office read FIREARMS IS NOT THE ANSWER SUPERIOR INTELLIGENCE IS.

The colonel was powerful-looking in a short, compressed way, like an attack hamster. He told us that three thousand NPA members had surrendered to him personally, so far.

Calida's office floor was littered with NPA weapons, the worst-looking arms cache I'd ever seen. There were battered Korean War–era Garand rifles, dozens of ancient gangster-style Thompson submachine guns, Philippine-built "short arms" with single-shot rifle barrels mounted on zip-gun-type pistol grips, a World War II paratrooper's grease gun, a British hand grenade, a USAF smoke bomb and a rust-crummied model 1894 Winchester lever action 30/30 left over from American occupation in President McKinley's time. It was death's flea market. Without a Cuba or any other Soviet butt boy to funnel in commie largess, the NPA are worse armed than an Oklahoma volunteer fire brigade.

"Isn't Alsa Masa just going to oppress the masses even worse than the NPA did?" said Kathleen, who didn't hit it off with the colonel.

"Neat guns," I said. The colonel and I got along fine.

I asked him what had made Alsa Masa such a pop sensation, besides, that is, his small but august self. Calida told me the NPA had grown paranoid and had begun to purge its own ranks. It was "a tactical error," as the colonel put it. Comrades began turning uncommunist quick. The former guerrillas had led Calida to the bodies of seventeen purge victims. He hoped there might be one hundred.

The colonel took us outside to see burlap bags full of dead people. An enlisted man dumped them on the parade ground. Dirty bones, with that particular smell of human morbidity, clunked dully on the ill-kempt lawn. A skull rolled across the grass and came to rest with its idiot eye holes pointed at the sky. "Later I will get coffins," said the colonel. "I will give them decent burial. This is propaganda."

Kathleen said, "I have reports that the Alsa Masa has been extorting money to support itself, intimidating certain groups, especially Chinese businessmen."

"No!" said the colonel. "That is *black* propaganda. We have intelligence officers, and we would know. But some Alsa Masa might ask some concerned groups to help. I do not call that extortion."

"What concerned groups?" asked Kathleen.

"Oh," said the colonel, "Chinese businessmen."

Calida leaned over and spoke confidentially to me. "We will disarm the Alsa Masa. But I have not told them yet. The government will have to give them livelihoods."

Which was, after all, what Commander Melody had said. The poor Cory government is going to have to get itself a tall stack of livelihoods from the World Bank or wherever they keep those things.

I told Calida about my visit with the NPA, Kathleen gasping at my indiscretion. "A scruffy bunch," I said. "But they seemed like pretty good guys. I gave them money." Which didn't bother Colonel Calida. He nodded in agreement. That was the decent thing to do.

"Three things that are their motives," he said. "First, the importance. Then the power of the gun. And only a tiny bit of politics. Just the leaders have the politics." He told me how he had the NPA leaders' radio frequencies. Sometimes he talks to them in

the hills. "I told them, 'Why don't you come down?' " Calida said.
" 'There are some beautiful girls in the city.' But it is against their
principles."

The colonel ordered a police officer to take me to see Alsa
Masa at work. The cop, Nick, was the largest Filipino I'd ever
seen—a sort of kitchenette-size Refrigerator Perry. He and I and a
very fat driver got in a battered Japanese micro taxi and drove off,
with chassis scraping the mud streets. Nick was thirty-four. He'd
been a policeman since he was sixteen. In a year and a half he'd be
eligible for his pension. His dream was to go to L.A. and be a
security guard.

All cities have slums but Davao *is* slums—filthy, jumbled
hovels spread like an architectural carcinoma along the mud flats of
the Davao River. The place grew up during Mindanao's ten-minute
logging and copra boom. The poor were drawn from all the dinky,
ungroceried hill towns. Then the jobs and money went away, but
the poor remained.

Nick took me to a squatter patch called Agdau. It used to be
known as "Nicaragdau," partly because the NPA ran it and partly
because Filipinos love any bad pun. Agdau was built right in the
water with splintered packing-crate catwalks from one stilt shanty
to the next. The Davao River—sewer, sink and the garbage collection service combined—flowed by underneath. On one bit of dry
land was Agdau's only solid structure, a tin roof covering a basket-
ball half court. I was promptly beaten in a game of H-O-R-S-E.
The tall kids in these precincts of malnutrition are four feet eleven
inches but do lay-ups like Air Jordan. If the NBA ever raises hoops
to twenty feet, the Chicago Bulls are going to have to take up field
hockey.

Nick summoned Pepe, who had been a member of an NPA
"Sparrow Squad" assassination team and was now an Alsa Masa
leader. Pepe was twenty-three but looked sixteen. Two of his boys
stood by with Thompsons. They looked twelve.

Nick hovered over Pepe like a large, blowzy, slightly dim
guardian angel. Pepe was smiling, cool and self-possessed. Nick
told me Pepe had joined the NPA at seventeen and worked his way
up from gofer to hatchet man to community organizer, the NPA
equivalent of Eagle Scout.

I asked Pepe why he'd turned against the NPA, and Nick translated a pat little rap about Cory, democracy, reconciliation and the rights of the people being violated.

"Tell him to get real," I said to Nick. Nick gave Pepe a smirk and a nudge.

"No drinking. No going to movies. No girlfriend," said Pepe. "No church," he added as an afterthought.

"I've lived here. I was a target of the Sparrows," Nick proudly interjected. "I survived by being security conscious and not committing crimes" (a rare thing for a Filipino policeman).

"Ask Pepe," I said, "if he ever tried to kill you when he was a Sparrow."

Pepe and the guys with the guns laughed and began talking, all three at once. Nick, a little abashed, translated: "We didn't try to kill him. We liked him. When he had money, he would buy drinks."

"Pepe," I said, "did the NPA really purge people, kill them because they thought they were spies?"

"Yes. Six in the *sitio*. One woman, five men." (A *sitio* is about equivalent to a city block.)

"Why?" I asked.

"A little intrigue only."

By now about fifty adults and every kid in running distance had gathered around us. I addressed the crowd, not hard to do since being a normal-sized American is like standing on a soapbox. "Alsa Masa okay?"

"Yes! Yes!" Lots of enthusiastic nods.

"The masses having fear of Alsa Masa?" I said in pidgin with charades.

Much laughter. "No! No! No, no, no." The little kids pressed in to touch the submachine guns.

I asked Pepe what the NPA leadership was like. He said, "Politics, lawyers, people who get orders from higher up." They seemed a vague bunch to him. Had he ever met any? "No." Was there ever any contact with NPA groups from other areas? "Only by higher up."

"When Pepe was a Sparrow," bragged Nick, "he killed twenty, maybe more—eight military and twelve others, civilian robbers."

"Jeeze," I said to Pepe. "Doesn't your conscience bother you? "The conscience bothered him before," said Nick, "but not since Alsa Masa."

"Pepe," I said, "have you gone to church?" He nodded. "Have you gone to confession?" He nodded. "Well, *what* in the hell kind of *penance* do you get for killing twenty people?!"

"The priest said I must be very sorry and say *many* Hail Marys."

Back in the only hotel in Davao with running water, Kathleen was taping an interview with a homely, skinny left-wing nun. The nun posssessed that bottomless indignation endemic to ideologues and had worked herself into a real bother about Alsa Masa. "Small kids are given already Armalites, and the grenades are like apples." She was writing a letter to Cory that would expose these things. I decided to hit the bar. Some people are worried about the difference between right and wrong. I'm worried about the difference between wrong and fun.

Holding forth in the hotel's dank but flashy cocktail lounge was Nonoy Garcia, once the top Marcos henchman in Davao and still the very picture of a corrupt pol. He was a barrel-chested, barrel-stomached guy with big gestures but the ability to order drinks all around with one tiny motion of a finger. "Come," said Nonoy, spotting me for some kind of journalist. "Sit down. Join us." He and his cronies were discussing bodyguards. In Davao it's fashionable to have former Sparrows for personal protection. These kids, none of them twenty-one, sat in the background, tiny and shy.

"My boy's only nineteen, and he killed ten people," said one of the cronies.

"Mine's eighteen," said another, "and killed a dozen." (That is, the man was saying, a dozen of his own friends and political allies.) The more people your Sparrow killed, the cooler it is.

When I told Nonoy my father had been a CB, he insisted I have dinner with him. The CBs are revered in the Philippines. In more than four hundred years of foreign and domestic mismanagement, the CBs seem to have been the only people who ever made anything work. Nonoy took me to a surprisingly clean Japanese restaurant, a sort of miniature Benihana's, as out of place in Davao as a kosher deli in Aman. Four very beautiful young women were waiting for us at the table. We talked about Cory a bit. Nonoy wasn't bitter. But from his own professional point of view she wasn't much good as a dictator. He thought she should have started some big, symbolic public-works projects and made other grand flourishes to get things hopping. "She has lost the momentum," he said.

Unfortunately, Nonoy probably had a point. What Cory had done so far in the Phillipines was magic, but a very mild kind of magic, like pulling a rabbit out of a rabbit hutch. However, a man must be made of sterner stuff than I am to meditate upon the fate of nations with so many pleasures of the flesh at hand. We ate about ten courses, drank enormously and went to Davao's only discotheque and danced with the young ladies until an hour that would make the IMF shudder about productivity in the Pacific Rim nations.

I wanted to nurse a hangover, but Kathleen wanted to see the war in the countryside. We hired a jeepney, and set off for the hills. A military outpost had been overrun three days before in Mandug, about thirty kilometers northwest of Davao. The leftist nun had told Kathleen that a pregnant woman was shot in retaliation while innocently washing her clothes in a stream.

Mandug was a pretty farm village with a range of hills behind it. We found the outpost on the first of the hills. It was a sloppy cluster of thatch huts and low stone walls with an open-air mess hall occupying the crest of the knoll. The whole affair looked to have been built by hippies or large ground-nesting birds. Government forces were back in control, the troops in usual Philippine battle dress—shower flip-flops, Michael Jackson T-shirts, brightly dyed bandanas around their heads and snips of red cloth tied to their rifles to protect them from bullets. And there was a spit-shined full-bird colonel there ready with a colorful yarn about the battle.

As befits a romantic nation, the Philippines are great romancers. Tales start out at Jack's bean-stalk height and get taller with every telling. Giannini, the Black Star photographer, swears he once saw a Manila newspaper story that began, "Miss Carmelita Torres was struck by an automobile on Rizal Boulevard and three of her legs were broken."

The NPA attackers, riding in a stolen jeepney and a commandeered truck and disguised as banana-plantation workers, came down the dirt road that runs beside the outpost.

"How many were there?" I asked the colonel.

"Oh, so many," he said, "a hundred."

"A hundred? In one jeepney and one truck?"

"Well, there were many more out there," said the colonel, waving his hand at the countryside.

The NPA apparently tried to encircle the position by stopping their jeepney at the outpost and sending their truck down the steep road to the base of the hill. "But," said the colonel, "our unit on patrol in the village spotted this truck already and fired upon the driver of it causing him to crash dangerously into a house."

The village was half a kilometer away, so this would have taken some good eyesight and better Armalite shooting. Moreover, the battle hadn't started, and there was no reason to shoot at a truck. However, a trail of mashed palm trees *did* lead straight off the road and into a small house with a large hole in the middle.

"Then what happened?" I said.

"The defenders of our outpost were attacked by surprise from the jeepney and returned fire, surrounded by superior numbers as the NPA shouted, 'You're looking for us? We are here already!' These NPA then, they were pinned down in the sleeping huts there for a fire fight of forty minutes after which our soldiers were forced to have decided, tactically, to retire with one killed and five wounded. But the NPA, they suffered, oh, twenty killed."

I solemnly wrote this all in my notebook. "How many NPA bodies have you, um, actually found?"

"Two."

I wandered around the outpost counting bullet holes and expended cartridges. There were no bullet holes at all in the sleeping huts where the NPA was supposedly under fire for forty minutes and only a few chips out of the stone wall around the mess tables.

This is what I'm pretty sure actually happened: Fifteen or twenty-five NPA came down the road, and the hayseed rebel driving the truck lost control on the hill and went off the road. Meanwhile, the remaining dozen NPA—the most a jeepney could hold—rushed the outpost all pumped up and firing their guns in every direction and probably inflicting their own two casualties on themselves. The completely surprised government troops, who were—five will get you ten—having a nap, hightailed it into the shrubbery. Then the NPA grabbed some guns. This is what most NPA actions are about. It's called an *agaw-armas*, a "gun-grab."

"So how many guns did the NPA get?" I asked the colonel.

"Two M-60 heavy machine guns, one M-30 light machine gun and four Armalites." He didn't mind that I hadn't believed a word he said. He could tell I liked a good war story, that was the important thing. Had he heard anything about a pregnant woman being shot? He said it might be true. The day before yesterday Scout Rangers—the Philippine equivalent of Green Berets—had come upon a group of NPA, and he'd heard a civilian had been killed. There was a lot of fighting, he said, around Fatima, the next village up the road.

Indeed, dozens of refugees were coming from Fatima, their possessions dragging on wooden travois behind the family caribous. But the colonel said he couldn't let us go there, the road might be mined by the NPA.

I'd have thought that twenty or thirty two-thousand-pound water buffalos would have cleared up the land-mine question. Kathleen and I stood in the tanning-salon sun with the colonel, considering. Filipinos don't argue. They "consider." And after, as it were, a considerable length of time, a truck arrived from the city, carrying rice and canned goods to Fatima. This allowed the colonel to change his mind without losing face. Now it would be okay to go. The food truck would set off any land mines, and we could follow behind it. But first, the soldiers must inspect the truck.

"It's a food blockade," whispered Kathleen. This seemed to be true. The soldiers said they had to take seven sacks of rice and two dozen cans of peas off the truck so there wouldn't be extra food for the NPA in Fatima. They stacked these by the side of the road, and the truck rumbled away. We started after it in our jeepney.

"Wait, wait," said the soldiers. "Are you going to Fatima? This food was supposed to go there." And they loaded the rice and peas into our laps.

In Fatima some families were evacuating, some families were

not evacuating and some families weren't sure if they were evacuating or not. They said one army officer had come and told them to stay put, and another army officer had come and told them to move. "What are you fleeing?" we asked. They weren't certain. "Where are you fleeing to?" They weren't positive. "Who's in charge here?" Hard to say. "Had there been any fighting?" Oh, yes, there had been a lot of fighting—in Callawa, the next village up the road.

Events move around a lot in the Philippine countryside. Whatever's happening is always happening one village away from where you are. "No fighting in this district then?" we said. Well, no. They thought it over. One eager fellow volunteered that the army had looted his house.

"They stole my pants, my scissors, my radio and my saw," he said. He was holding a large cross-cut saw in his hand. I stared at the tool. "Well, they gave the saw back," he said.

We asked if anyone had heard about a pregnant woman being shot. Yes, yes. It was an awful thing, terrible, very bad. They were all sad about it. "Did you know her?" No, they'd heard it on the radio.

We drove on toward Callawa. We were in communist-held territory now. We knew that because a large banner across the road said so. The hills were rising into mountains here and covered with balsam trees. When the road crossed the head of a deep ravine, we could see the amber Davao River twisting through rice fields below us like a gold-link bracelet dropped on a putting green.

Five kilometers from Fatima we came up on a grizzled old man carrying a wooden hoe and leading a caribou. Man and beast could have belonged in any of the past dozen centuries except the man was wearing flare-leg double-knit slacks and an earth-smeared Ban-Lon shirt as though dressed for some game of peasant golf. When we asked him about the pregnant girl, the old man was matter-of-fact. Yes, sixteen rebels had stayed at his house, more in two other houses nearby. About nine o'clock Sunday morning, while the rebels were having breakfast, the Scout Rangers fired on the houses. One woman with the NPA was killed, hit in the forehead and leg. Yes, she was pregnant. The rebels fired back briefly "but had short arms only." Then they fled.

"Put a sock in it, buddy," I wanted to say. For all he knew,

Kathleen and I were Fawn Hall and Ollie North, Far East division. But *omerta* is not a Philippine concept.

The old man wasn't, however, eager to lead us back to his home. He said someone would show us the way in Callawa, if we wanted.

Callawa looked like everyplace else in the Philippines, sort of cute, sort of ratty, with Latin stucco false fronts on southeast Asian thatch-and-bamboo buildings. The food blockade didn't seem to be working very well here either. Our driver immediately began loading his jeepney with cheap local produce.

The town's largest landowner invited us to lunch. Yep, he said, Callawa was a red area. The army never came here because people would tell the NPA on them. He laid out an enormous spread—rice, sardines, pork chops, mangos, jackfruit, coconut milk, caramel pudding and three kinds of bananas.

"Great bananas," I said, "not like what we get back in the States."

"Yep, we feed those to the caribou," said our host.

I asked him if he'd been bothered by the NPA, and he said of course he had; they considered him a rich man. He said he paid the NPA a tax, "part out of fear, part out of pity. I bargained with them."

"How much did they want?" I asked.

"Ten thousand pesos a month."

"What do you give them?"

"Three hundred." This is probably one reason the NPA is communist—because they're such lousy businessmen. If I couldn't negotiate a better deal than that while holding somebody at gunpoint, I'd be a goddamned communist too.

While we were having lunch, an ambulance and a car from a Davao funeral parlor arrived in town. The pregnant woman's family had come to get her body. A guide was found, and a procession of a dozen people started into the countryside, carrying a stretcher, shovels and plastic sheets. The parents were about sixty, the father stoic, the mother in steady, quiet tears.

We walked for an hour, across a banana plantation and up onto grassy slopes. A cousin, a young man in his twenties, told me the dead woman had been married only a year. She was twenty-six and six months pregnant. Her husband was in the NPA, and she was a member of the Urban Poor Coalition in Davao, a pro-NPA group harassed by Alsa Masa. She and some thirty other coalition members had fled to Callawa, where she met with her husband. She hadn't seen him in several months. The cousin told me all this as though politics were something like a flu epidemic or a car wreck.

Kathleen and I found the three crude plank houses where the NPA had stayed. There were chickens and a puppy in one door yard and bullet holes in all the buildings but no humans. Most of the bullets had struck the houses too high to hit anyone. They'd gone through the flimsy constructions, in one side and out the other. But in one house there was a sleeping pallet in a corner and several bullet holes just where you'd prop a pillow against the wall.

Everything in the scene spoke of idiocy. The NPA had two or three dozen people cooped up and hadn't secured a perimeter. The houses were sited so that four or even three Scout Rangers could have surrounded them and forced everyone to surrender—or killed them all. But, instead, the Scout Rangers had obviously stood away and just let blast, not even bothering to aim. They'd killed one pregnant girl, and all the rest had escaped in broad daylight. We could see where the NPA group had run across a plowed field; they'd dropped a cheap pistol holster, some propaganda leaflets and an empty cartridge box.

The grave was a hundred yards away, marked with a cross of lashed sticks. It was by the side of a path on a high, broad meadow in a nimbus of hills. The undertaker's men began to dig. The mother yelled, "Where are the masses when we need them? How could they leave her like this?"

The undertaker's men dug carefully, holding their shovel blades almost parallel to the ground and tossing aside little scoops of soil. They wore bandanas across their faces. Everyone else breathed through handkerchiefs. The smell was already as strong as a vision. There is no odor like the odor of a dead human. It's a saccharine putrescence—rotting meat and prom corsages, a sweet, gagging stink. It penetrates clothes and skin. No matter how many times you shower, no matter how many times you tell the poor laundry girl at the hotel to take your clothes back and wash them again, the scent returns like a worry or an evil thought. It's not even such a bad smell, no worse than whiskey vomit, but the reek of our own death goes like a shock to some early, unevolved ganglion just at the head of the spine, to the home of all wordless, thoughtless fear.

The first part of the body to come unearthed was a knee, swollen black and round as the crown of a hat. When the mother saw this, she screamed and fell, not in a faint but attacking the ground with her fists and forehead and screaming something, screaming everything, I guess, there is to scream. It took three of her family to pull her away. They led her into the shade, where she sat splay-legged and cried, open-faced and open-lunged, making a sound I'd never heard from an adult, a rhythmic sobbing louder than a yell, the sound infants make, meant to wake the world.

The undertaker's men kept at their work, clearing the dirt from two bloated sausage arms and from the mound of pregnant belly and then from the face. The features had swollen and begun to liquify into a wide, smooth, sickening bruise—with the face of a young girl disappearing into slime, beauty haunting horror. They pulled at her hips, and the body came free, stiff, distended, over-ripe inside its ghastly skin, hair trailing clots of sod. What ideology has that oozing face for a price? What abstraction is worth that smell?

I convinced Kathleen to fly to Negros the next day, to visit a sugar-planter friend of Tina's family. Maybe there'd be a vast, tile-roofed hacienda with servants to bring lots of drinks to banish the memory of that dead girl and gardens out to the horizon to look at to make her face go away and a swimming pool, a huge swimming pool, to splash chlorine up our noses.

But no such thing. Instead, we met Ed Alunan, who had given up a singing career in Manila to save his mother's estate from bankruptcy. He lived in a city apartment. The estate, like many of the "big" land holdings in the Philippines, was just a couple hundred hectares of cane with a peasant village in the middle where the "haciendero" families had lived for generations. Ed drove us there in a dented Japanese car.

The Alunans were turning over 10 percent of their land to Cory's land-reform program. Each family on the estate would get a garden plot to grow cash crops. Tina told me later that Ed was in trouble with both the left and the right—with the NPA because he was a landowner and with the landowners because he supported reform. "He'll get shot, already," she said.

Ed had had some difficulty convincing his hacienderos that the garden plots were a good idea. "We don't want our children to be tied to the land," they'd said. "We want them to go to the city. We want them to go to school." Ed was at pains to show them the gardens were an investment, a way to have something of their own so they could pay for their children's schooling.

He sent for specialists from the government's Land Reform Ministry. The specialists told the villagers how they could buy the land for a very modest price with a low-interest government loan that could be paid back over many years and so forth. The villagers listened politely. When the specialists were finished, they asked their audience, "Are there any questions?"

"Yes," said the hacienderos. "Does Ed know you're doing this?"

Ed had to go back to the estate and explain that he'd invited the government specialists to come. The villagers nodded and listened to the whole land-reform proposal again.

"Are there any questions?" said Ed.

"Yes," said the hacienderos. "Does your *mother* know you're doing this?"

But they'd gotten the idea at last, said Ed. And now they were full of enthusiasm and had all sorts of progressive projects under way.

"Like what?" said Kathleen, looking askance at the estate's primitive houses and boodle of naked children.

"They came and asked if they could decorate the threshing floor on Saturday nights," said Ed, "and hire a fellow with a cassette deck and get all the other hacienderos in the area to come and dance and buy beer."

So maybe there's hope for the Philippines. I'm sure there is. There has to be hope for people whose first step out of peonage is to start a discotheque.

Christmas in El Salvador

. . . .

DECEMBER 1985

This little country had been nothing but in the news since 1979— linchpin of something-or-other, vital this-and-that. Every liberal crybaby had been screaming about the death squads. Every conservative bed wetter had been hollering about the communists. For all I could tell we were going to go to war down there. And I didn't even know what it looked like.

I thought El Salvador was a jungle. It isn't. El Salvador has the scenery of northern California and the climate of southern California plus—and this was a relief—no Californians. My flight came in over the cordillera that separates El Salvador from Honduras. The mountains were crisp and pointy like picture-book Alps but forested to the peaks. We flew across a wide, neatly cultivated valley and then turned east above the spectacular volcanic cones that divide the central valley from beaches as beautiful as any I've ever tried to avoid at Christmastime. The airport was in the coast littoral, among green fields. Tidy lines of palm trees stood along the roads.

Where do we get our information about these places? From a president who can't remember which side Iran is on? From news media so busy being terse and fair that the guerrillas might as well be fighting on the Oprah Winfrey show? I want to know what it smells like. Are the girls pretty? Do they have little plastic Santas in the dime stores? (You bet they do, also sandbagged gun emplacements with red-foil Christmas-tree silhouttes on the front.)

I got a taxi into San Salvador. It was a little Toyota station wagon whose driver had filled the rear window with blinking lights, dangling Wise Men and FELIZ NAVIDAD in glitter letters. The road to town runs forty kilometers up through the lava-soil hills. The sun set with dispatch. The night was warm, but with a dry, cool breeze. People were sitting down to dinner in the thatched houses by the roadside. There was an autumnal, back-to-classes, college-football scent from the burning cane fields.

Nothing particularly sinister was on view, unless you count armed men—though every Latin country seems to have plenty of these. In the capital, some of the architecture was a shambles, but not from war, just from the earthquakes that level everything periodically.

I expected to see gross, barbaric haciendas owned by the oligarchy, the so-called Fourteen Families, who control more than half of El Salvador's industry and agriculture. But San Salvador's richest suburb, Colonia Escalón, looked like the second-string good parts of L.A. It could have been Sherman Oaks with walls around the yards.

The wealthiest 20 percent of the population gobbles up 66.4 percent of El Salvador's personal income. Maybe this is unfair, but it still didn't look like any oligarch had enough worldly goods to scare Barry Manilow's accountant. Rapacious as they may be, there's only so much to squeeze from a primitive agrarian country smaller than Vermont. Down at the shore, I was shown a beach house being built by some fabulously corrupt general. It wouldn't have passed muster as a garage in Malibu Colony. It was interesting to think about the rich U.S. liberals, the Jane Fondas, the Norman Lears, the Shirley MacLaines, whining about exploitation in Central America while sitting in houses four times as large as any owned by the *Fourteen Families.*

The middle class—usually described as "infinitesimal" or "statistically almost nonexistent"—appeared to be all over the place, honking their horns in dusty Jap cars and dented mini-pickups. At rush hour, San Salvador seemed to be populated not by 1 million people but by 1 million New York cabdrivers, though Salvadorans speak more English than New York cabbies. All of the well-off people and many of the poor have been to the United States.

El Salvador is not nearly so filled with litter, filth and begging as Mexico. The beach town of La Libertad is supposed to have the best surfing east of Waimea Bay. There are some impressive Indian ruins at Tazumal and Chalchuapa. And TACA, the national airline, lost my luggage, just like airlines do in regular vacation spots.

I went to get some clothes at a new, upscale shopping center. It looked like a mall in Dayton. Because I'm obviously *norte-americano*, a half dozen people stopped and introduced themselves. What part of the States was I from? And how was the Ohio State football team doing? It was a handsome crowd. The conquistadors weren't as civilized as our own founding fathers; they fucked the Indians before they killed them. Now everybody in El Salvador is a slight mix, a sort of Mestizo Lite, Iberian of feature but prettier colored. The women are heartbreaking.

The scene at the mall was less exotic than the Cuban parts of Miami, except for one mystifying detail. I could find no jeans shorter than thirty-two inches. I'm five feet nine, a hand taller than most Salvadorans, and my inseam measurement is only thirty inches. A salesgirl borrowed a needle and thread from a sewing shop next door and basted my new trousers at the cash register. This is a country of beautiful eyes and bad pants cuffs.

You can go to El Salvador, for the moment at least, and see nothing too dreadful, just some assorted anomalies. The soldiers guarding the highway to the airport were dressed in full camouflage but also in Day-Glo-orange road-crew vests. It must have been tough choosing between guerrilla sniper fire and the way the average Salvadoran drives.

But when you pick your hotel, you pick according to the kind of fear you prefer. The Sheraton, outside town on the hip of the San Salvador volcano, houses U.S. military trainers, State Department and CIA types and oligarchs home on a visit after taking their bank accounts out for air in Miami. Behind the hotel, running down the volcano into town, is one of San Salvador's dozens of slum-filled ravines, or barrancas. This one is known locally as Calle Ho Chi Minh (Ho Chi Minh Street). The hotel security guards are probably useless against the left-wing guerrillas who trundle up and down the barranca. And the guards are probably in league with the right-wing death-squad boys who hang out at the bar. In January 1981, two U.S. agrarian-reform advisers were gunned down in the Sheraton dining room by *pistoleros*, who escaped through the lobby at a slow walk. A month before, a U.S. freelance journalist had been *desaparecido*ed there. Gossip has it he was in the bar and asked somebody who happened to be an *esquadrón de muerte* member how to get in touch with the guerrillas.

The Camino Real, closer to downtown, houses the press. It's a friendlier place, but if you make the mistake of buying the reporters drinks, they'll tell you stories of kidnapping, torture and assassination that will make your guts run like a white-water raft trip.

In the past seven years, nearly twenty thousand of El Salvador's 5 million people have been murdered by the death squads. And the army and the guerrillas are bidding fair to kill the rest. Something like fifty thousand people are dead from the civil war, five hundred thousand are homeless, and another five hundred thousand are on the lam in the United States.

There's another kind of horror, not as dramatic but a lot more pervasive. At any given moment, nearly half the Salvadoran work force is unemployed. And most of these who are employed receive less than the minimum wage, which is pretty minimum. Per capita annual income is $710. The poorer half of the population has a daily calorie intake that is a third less than what the Organization of American States considers healthy. Eighty percent of their children suffer from malnutrition.

Much of this poverty is hidden. It's out in the countryside in places ignored by central government since before the Spanish conquest. And the rest is tucked into the barrancas, because rich Salvadorans, unlike the rich in Rio de Janeiro, Caracas and most of Latin America, have the sense to live on the hillsides and keep the gully bottoms and ravines for the squalor.

It's hard to fathom another society, especially a troubled one, hard to figure its contradictions, measure its attitudes, see it in its underpants. I thought I had an insight at the Mercado Central, the market in downtown San Salvador where peasants and artisans bring their goods. It is a massive, newish cement building that looks like a parking garage for trolls. The two floors are low ceilinged and lit by a desultory scattering of single fluorescent tubes. And the place is packed, a thrashing minnow seine of small, tan people.

Coming in from the blinding sunshine, I felt a gestalt hit me, a Jungian race vision—the cruel Pipils and Mayas flaying victims to the sun, strange, hairy man-horse conquistadors, the forced labor *repartimientos*, the Inquisition, the *esquadrones de muerte*—the odor of the charnel house struck me full in the face. But actually I'd walked into a hanging side of beef.

The market was a jolly enough place, once I'd disentangled myself from the cow. The interior was labyrinthed with aisles a foot wide, the floor piled and the ceiling hung with things to eat. There were eggs in six-foot ziggurats, baskets of live chickens, cheeses like snow tires, peppers in bundles cute as country-kitchen wallpaper and stacks of fruit like Brazilian nightclub-dancer hats. And everywhere were young country girls with breasts as beautiful as little melons and baskets on their heads full of melons as beautiful as little breasts.

One stall had trussed-up armadillos and a basket of iguanas, lips sewn shut, foreclaws tied behind their backs—minor death-squad victims in the food-chain civil war. On the steps down to the street, an old peasant woman squatted with dozens of little hand-made clay figurines, like crèche figures. They were all soldiers.

But the one real insight I had at the market was the crowd, not its appearance or its behavior but its fact. This country is full, stuffed, gorged with people.

The next day I drove into the central valley which is formed by the Lempa River. People were living everywhere. El Salvador has more people per square mile than Haiti, and only twenty percent of the land would be used by U.S. farmers for anything but dumping wrecked cars.

The crowding, like the poverty, is a subtle, bucolic thing. I didn't really understand it until I tried to find a half-private place to take a leak. Anywhere I went I'd get an audience of little *camp-esino*-ettes—who'd never seen a *norteamericano* trouser snake before. (I may say none of them looked very impressed.)

In El Salvador, there are no Ethiopian concentrations of starving masses to advertise for a rock concert, no skeletal infants to act as poster children for the professional lovers of misery. The malnutrition is what's called first degree, which means the kids are 10 to 24 percent underweight. They're still cute. Small, but cute. Dead sometimes, but cute. This is the kind of nearly invisible poverty that, in fact, most of the world is mired in. It looks quaint from inside a car.

What feeds this countryside is not the truck produce I saw in Mercado Central but labor-intensive cash crops—coffee, sugar, cotton. But to get land for cash crops, landlords have been evicting tenant farmers and squatters and stealing property from the Indians for a hundred years. This is the same thing British landlords did to the Irish in the nineteenth century, and it's had the same lively results.

It was the issue of land reform that sparked the current civil war. A semi-progressive military coup in 1979 brought in a government that tried to redistribute the big estates, the *fincas*, and to raise the agricultural minimum wage. The terrified oligarchs took to using death squads. The leftist advocates of these reforms took to the hills.

But the conflict would have been no great shakes if there hadn't been five generations of rural grudges and deprivations behind it. And there won't be any tidy resolution, no matter what ideology wins out. About half of El Salvador's people depend on agriculture for their livelihood. To give each of these families nine hectares (about twenty acres—the minimum acreage needed to support life even as rural Salvadorans know it) would take six times more crop land than the country has.

I was traveling with a translator—I'll call him Alberto—a well-educated and strictly non-political young man. "Where does the government get all its soldiers?" I asked Alberto. "Is there a draft?"

Alberto looked to be about draft age. "Oh, yes," he said. "There's a draft. In everyone's identity book there is a page where it's marked whether you have fulfilled your military obligation. The army often goes to big dances and festivals and such things and surrounds the places. When the young men come out, their identity books are checked. If they have not done their service, they are loaded immediately on buses and taken to the training camp."

"Were you drafted?" I asked.

"Oh, no." He looked surprised. "They only do that out in the country."

There were soldiers everywhere along the highway. Some looked professional; others dragged their guns by the barrels like rag dolls. In between the numerous military roadblocks we saw dozens of burned produce trucks—victims of rebel economic sabotage. The government operates its roadblocks by day, and the guerrillas operate theirs by night so that Salvadorans have twenty-four-hour roadblock service.

We drove on north to La Palma, in the mountains, almost to the Honduran frontier. Until recently this was a rebel stronghold. There were more bullet holes here than any place I've ever seen, more per square foot than in an average Michigan stop sign. One thing about adobe: it takes a bullet hole beautifully. The bullet leaves a nice aureole of missing plaster around the impact point, like in a Sgt. Rock comic, and not like bullet holes usually look, which is as if somebody used a Black & Decker drill.

La Palma has no palms. It's too high and cool. But it has handsome pine trees. To the north is the crest of the mountain range, with cloud-diademed peaks. To the south, all El Salvador is laid out like the Land of Counterpane. The town itself is the image of that tile-roofed mountain fastness where we all think we'll spend our meditative years. Or so it seemed until I stuck my head into the corner cantina. In the El Salvador hinterland there's nothing to eat but coarse tortillas, bad beans and worse rice. There's no clean drinking water. And there's no place to shit but the yard. Nothing except the grip of poverty is stronger than the smell.

A couple days later, Alberto and I drove west, to the far side of the San Salvador volcano, where the *esquadrones de muerte* dump their victims. I asked Alberto, "Just exactly what kind of people do the death squads kill?"

This had never been clear to me. And the word *leftist* was no help. Depending on who's talking in Latin America, *leftist* can mean anyone from Kim Il Sung to George Shultz.

"It started with labor-union organizers," said Alberto, "and then just sort of expanded."

We talked for a while about politics in the abstract, the only way Alberto would talk about politics. I told him about my own ventures into activist loudmouthing when I was in college.

"Oh, you'd be dead," said Alberto, and he gave me one of those encyclopedic Latin shrugs. "It is an autocratic tradition of government. There is no mechanism for dissent. What else can they do?"

The people who perform the actual killings are, as far as I could figure, militia members, low-ranking policemen and a few plain bully boys. They hang precariously to lower-middle-class status, a couple of steps down the social ladder from the students and intellectuals they abduct, a step up from the *campesinos* they slaughter. The *esquadrones de muerte* are cut from the same cloth as the scared, fanatic lumps who, twenty-five years ago in our own country, were dynamiting black Sunday schools and burning freedom-rider buses. In the U.S. today they're selling GOD, GUTS AND GUNS MADE AMERICA GREAT bumper stickers at swap meets. In El Salvador they have more career opportunities.

The dumping ground is called El Playón, "the Big Beach." The name is a local drollery. El Playón is a huge cinder field deposited by an eruption of the San Salvador volcano. The lava fell in irregular, sharp-edged chunks, brittle and black, and covered hundreds of acres. The flat color absorbs the light. The porous stone absorbs the sound. Nothing grows or lives on El Playón except vultures, which have the same angles and colors as the lava and look like pieces of it made animate with horrid heads and necks.

The cinders are piled like sea chop, in pointed crests—the wide river Styx frozen in a moment of bad weather. El Playón has been used as a garbage dump for decades and smells no better than it looks. But there's a more viscerally disturbing odor. I walked fifty or sixty feet out into the cinders and saw a pair of skeletons, rib cages intermingled. The skeletons had no skulls or finger bones. This is to prevent identification, sometimes. Or sometimes the head goes on somebody's doorstep. "Haircut and a manicure" it's called.

The bones weren't hard to look at. They were clean from the birds and the sun—theatrical, really. But walking back to the car, I saw matted clothes by the path, a sport shirt and jeans—teenage clothes, slim fit and narrow in the hips. And then I was sick and shocked.

And scared, too. I had to keep myself from running. I got us out of there as fast as I could and off to look at some dumb Maya pyramid. Alberto said, "The last time I was here there were bodies in garbage sacks."

How can these things happen in a place that looks like Santa Barbara? A place that's just a quick jaunt down the Pan American Highway? A place that was settled by Christian Europeans a full ninety-five years before the Massachusetts Bay Colony?

A social system like El Salvador's is not won on a TV game show. It takes time and effort to create something like this. The first thing the Spanish did when they arrived in the country was fight—with each other. Pedro de Alvarado, leading an expedition from Guatemala, met up with Martín de Estete, leading another from Nicaragua. And they blazed away.

The native city-states, mostly Pipil (cultural kin to the Aztecs) and Maya, were already in decline. These city-states were based on a huge underclass of landless serfs, and either the serfs had rebelled or the topsoil had eroded until it couldn't feed them. Whichever, the Pipils and Mayas were in a very modern condition when the Spaniards found them in 1522.

Spain, in the early sixteenth century, was fresh from a messy national unification. The Spanish crown was determined to maintain centralized control over its new American provinces. For more than three hundred years, virtually every administrative post above small-town mayor was held by a native Spaniard. Even the Creoles, the locally born people of pure Spanish blood, were not eligible for office, much less the mestizos or the Indians. So El Salvador, like the rest of Spanish America, arrived at independence with an experienced group of public administrators numbering none. And Simón Bolívar died saying, "America is ungovernable. . . . He who serves a revolution ploughs the sea."

Not that experienced administrators would have necessarily
helped. The historian C. H. Haring points out that there are two
kinds of colonies. He calls them farm colonies and exploitation
colonies. Farm colonies are refuges where Pilgrims, Quakers and
other fruitcakes can go chop down trees and stay out of everybody's
hair. But exploitation colonies are places for wastrel younger sons
and sleazed-out noblemen to get rich on gold or slave-labor planta-
tions. Farm colonists are interested in forming their own permanent
institutions. Exploitation colonists are interested in getting home
and spending their money. For this reason New England, Canada,
Costa Rica and parts of Argentina are reasonably nice places,
while Mississippi, Jamaica, Mexico and most other sections of our
hemisphere are shit holes. El Salvador is a shit hole.

The 1821 Salvadoran Declaration of Independence reads, in
part, "If we do not issue a proclamation for independence, the
people themselves might, in fact, do it." The country didn't even
know it was independent for a couple of days, because independence had been declared up the road in Guatemala. Two political
parties promptly emerged: the Liberals, or Cacos ("Thieves"), and
the Conservatives, or Bacos ("Drunks").

El Salvador's first war was fought with Guatemala a few
months after independence. Guatemala wanted El Salvador to join
in a union with Mexico and so did El Salvador, but not on
Guatemala's say-so. Since then, El Salvador has been involved in
forty-two armed conflicts with its neighbors, culminating in a 1969
invasion of Honduras over a soccer match.

Changes in government have been frequent and confusing. In
1839, U.S. envoy John L. Stephens spent seven months looking for
someone to present his credentials to. And the changes in government have rarely meant improvement. From 1931 to 1944, El
Salvador had a dictator named General Martínez, who, among
other things, put colored cellophane over the San Salvador street
lamps to cure a smallpox epidemic.

Every now and then things get out of hand. Now, for instance,
or in 1932, when a secret communist rebellion screwed up so badly
that its schedule appeared in the daily paper. Only some Indians in
the western half of the country actually rebelled. In Juayúa, they
cut the hands off a local policeman and killed the town's richest

man, a liberal philanthropist. Then they got drunk. The air force arrived two days later and bombed the town. Then the army came—between eight thousand and ten thousand Indians were killed, all the government troops had ammunition for.

President of the moment is José Napoleón Duarte, who was installed in 1980 after the military forced out the semiprogressive junta it had installed the year before. Duarte is a moderate, which, in El Salvador, is like being in a game of tag where everyone is it but you.

A British pilot working for TACA told me a story about Duarte. The pilot made an unusually hard landing one time when the president was aboard. The plane bounced several times. As Duarte was getting off, the pilot apologized. "Don't worry," said Duarte. "When people see I was on the plane, they'll blame me."

Or they'll blame the United States. The pilot and I were having dinner at an outdoor cafe called Chili's. I happened to look up from my food while the pilot was telling his story, and there was a bullet hole in the iron grillwork by my head, right at eye level. The pilot and I were sitting at the same table where four U.S. embassy Marine guards had been sitting the previous summer when they were shot by guerrillas from the Central American Revolutionary Workers' Party. The rest of the bullet holes had been covered with neat squares of masking tape and painted over.

Are these guerrillas, "the Gs," as they're called, the good guys? They make a point, I was told, of not harming the common people (though they got quite a few besides the Marines that night at Chili's). The Gs mostly sabotage the economy. I guess this is all right if you're a common person who doesn't need money or food. Also, the guerrillas seem to be better at killing embassy guards and the like than at getting rid of the death squads. The death squads are a powerful tool of right-wing terror. But they're also a powerful tool of left-wing recruitment. In the ugly air of El Salvador, you begin to wonder about things like that.

While I was there, the Gs were trying to disrupt the coffee harvest in the eastern provinces, but they weren't keeping regular hours. I never saw a guerrilla.

I did, however, see their press agent. I'm making a joke, actually. David Fenton, head of Fenton Communications, is a New

York–based public-relations executive specializing in efforts to make the world—especially the Third World—a better place. His firm is a sort of grown-up version of the mimeograph machine in the old Vietnam Moratorium office. I talked to Fenton after I got back to the United States. He emphasized that he is hired by U.S. citizens and U.S. foundations, *not* by the rebels, to "tell the other side of the story in Central America."

"I don't think the rebels are entirely Marxists," Fenton said. "Personally, I'm a social democrat." I asked him what he could tell me about El Salvador. He said, "There are two things people have to understand about El Salvador: One is the culture of violence. Two is what average daily poverty is really like. Poverty and violence."

"Violence and poverty: those are the two things you have to understand about the country," the briefing officer at the American embassy in El Salvador told me. The embassy officer did not think the Gs were social democrats. He noted they weren't getting their guns from Sweden or the British Labor party. He gave me a three-page list of attacks on the U.S. Embassy, apparently a routine handout, like a communion card. But not all the attacks had been launched by the left.

"When we first got involved here," said the embassy officer, "the right wing regarded us as pinko wimps, the left as pig imperialists."

"And things are better now?" I asked.

"Yes." He told me that death-squad activity had been curtailed. (Though Fenton later gave me a list of people who have disappeared since Duarte was elected.) He told me that the Gs were on the defensive and that the army seemed to be backing Duarte's attempts at reform.

"How about the economy?"

He sighed and said there wasn't enough land, wasn't enough industrial base. Natural resources are zilch. El Salvador needs a Singaporean high-tech solution. But the death squads murder the college-educated, and the Gs kidnap the entrepreneurs and chase capital out of the country.

"Well?" I asked.

"If everything goes the best it possibly can, they will be killing each other for another ten years."

I went out for a night on the town with the briefing officer,
some other embassy people and some U.S. reporters. We went to
the Zona Rosa, San Salvador's Montmartre or Bourbon Street. It's a
tepid three-block area, site of Chili's and half a dozen other cafes,
one discotheque and a few restaurants.

We drove there in an embassy car, a fully armored Chevy
Blazer with bullet-proof glass so thick the passing scene was pulled
like taffy and oncoming cars were foreshortened until they looked
like Robert Crumb cartoons. Besides the glass and body armor, the
Blazer had run-flat tires and a device beneath the back bumper
that, if you turn a special key under the dash, sets off a flash-and-
concussion grenade. I understand it's very effective. A Salvadoran
driver turned that key by accident once and flattened the embassy
parking lot.

We had an armed chauffeur and a guard with an Uzi riding in
the front seat. A pistol hung from a holster on the door pillar, and
there was another on the back-seat floor. When we got to the Zona
Rosa, the electric door locks clicked open and the guard stepped
out and surveyed the area, machine gun at port arms.

A band at one of the cafes was playing "For What It's Worth,"
by Buffalo Springfield ("Paranoia strikes deep/Into your life it will
creep . . . "). We ate at a restaurant called Ciao, which looked
exactly like a restaurant called Ciao would look in Atlanta—pink
and black art deco with neon highlights—but we sat well back from
the windows in case of grenade attacks.

The briefing officer described the security arrangements at his
house. He has a lethargic, twenty-four-hour armed guard outside
and a German-shepherd watchdog who's afraid of loud noises. He
said his best hope was that the Gs would stumble over the sleeping
guard. The guard would wake up and drop his gun. The gun would
go off and scare the dog. The dog would run indoors to hide under
the bed. And that would alert him in time to get out the back way.

A reporter asked me if I was going to turn this into a whole
book, like Joan Didion did after her two rather uneventful weeks
here. Didion's book, *Salvador*, is something of an in-country laugh-
ingstock. One heavy-breathing passage describes an incident in a
posh neighborhood in San Salvador, where Didion reaches into her
purse for something and suddenly hears the noise of all the armed
guards on the street releasing the safeties on their guns. This set

everyone at the table laughing uproariously. It seems no one in El Salvador has *ever* used the safety on a gun.

I said, no, no book for me. I said I was having trouble sorting out Salvadoran politics. Some of the principal supporters of the guerrilla front, the FMLN-FDR, were President Duarte's political allies when he was an opposition figure in the Seventies. And some of Duarte's present allies have reputed connections to the death squads, which were killing his supporters during the 1982 elections for the national legislature. Meanwhile, the army has supported torture-happy paramilitary organizations, engineered left-leaning coups and emerged as a force for social compromise, sometimes all at once. Was there, maybe, something I could read to get all this straight?

"Yes," said another embassy officer. "*The Valachi Papers.*"

Several days later, on Christmas Eve, real havoc broke loose. From the balcony of my room at the Sheraton, I could see the entire city. There were powder flashes and staccato bursts in every neighborhood. Rockets whistled. Huge explosions illuminated the surrounding hills. A dozen blasts came inside the hotel compound itself. Bits of debris flew past my head. The brazen face of war? No, firecrackers.

Everybody in Latin America likes to set off firecrackers on Christmas Eve, but nobody likes it more than the Salvadorans. They have everything—cherry bombs, M80s, defingering little strings of one-inchers and items of ordnance that can turn a fifty-five-gallon oil drum into a steel hula skirt. The largest have a warning printed on them, that they shouldn't be lit by drunks. I am no stranger to loud noise. I've been to a Mitch Ryder and the Detroit Wheels concert. I once dated a woman with two kids. But at midnight on Christmas Eve—with the windows shut, the air conditioner on, the TV turned up and the bathroom door closed—I couldn't hear myself sing "Wild Colonial Boy" in the shower. On Christmas Day I saw people raking their yards, gathering mounds of spent gray firecrackers as large as autumn leaf piles.

You'd think after six years of civil war and 464 years of civil unrest, more explosions would be the last thing the Salvadorans would want. Or, maybe, the thing they want most.

At Sea with the America's Cup

I hear the America's Cup race was the most spectacular sporting event of the decade. You could have fooled me. I was right there in the middle of it on the official press boat, the *Sea Chunder*, getting bounced around and shook silly. I had a psychopathic strangler's grip on the railing and was staring out at the horizon like some idiot Ahab who'd run out of whale bait. All I could see was a whole bunch of ocean and wet, messy waves. Though, as it turned out, I was facing the wrong way, and had to clamber and stumble and crawl on all fours over to the *Sea Chunder*'s other railing. There was a whole bunch of ocean on that side, too, if you ask me.

Way off in the distance, or so I was told, were *Stars & Stripes* and *Kookaburra III*. They looked like two dirty custard-pie slices stood on end. First one tipped one way, then the other tipped the same way, then the first tipped the other way and so did the second.

"Awesome!" "A brilliant tacking duel!" "Superb seamanship!" said the professional boat reporters from *Dinghy & Dock*, *Flaps Afloat* and other important journals of the sport. I don't think I'll

ever be a real boat reporter. My Rolex isn't big enough. Also, I
don't have the color sense. You have to wear orange Top-Siders and
a pair of electric-blue OP shorts and a vermilion and-yellow-
striped Patagonia shirt and a hot-pink baseball cap with the name
of somebody's boat on it in glitter, plus Day-Glo-green zinc oxide
smeared down your nose and around your lips like a radioactive
street mime. I do have one loud necktie with little Santas that I
wear at Christmas, but this isn't enough to qualify. And professional boat reporters love to hang bushels of stuff around their
necks—press passes, dock passes, ball-point pens that float, cameras, binoculars and Vuarnet sunglasses on those dangle cords that
are supposed to look so cool nowadays but which remind anyone
over thirty-five of the high school librarian. Good luck to these men
and women if they happen to fall over the side.

Falling over the side, however, was something the boat reporters were disappointingly bad at. While the *Sea Chunder* bucked
like a fake Times Square sex act, the boat reporters assumed poses
of studied nonchalance, talking boat talk in loud and knowing
voices.

It's no use my trying to describe this America's Cup business
if you don't understand boat talk. Everything on a boat has a
different name than it would have if it weren't on a boat. Either this
is ancient seafaring tradition or it's how people who mess around
with boats try to impress the rest of us who actually finished
college. During the brief intervals on the *Sea Chunder* when I
wasn't blowing lunch, I compiled a glossary:

Fore—Front.

Aft—Back.

Midships—You don't know "fore" from "aft" and had better stay
where you are.

Bow and Stern—These also mean front and back. Yet although
you can go back to the front of a boat, you cannot go aft to the bow
(which shows that even boat people get confused by boat talk).

Port—Left. Easy to remember because port wine is red and so's
your face if you say "left" instead of "port" on a boat.

Starboard—Right. Not so easy to remember.

Leeward—The direction to throw up in.

P. J. O'Rourke

. . . .

Windward—The direction not to.

Avast—A warning that you're talking boat talk or are about to start.

Ahoy—Ditto.

Deck—The floor, except it's also the ceiling and this can be perplexing during bad weather when you're not sure which one you're standing on.

Bulkhead—A wall.

Hatch—A door.

Companionway—A staircase.

Gangway—When you're moving along a wall, trying to stay on the floor, and you go through a door and fall down a staircase, you yell "Gangway!"

Sheets—Ropes and not the things that look like great big bed sheets, which are sails, even though the sheets tend to sail all over the place and the sails are really just big sheets.

Jibs, Mains, Mizzens, Jenoas, and **Spinnakers**—What you're supposed to call the sails if you're hep.

Cleats, Battens, Booms, Stays, Yards, Gaffs, Clews and **Cheek Blocks**—Things on a boat and you don't know what the hell to call them.

But none of this will help you with the most difficult part of boat talk which is how to spell yacht. I've tried "yacth," "yatch," "ychat" and "yot." None of them look quite right.

Meanwhile, out in the shark-semi-infested Indian Ocean (most of the sharks were back on the Fremantle docks selling Kookaburra sweatshirts for $65), the most spectacular sporting event of the decade dragged on.

If the wind is blowing like stink and everything is working right, a twelve-meter sailboat can go eleven and a half or twelve miles an hour, the same speed at which a bond lawyer runs around the Central Park Reservoir. The *Sea Chunder*—a lumbering diesel the size and shape of a Presbyterian church—can run rings around any twelve-meter ever built. So can a rowboat with a twenty-horsepower Evinrude on the back. The America's Cup is like driving your Lamborgini to the Gran Prix track to watch the charter buses race.

Stars & Stripes and *Kookaburra III* dawdled out to this thing, a

143

buoy, that was floating in the water and from there sailed 3.64 miles to another thing, then turned around and did that seven more times. This took five hours at the end of which everybody was drenched and sick and sunburned, especially me.

Of course they couldn't do it in just any old boat or it might have been over in twenty minutes and cost only a hundred bucks, and what kind of fun would that be? They had to have special twelve-meter boats, which cost $1,000,000 apiece and don't even have a toilet. They also don't have a fridge full of tall cool ones or any tanned wahines in string-knit bathing-suit bottoms.

A twelve-meter is not twelve meters long or twelve meters wide or even wrecked and sunk and twelve meters under the water, no matter how good an idea that would be. A twelve-meter is a boat that conforms to a complex design formula:

$$\frac{L + (2 \times d) + \sqrt{s} - F}{.75\pi} = 12$$

In layman's terms this means length (L) of the boat owner's insider-trading securities-fraud-trial transcript plus all the dollars (d) in the world times 2 plus the square root of the Ralph Lauren designer sheets ($\sqrt{s}$) ruined by the crew members sleeping with the spoiled rich girls who follow boat races around minus the number of ugly and embarrassing free (F) boat visors given away by the boat's principal sponsor divided by all sorts ($.75\pi$) of snits and quarrels over the rules.

The race ended at last and somebody won, but the *Sea Chunder* was still going UP and *down* and UP and *down* and UP and *down* and oh, God, I had to get to a bathroom, I mean "head." I worked my way along the "deck," holding onto the "bulkhead" and I had just made it to the "companionway hatch" when we hit an extra-messy wave. Blaauuuuughhh. "Gangway," indeed.

There are a lot of mysterious things about boats, such as why anyone would get on one voluntarily. But the most mysterious thing is why rich people like them. Rich people are nuts for boats. The first thing that a yo-yo like Simon LeBon or Ted Turner does when he gets rich is buy a boat. And, if he's a high-hat kind of rich—that is, if he made his money screwing thousands of people in arbitrage

instead of screwing hundreds selling used cars—he buys a sailboat. I don't know about you, but if I got rich I'd buy something
warm and weatherproof that held still, like a bar. But not your true
cake-eater; he has to have a breeze bucket, a puff-powered moola
scow, a wet-ended WASP Winnebago.

Although I don't know why rich people like boats, I do know
that many of them deserve no better. And it's all right with me if
they spend the privileged hours of their golden days cramped and
soggy and bobbing at a clam's pace from Cold Hole Harbor, Maine,
to Muck Cay in the Bahamas to Cap de Tripe on the Riviera to
Phooey-Phooey in the Solomon Islands. And then there's Fremantle, Western Australia.

Fremantle doesn't seem to fit the mold. I mean, the place is
okay, and I was glad to be there as opposed to being on the *Sea
Chunder*. But Fremantle is Dayton-on-the-Sea. In fact, Western
Australia is Ohio with one side of its hat brim turned up. As soon as
I got on solid ground, I went over to the famed Royal Perth Yacht
Club. It looked like a cinder-block drive-through bottle store.
(Cinder-block drive-through bottle stores are the main architectural
features of the greater Perth-Fremantle metropolitan area.) Then I
visited the Fremantle docks where the twelve-meters are parked.
Welcome to Hoboken, circa 1950. I expected Marlon Brando to
saunter out at any moment and have the climactic fist fight in *On
the Waterfront*. God knows how the America's Cup race wound up
out here. Somebody told me it had to do with Australia cheating in
1983 and putting tail fins on their boat bottom, but that sounds
unlikely. I think the International Sailboat Racing Politburo, or
whatever it's called, got Fremantle mixed up with Fort-de-France
and thought they were going to Martinique. In Western Australia
they don't even know how to make that vital piece of sailboating
equipment, the gin and tonic. If you don't watch them, they squirt
Rose's Lime Juice in it.

Australia is not very exclusive. On the visa application they
still ask if you've been convicted of a felony—although they are
willing to give you a visa even if you haven't been. Australia *is*
exotic, however. There are kangaroos and wallabies and wombats
all over the place, and even the Australian horses and sheep and
house cats hop around on their back legs and have little pouches in

145

front. Well, maybe they don't. Actually I never saw a kangaroo. I saw kangaroo posters and kangaroo postcards and thousands of kangaroo T-shirts. Kangaroos appear on practically every advertising logo and trademark. You can buy kangaroo-brand oleo and kangaroo bath soap, and get welcome mats, shower curtains and beach towels with kangaroos on them and have kangaroos all over your underpants. But, as for real live kangaroos, I think they're all in the Bronx Zoo.

While I was visiting every bar in Fremantle, trying to recover from my *Sea Chunder* ordeal, I heard the Australians talking about how much they drink and punch each other. True, Australians do drink mug upon mug of beer. But these are dainty little mugs that hardly contain enough beer for one serving of fish-fry batter back where I come from. I could tell the Americans by the way they ordered four or six of these baby brewskis at a time. And the only fight I saw was between two U.S. boat groupies because one threw the other into a swimming pool and ruined his favorite pair of purple boat socks with little pom-poms on the heels.

Australia was like "Australia Nite" at the Michigan State Phi Delt house. The big excitement was driving on the wrong side of the road. Not that I drove on the wrong side. I was over on the right where I was supposed to be. But the Australians were on the left and coming straight at me. After ten or twelve of those lime juice G&Ts, this got very exciting.

I also went to the exciting Royal Perth Yacht Club Ball. The ticket prices were exciting anyway—$300 a pop. The invitation said black tie so I called South Perth Formal Hire and Live Bait and got a polyester quadruple-knit dinner suit with foot-wide lapels and bell bottoms in the Early Sonny Bono cut. When I arrived at the dance, I was too embarrassed to get out of the car, especially since it was 100 degrees and I was sweating like a hog and the polyester had made my whole body break out in prickly heat. But nobody else in Western Australia owns a tuxedo either. Every guy there was wearing a rented one exactly like mine. We all spent the evening itching and squirming and scratching ourselves like apes.

The R.P.Y.C. buffet, booze-up and fox-trot exhibition had 2,500 guests. This was more than the Royal P's dinky clubhouse or even its parking lot could hold. So the ball was given in an old wool

barn that had been decorated to look like, well, an old wool barn.
And there was no air conditioning. Lanolin, ahoy.

At least the Australians weren't dressed the way they usually
are, which is in kangaroo T-shirts, khaki short shorts, work boots
and black mid-calf socks. You could tell this was genuine Perth
and Fremantle high society because hardly anybody yelled,
"G'day, Mate!" They yelled, "Ciao, Mate!" instead.

Australians are friendly, very friendly. I couldn't spend three
seconds eating my dinner without one of them butting in at the top
of his lungs, "G'day, Mate! Eatin' are ya? Whatzit? Food? Good on
ya!" Followed by an enormous backslap right in the middle of my
mouthful of boiled lamb brisket (which is either the national dish or
just what everything in Australia tastes like). The Australian language is easier to learn than boat talk. It has a vocabulary of about
six words. There's *g'day,* which means "hello." There's *mate,* which
is a folksy combination of "excuse me, sir" and "hey you." There's
good on ya, which means "that's nice" and *fair dinkum,* which
doesn't mean much of anything. Australian does have, however,
more synonyms for vomit than any other non-Slavic language. For
example: "liquid laughter," "technicolor yawn," "growling in the
grass" and "planting beets." These come in handy for the would-be
boat reporter or the would-be Yacht Club Ball society columnist,
for that matter.

Stars & Stripes captain and future White House guest Dennis
Conner was there, also in a bad tux. He looked like a poster child
for the Penguin Obesity Fund. Dennis is supposed to be something
of a personality, but with 2,499 other drunks with skin rashes all
around it was hard to tell.

In the middle of the wool-barn dance floor, flanked by armed
guards, was the America's Cup itself. The America's Saucer, the
America's Dinner Plate, the America's Soup Tureen and the America's Gravy Boat that go with it are presumably held by other yacht
clubs. It must be quite a place setting when it's all put together.

I was milling through the crowd of Cup admirers when I
bumped into Jimmy Buffett, on tour in Australia and looking, as
usual, like a one-man Spring Break. I've known Buffett since he
was playing for Coppertone handouts on the beach at Key West.
He's a sterling character and so forth, except he's under the

misapprehension that sailboats are fun. He nearly drowned me in a sailboat one time when we almost collided with a supertanker off Miami Beach. It was a Gulf supertanker, but it came so close all we could see was the *U.* Anyway, Buffett had written the *Stars & Stripes* fight song "Take It Back" and was in a tizzy of spectator enthusiasm.

"Oh, come on," I said. "This is about as interesting as watching George Bush get ready for bed."

"Goddamn it, P.J.," said Buffett, "you dumb-ass Yankee landlubbing typewriter skipper with your phony-baloney job making fun of everything—this is the most spectacular sporting event of the decade." And he promised to explain twelve-meter racing to me so that I'd feel about the America's Cup like David Hinkley felt about Jodie Foster.

Buffett and I went off to show the Australian bartender what he could do with his Rose's Lime Juice. And before you could say, "G'day, Mate! Got a fair dinkum hangover? Good on ya!" We were back on the *Sea Chunder,* flopping around like tropical fish on the carpet.

This time I had a better view of the action, not that there was any. "Look!" yelled Buffett, "They're jibing! They're heeling! They're running! They're reaching! Oh, my God, they're jibing again!" All of which seemed to mean that they weren't doing much.

A twelve-meter is a big boat, some sixty-five feet long, with eleven people sailing it all at the same time. But, no matter how much fooling around they do with the ropes and the steering wheel and stuff, the boat just keeps piddling along in the water. Now and then they put up a spinnaker—a great big sail that looks like what happens when a fat girl in a sun dress stands over the air vent at a Coney Island fun house. The purpose of the spinnaker is, I believe, to give the sponsor some place where he can put the name of his company in really gigantic letters.

"Jimmy," I said, "I could probably get into this if they'd *arm* these twelve-meters. You know, maybe twin-mount .50-calibers right up in the pointy part at the front—with tracer bullets."

"P. J.," said Buffett, "shut up."

Fortunately, there was a wild-ass drug scene on the *Sea Chunder.* I was popping fistsful of hyoscine hydrobromide (marketed under the Barf-No-Mor label). Enough of this in your system and you get seriously bent. Your vision goes zoom lens and begins doing *Top Gun* special effects, aboriginie didjeridoos start playing in your brain, your temples inflate and your mouth tastes like Lionel O-Gauge track. You don't feel like throwing up. But you do feel like wetting yourself and raping the first mate and eating all the colorful boat clothes. Sailboat racing can be interesting. So was Altamont.

I went downstairs to the *Sea Chunder*'s first floor and had twelve beers to cool out and make myself regular sick instead of hyoscine hydrobromide sick. Also, I figured it was important not to see any more of this America's Cup stuff sober, or I might start thinking about how many starving Ethiopian kids you could feed with just one of these twelve-meters. Of course, that's ridiculous. You can boil *Kookaburra III* for as long as you want, and starving Ethiopian kids still won't eat it.

I spent the rest of the race in the *Sea Chunder* bar watching "Dialing for Dingos" on local TV. Eventually I heard Buffett outside hollering, "We won! We won!" And I guess we did. That's nice. We now have a new national hero, size extra-large. I like it that Dennis Conner, 1987 Athlete of the Year, can't touch his toes or even see them. And twelve-meter racing is the perfect sport for the Eighties—snobbish, expensive and high-tech in a pointless way. You have to be rich even to afford to go see it. I'm sure there are two dozen Hollywood mudsuckers slithering around L.A. this moment pitching twelve-meter movie ideas. "Like *Karate Kid*," they're saying, "but with boats."

Already a great national debate has started about where the next America's Cup race should be held. Let me be the first to suggest Aspen. I'll bet these twelve-meters go like a bitch downhill.

149

Intellectual Wilderness, Ho—A Visit to Harvard's 350th Anniversary Celebration

. . . .

SEPTEMBER 1986

I always envied the fellows who went to Harvard. Wouldn't it be swell to be on the Crimson gravy train? I'd probably be a government big shot by now, undermining U.S. foreign policy, or a CEO running some industry into the ground. I'd have that wonderful accent like I'd put the Fix-A-Dent on the wrong side of my partial plate. And I'd have lots of high-brow Ivy League friends. We could have drinks at the Harvard Club and show off our Ivy League ability to get loud on one gin fizz. There, but for low high school grades, middling SAT scores, a horrible disciplinary record and parents with less than $100 in the bank, go I. How sad.

Or so I thought. I'm cured now. I just came back from Harvard's monster gala 350th Anniversary Celebration, and thank you, God, for making me born dumb. I went to a state college in Ohio. Therefore, I will never have to listen to dozens of puff buckets jaw for hours about how my alma mater is the first cause, mother lode and prime mover of all deep thought in the U.S.A. I'm not saying the puff buckets are wrong. Harvard *is* the home of American ideas; there have been several of these, and somebody has to take the blame for them. But it ain't the likes of me. Us yokels who majored in beer and getting the skirts off Tri-Delts bear no responsibility for Thoreau's hippie jive or John Kenneth Galbraith's nitwit economics or Henry Kissinger's brown-nosing the Shah of Iran. None of us served as models for characters in that greasy *Love Story* book. Our best and brightest stick to running insurance agencies and don't go around cozening the nation into Vietnam wars. It wasn't my school that laid the educational groundwork for FDR's demagoguery or JFK's Bay of Pigs slough-off or even Teddy Roosevelt's fool decision to split the Republican Party and let that buttinski Wilson get elected. You can't pin the rap on us.

But I was still full of high, if slightly green-eyed, expectations when I arrived at Harvard on Wednesday, September 3rd. I was just in time for something the Official Program called "Harvard's Floating Birthday Party," though it took place on a patch of muddy grass between Memorial Drive and the Charles River and didn't float at all. According to the Program notes, there were to be "a 600 foot illuminated rainbow, laser projections . . . appearances by the Cambridge Harmonica Orchestra . . . The Yale Russian Chorus, the clown Mme. Nose; the one-man riddle and rhyme show, 'Electric Poetry,'" and other sophisticated delights.

The laser projections looked like Brownie Scouts at play with flashlights and colored cellophane. The illuminated rainbow looked like a McDonald's trademark. "Electric Poetry" turned out to be one of those two-bit Radio Shack things where you can program messages to crawl along rows of little light bulbs. It flashed such verses as, "Be your best/Pass this test/Divest/Your funds from South Africa." I searched in vain for the clown Mme. Nose.

The Yale Russian Chorus, however, was performing or maybe that was the Cambridge Harmonica Orchestra or perhaps the Oxford Nose Harp Ensemble. I listened, but I couldn't be sure. It was raining, but this did not deter the spectators who arrived by the hundreds to stand lax-jawed in bovine clusters, occasionally fingering their alumni badges. Here was America's power elite, all wet with no idea what they were doing. You can take it for a symbol if you like. I couldn't take it at all and went to the nearest bar.

There was a modern-dance performance that night called "Gym Transit"—part of Radcliffe College's contribution to the 350th festivities. The Program notes described it as "celebrating the art of sport and dance." I admire phrases like this with a whole bunch of concepts that, if you have a Harvard education, you can just jumble together any old way. I'll bet "Gym Transit" could also be described as "dancing the celebration of art and sport" or "sporting the dance of celebration art" or "making an art of sport dance celebration." It was hard to pass this up, but after six drinks I managed.

The next morning was the great Foundation Day convocation, which President Reagan wasn't addressing. You may remember the press flap. Harvard wanted the president to give a 350th birthday speech as Franklin Roosevelt had done at the 300th and Grover Cleveland at the 250th. But Harvard didn't want to give the president an honorary degree. I guess they felt Reagan was a nice man and, no doubt, important in his way, but not quite Harvard material. Once again they're right. Ron would have dozed off during "Gym Transit" even quicker than I. So the president, God bless him, told Harvard to piss up a rope. And Harvard had to go shopping for someone else. I'm sure they were looking for a person who embodied democratic spirit, intellectual excellence and the American ethos, which is why they picked Prince Charles.

The Convocation opened with prayers by Chaplain of the Day Rabbi Ben-Zion Gold, director of the campus B'nai B'rith Hillel Foundation. Rabbi Gold graduated from Roosevelt University in Chicago and sounded like Shecky Green, and running him first out of the gate seemed a kind of cruel joke. The Ivy League has never been famously hospitable to Jews. And Harvard has been almost as important to the American Jewish community as the pork-sausage industry. There followed eleven speakers and three anthems sung mostly in foreign languages. The temptation to rattle on at length was resisted by no one. I whiled away the time in the half-empty press section by defending myself from a horde of yellow jackets that had descended on Harvard Yard and by deciding which member of the Radcliffe Choral Society I would take with me to a desert island if I had to take one of them, and fortunately I do not. The choral society looked like the Harvard football team with mops on their heads. Indeed, since Harvard football is played as though the team spends its practice sessions singing in a choir, this may have been the case.

Every now and then I'd catch some fragment of a speech. I remember the adenoidal-voiced professor of classical Greek, Emily D. T. Vermeule, dumping on Homer. She quoted the *Odyssey* where Homer had the minstrel Phemius, begging Odysseus to spare his life, say, "I am self-taught. God planted all the paths of poetry in my mind."

Professor Vermeule took a dim view of this. "He spoke in pride," she said, "that only God was his tutor; in vanity, for his original genius; in fear, that death might take his irreplaceable gift of words. He was wrong. . . . Harvard," Professor Vermeule said, ". . . is not self-taught, and is rightly proud of that." Poor Homer, you see, probably couldn't even get into Yale.

By the time Prince Chuck got to the podium the show was running almost an hour behind schedule. "The suspense of this momentous occasion has been killing me," said the Prince. "It's exquisite torture for the uninitiated. Fortunately, all my character-building education has prepared me for this." Charles seemed as confused as I was about what he was doing there. "I thought that in Massachusetts they weren't too certain about the supposed benefits of royalty," he said and noted that he hadn't "addressed such a large gathering since I spoke to forty thousand Gujarato buffalo farmers in India in 1980 . . . "

The rest of the speech was a sweet little well-pronounced thing about development of character being more important in education than mastery of technology. The audience clapped at odd moments, and it was a while before I figured out they were applauding anything that could be construed as a warning against atomic energy and bombs and stuff.

The 350th Anniversary Celebration went on for four days and included a mind-numbing and butt-wearying number of events. There were two other convocations, eighty-three academic symposia, forty-three exhibitions and sixteen performing arts events, plus heaps and piles of private lunches, cocktail parties, dinners and receptions. The symposia ranged from over-reach ("The Universe: The Beginning, Now and Henceforth") to under-reach ("Films as an Art Form") and included the dumb ("Feminist Criticism and the Study of Literature: What Difference Does Difference Make?"), the very dumb ("Taking Charge of Your Life") and the hopelessly oxymoronic ("The Role and Social Value of the Large Law Firm"). One symposium was called "Beyond Deterrence: Avoiding Nuclear War" and billed itself as "An examination of the use of nuclear weapons." For doorstops? Another was titled "Homer at Harvard," so maybe they're claiming the old hexameter-basher as one of their own after all.

The list of exhibits looked worse yet, for instance, "Artifacts of Education" at the Gutman Library, which I assume was old pen nibs and gum under seats. I actually saw only one exhibit, a massive display on "A New Approach to the Treatment of Advance Periodontal Disease," complete with color photographs, which I had to walk by to get to the free press lunch.

I felt I should go to at least one symposium too. I picked "The International Negotiation Process: Can We Improve It?" figuring this was as likely a place as any for eggheads to go wrong. But, in its ability to disappoint, as in all other fields, Harvard excels. The eggheads didn't go wrong. They didn't go anywhere. They yammered for two hours about US.-Soviet treaty bargaining, saying nothing about negotiation I couldn't have learned from a Kansas City divorce lawyer.

The moderator, Professor of Law *emeritus* Louis Sohn, had an accent so thick I could understand almost nothing he said. The gist of that almost nothing was that there are three kinds of negotiation: one-on-one, mediation by a third party and submission of dispute to an international tribunal. Professor Sohn said one of these doesn't work very well with the Soviets and the other two don't work at all.

The first panelist, Arthur Hartman, U.S. ambassador to the Soviet Union, pointed out that Russians are very Russian. He also pointed out that communism is totalitarian and we can't count on *Pravda* investigative reporters to catch the Soviets cheating on arms agreements. And he railed briefly against congressional tendency to legislate the negotiating process instead of letting the executive branch screw things up on its own.

154

P. J. O'Rourke
· ·

The second panelist was former Attorney General Elliot Richardson. Richardson is one of those fixtures of the political scene that nobody knows quite what to do with. A job negotiating the boring International Law of the Sea Treaty was fobbed off on him a few years back. It must have made a big impression. Richardson brought the discussion around to sea law at every opportunity. Among his many insights (each illustrated with a law-of-the-sea example): The Soviets act in their own self-interest; the Soviets get peeved when reminded that they're not really a super-power but a sort of overgrown Bulgaria; and "If we are to succeed in negotiating, we must understand their position . . . and we'd better understand our position, too."

The third panelist was Howard Raiffa, a professor at the Harvard Business School and an expert on decision analysis and negotiation. He said a number of things, or I assume he did. I had temporarily dozed off.

Batting clean-up was Roger Fisher, another Harvard Law School prof and author of the best-selling *Getting to Yes: Negotiating Agreements Without Giving In*. Professor Fisher was cute and glib and quotable, saying things like, "Asking who's winning a negotiation is like asking who's winning a marriage," and, "When it comes to arms negotiations, we can be equally insecure for less money." Fisher could probably get a job in the real world if he tried.

A question-and-answer period followed. I asked myself the question, "What am I doing here?" and left.

That night I went to Boston and got hammered and missed the only interesting thing that happened during the anniversary. A weedy group of sixty or eighty anti-apartheid protestors had been popping up here and there all through the ceremonies, squeaking, "Divest Now" and waving placards saying "There's blood on your portfolio." Being a veteran of the pressing issues and real riots of the 1960s, I had paid them no mind. But on Thursday night the do-gooders nerved themselves and blocked the entrances to the 350th Anniversary Dinner, a $20,000 black-tie fête for several hundred of the university's most influential alums. There was a good deal of shouting and even some pushing and wrassling between alumni and protestors. According to the *Harvard Crimson* student newspaper, "Hugh Calkins '45 . . . led a small contingent of alumni who tried

to make their way through the blockade in front of one door. The
activists physically repelled them . . . . At another entrance . . .
an alumnus successfully climbed through several rows of arm-
linked protestors who attempted to push him down the steps. As he
physically struggled against the activists, the alumnus called them
'assholes' . . ."

Mercifully for the protestors, this wasn't Georgia Tech. Cambridge police officers reportedly said they were ready to arrest the
protestors and only had "to be given the word." President of
Harvard, Derek C. Bok, cancelled the dinner instead. I was unable
to determine the whereabouts, during these events, of Professor
Fisher and his *Negotiating Agreements Without Giving In*.

On Friday morning Secretary of State George Shultz addressed the second convocation. This was almost as long and
involved as the Prince Jug Ears get-together, and the security
arrangements verged on the maniacal. A UPI reporter told me he'd
counted fourteen different law enforcement agencies so far. While
we sat in Harvard Yard, nearly a dozen Secret Service agents
roamed the aisles staring intently at us. Outside, the protestors
were back but this time double-teamed by cops. They carried signs
protesting not only apartheid but also aid to Israel, involvement in
El Salvador, and aggression against Nicaragua and Cuba; one sign
said "Remember John Reed," the pro-Lenin U.S. reporter (and
Harvard grad) buried in the Kremlin wall. Inside, a few protestors
had scattered themselves through the audience. About every five
minutes one would bob to his feet and yell. Then police and Secret
Service agents would come and stand in front of him and glower
until he sat down.

Just as the convocation got under way, a low-flying plane
began to circle the Yard dragging a banner with the message "US/
HARVARD OUT OF SOUTH AFRICA SANCTIONS DIVEST
NOW." This drowned out the Call to Order and a long-winded
prayer by the Chaplain of the Day (a Mick, this time) and part of an
address by the Mayor of Cambridge—so disrespect for freedom of
speech has its rewards. Governor Dukakis spoke next and did some
Kennedy quoting. He was followed by Tip O'Neill, who seems
determined to break Sarah Bernhardt's record for farewell appearances. It's not often that I have any fellow-feeling for the Buddha of

Bureaucracy, but I must hand it to Mr. Speaker; he began by saying he remembered Harvard Yard very well—at fourteen he cut the lawns here. And he went on to point out that when he was first starting in politics and Harvard was celebrating its 300th Anniversary, only 3 percent of high school graduates got a chance at college, leaving it unsaid how it's no thanks to Harvard that more do today. The rest of Tip's speech was, of course, blathersgate, and was followed by a bland student oration and a bad poem by Seamus Heaney, professor of Rhetoric and Oratory.

Finally, they got around to George Shultz. "This magnificent institution stands for a great tradition of intellectual openness, free inquiry and pursuit of truth," Shultz said, while protestors in the audience tried to drown him out. He talked about the advantages free nations have over communist societies in the "Information Revolution." "How can a system that keeps photocopies and mimeograph machines under strict control exploit the benefits of the VCR and personal computer?" Shultz asked the unresponsive audience.

Shultz proposed that freedom is a revolutionary force, and there were mixed noises when he mentioned resistance groups in Afghanistan, Angola, Cambodia and Nicaragua. "In South Africa, the structure of apartheid is under siege as never before," he said.

"Not by you," screamed someone in the crowd, and there was scattered applause.

"Today the validity of the idea of democracy is the most important political reality of our time," said Shultz and received some yells of dissent. Shultz spoke cogently against government central planning—no response. Shultz argued persuasively that "America's weakness makes the world a more dangerous place"— no response. Some conservative listeners bestirred themselves at the mention of the Libyan air strike. Others booed. ". . . [A] better future is likely to take shape if, and perhaps only if, America is there to help shape it," said Shultz—no response.

Shultz made an attack on the neo-isolationism that has formed the basis for liberal foreign policy since the early seventies. He condemned "the illusion that we can promote justice by aloof self-righteousness, that we can promote peace by merely wishing for it." There was no response to that either. He damned economic protectionism and got some hand claps until he said, "Another form of escapism is self-righteous moralism," and the booing began again. Then Shultz went into the debate about congressional cuts in the foreign affairs budget, but this seemed too deep for the audience and they quit booing or clapping and started rifling through the program notes trying to figure out where lunch was.

"Those who built a college at the edge of a boundless forest were not fearful, timid people," said Shultz at the end of his speech. "They did not shirk their responsibilities. They were practical men and women. They were earthy and realistic. . . . Let us honor that tradition." Maybe George was mixed up. Maybe he thought this was the 350th Anniversary of Ohio State.

In Whitest Africa

DECEMBER 1986

I'd been told South Africa looks like California, and it looks like
California—the same tan-to-cancer beaches—the same Granola'd
mountains' majesty, the same subdeveloped bushveldt. Johan-
nesburg looks like L.A. Like L.A., it was all built since 1900.
Like L.A., it's ringed and vectored with expressways. And its best
suburb, Hyde Park, looks just like Beverly Hills. All the people
who live in Hyde Park are white, just like Beverly Hills. And all
the people who work there—who cook, sweep and clean the
swimming pools—are not white, just like Beverly Hills. The only
difference is, the lady who does the laundry carries it on her head.

I was prepared for South Africa to be terrible. But I wasn't
prepared for it to be normal. Those petty apartheid signs, NO DOGS
OR NON-EUROPEANS, are rare, almost tourist attractions now.
There's no color bar in the big "international" hotels or their
restaurants or nightclubs. Downtown shopping districts are inte-
grated. You see as many black people in coats and ties as you do in
Chicago. If I'd really tried, I could have spent my month in South

159

Africa without noticing any hint of trouble except the soldiers all over the place. South Africa is terribly normal. And this is why, I think, we get so emotional about it.

Everywhere you go in the world somebody's raping women, expelling ethnic Chinese, enslaving stone-age tribesmen, shooting Communists, rounding up Jews, kidnapping Americans, setting fire to Sikhs, keeping Catholics out of country clubs and hunting peasants from helicopters with automatic weapons. The world is built on discrimination of the most horrible kind. The problem with South Africans is they admit it. They don't say, like the French, "Algerians have a legal right to live in the sixteenth *arrondissement,* but they can't afford to." They don't say, like the Israelis, "Arabs have a legal right to live in West Jerusalem, but they're afraid to." They don't say, like the Americans, "Indians have a legal right to live in Ohio, but, oops, we killed them all." The South Africans just say, "Fuck you." I believe it's right there in their constitution: "Article IV: Fuck you. We're bigots." We hate them for this. And we're going to hold indignant demonstrations and make our universities sell all their Krugerrands until the South Africans learn to stand up and lie like white men.

Forty miles from Jo-burg is Pretoria, the capital of South Africa. It looks like Sacramento with soldiers, like Sacramento will if the Chicanos ever rebel. And on the tallest hill in Pretoria stands the Voortrekker Monument, a 120-foot tower of shit-colored granite visible for twenty miles in every direction. The Voortrekker Monument is to the Afrikaners, the controlling majority of South African whites, what the Salt Lake City Tabernacle is to Mormons. It commemorates the Great Trek of the 1830s when the Boers escaped such annoyances of British colonial rule as the abolition of slavery and pushed north into the interior of Africa to fuck things up by themselves. The Voortrekker Monument's rotunda is decorated with an immense, heroic-scale bas relief depicting the entire course of the Great Trek from Bible-kissing sendoffs in Cape Town to the battle of Blood River in 1838 when 3,000 Zulus were killed *vs.* 0 dead Boers.

It was with unmixed feelings about Afrikaners that I climbed the wearyingly dramatic steps to the monument. One stroll through central Pretoria and one walk through the memorial's parking lot

were enough to see that they're no-account people—dumpy women
in white ankle socks and flower-print sundresses, skinny, quid-
spitting men with hair oil on their heads and gun-nut sideburns.
Their language sounds like a Katzenjammer Kids cartoon: *Die
telefoon is in die sitkamer* ("The telephone is in the living room").
Die dogter ry op n' trein ("The daughter rides on the train"). And
their racism is famous for its high degree of international de-
plorability. Liberal pinkteas, unreconstructed Stalinists, cannibal
presidents of emerging nations and fascist military dictator swine
all agree on this point.

Therefore my heart sank when I saw the Great Trek sculpture.
It was, God help me, "Wagon Train" carved in stone. There was no
mistaking the pokey oxen and Prairie Wagoneers parked in a circle
for a combat-ready campout. The gals all had those dopey coal-
scuttle bonnets on and brats galore doing curtain calls in their
skirts. The fellers all wore Quaker Oats hats and carried muskets
long as flagpoles. Horses pranced. Horizons beckoned. Every man
jack from Ben Cartwright on down stared off into the sunset with
chin uplifted and eyes full of stupid resolve. Every single give-me-
a-home-where-the-buffalo-roam bromide was there, except the buffalo were zebras, and at that inevitable point in the story where one
billion natives attack completely unprovoked, it was Zulus with
spears and shields instead of Apaches with bows and arrows. The
Zulus were, of course, doing everything Apaches were always
depicted as doing before we discovered Apaches were noble ecolo-
gists—skewering babies, clobbering women and getting shot in
massive numbers.

South Africa's bigoted, knuckle-headed Boers turn out to be
North America's revered pioneer forefathers. And here I was, a
good American descendant of same, covered with gore from Indian
slaughters and belly stuffed to bursting by the labor of kidnapped
slaves, ready to wash up, have a burp and criticize the Afrikaners.

Now, if the horrible Afrikaners resemble us—or me, anyway—what about the English-speaking white South Africans?
They're better educated than the Afrikaners, richer, more cos-
mopolitan. They dress the same as Americans, act the same as
Americans and, forgiving them their Crumbled Empire accent,
speak the same language. What are they like?

I'd heard about the sufferings of the blacks in South Africa. I'd heard plenty about the intransigent racists in South Africa. And I'd heard plenty more than enough about the conscientious qualms and ethical inconveniences that beset whites who go to South Africa and feel bad about the suffering blacks and intransigent racists there. But I'd never heard much about the middling sort of ordinary white people with Mazdas to keep Turtle Waxed and child support payments to avoid, the ones who so resemble what most of us see when we brush our teeth. What's their response to the quagmire of apartheid? How do they cope with the violence and hatred around them? Are they worried? frightened? guilty? bitter? full of conflicting emotions?

I stayed a month in South Africa, traveled five thousand kilometers, talked to hundreds of people and came back with a two-word answer: they're drunk.

The South Africans drink and open their arms to the world. Before I left the States I phoned a lawyer in Jo-burg, a man I'll call Tom Mills, a friend of a friend. I called him to see about doing some bird hunting. (Just because you're going to a place of evil and perdition is no reason not to enjoy it.) And when I called him back to tell him what hotel I'd be staying in, Tom said, "The hell you are. We've got a guest house and a swimming pool. You're staying with us." This was a sixth-generation white African, no radical or pal of the African National Congress. He knew I was an American reporter and would do to South Africa what American reporters always do and which I'm doing right here. And he didn't otherwise know me from Adam. But Tom insisted. I was his guest.

"It isn't like you thought it would be, is it?" said Tom as we walked around the lawn with enormous whiskeys in our hands. "It's like California, isn't it?" Except the sparrows are chartreuse and the maid calls you Master. "That doesn't mean anything," said Tom. "It's just like saying 'boss' or whatever." And that barking noise, that's jackals on the tennis court. "Mind your step," said Tom. "This is where the yard boy got a cobra in the power mower."

The South Africans drink and make big plans. Tom's plan was to put a property qualification on the vote. "Do away with apartheid and the Group Areas Act and all that. Let anybody have whatever he can afford. If he can afford political power, let him have that, too. That's about how you do it in the States, isn't it? It doesn't change things much."

Tom's friend Bill Fletcher had a plan for splitting up the whole country into little cantons, like Switzerland's, and federating it all back together again some way or other—*togetherheid*.

Tom's wife had another plan, which I forgot. We watched the TV news and mixed more drinks. Down in the black townships the "comrades" and the "fathers"—the young radicals and older moderates—were going at it with necklacings and machetes. But this wasn't on the news. New regulations had been issued by the government that day, forbidding any media coverage of civil disturbance. The lead story was about sick racehorses.

The South Africans drink and go on the offensive. Tom and Bill and I and some other bird hunters went to Jim Elliot's house for drinks. Jim was a dentist with a den made up almost entirely of animal heads and skins and other parts. The bar stools were elephant feet. "A man can live like a king in this country!" said Jim, petting a Labrador retriever named Soweto. "Like a goddamned king! I've got my practice, a house, a couple of cars, a shack down on the beach and the best goddamned hunting and fishing in the world. Where else could I live like this?" He hauled out a five-kilo bag of ice. "I know you Americans like your ice." He stuffed in as many cubes as my big glass could hold and filled it with Scotch to the brim.

"The blacks live better here than they do in the rest of Africa, I'll tell you that," said Bill Fletcher.

"We like the blacks," said Tom. "They don't deserve to be treated the way they are."

"We all like the blacks," said Jim.

"Though they're a bit childish," said someone and told a story about the new maid at his house who tried to make tea in the steam iron.

"But they don't deserve to be treated the way they are," said Tom. And he told how last year he'd seen a white motorist run into a black man and knock him across the road. The motorist stopped but wouldn't get out of his car. Tom called an ambulance and tried to get the white man to help, but the man just drove away. "He was a British tourist," said Tom with some satisfaction.

Later Jim said, "We fought alongside everybody else in World War I and World War II, and now they all turn their backs on us. The minute we're in trouble where are our friends?"

And a good deal later somebody said, "Thirty days to Cairo," by which he meant the South African army could fight its way up the whole length of Africa in thirty days. It's probably true. And it would certainly put the South African army thirty days away from where it's causing trouble now. But I didn't point that out.

The South Africans drink and get serious. Tom and I were shooting doves and drinking beer with a Greek car dealer named Connie. Connie had lived in the Belgian Congo and had been trapped there with his wife and little children in the horrors of '60 and '61. Sitting out in a grain field at sundown, Connie talked just a little, just obliquely about people mutilating each other, about the rape of nuns "by the very ones which they were ministering," about cattle left alive with their legs cut off at the hocks. "It makes me shaking to even think what I saw."

That night Tom and I drank with Carlo, who'd come out to Africa in 1962, a teenager from a little village in Sicily carrying his mother's whole savings, one English pound and fifty pence. He'd made his way to Angola, "so rich, so beautiful. You put a dead stick in the ground, it would grow." He'd prospected for minerals, gotten rich, started a big-game hunting operation that had, at last, eighteen camps. Then the Portuguese left. He talked about corpses hanging in the trees, about men castrated and fetuses hanging out of the slit bellies of women and, like the Greek, about cattle with their legs cut off. He abandoned all his mineral claims, dynamited his hunting camps—"not even the stones were left in one piece"— and came to South Africa to start over.

I wondered what I'd think if I were South African and looked at the rest of Africa and saw nothing but oppression, murder, chaos, massacre, impoverishment, famine and corruption— whereas in South Africa there was just some oppression and murder. "You think the blacks can't govern themselves?" I said to Carlo.

He shrugged. "It was the East Germans, the Cubans who did the worst things I saw."

"You know Jonas Savimbi?" he said, naming the head of the

more-or-less pro-Western UNITA guerrillas fighting Angola's Marxist government. "I would cut my arm off, here, to put Savimbi in power." And he pointed to the same place on his limb as the cattle had been mutilated on theirs.

South Africans drink and get nostalgic. I spent the Christmas holidays on the Indian Ocean in Scotboro—a sort of Southampton or Hilton Head with its peak season at South Africa's midsummer Yuletide. There were a lot of old people there, members of the "Whenwe Tribe," so called because most of their sentences begin with "When we were in Nyasaland. . . ," "When we were in Bechuanaland. . . ," "When we were in Tanganyika . . ." It seems Africa was a paradise then, and the more that was drunk the more paradisical it became. Though it must have been an odd kind of Eden for some of its residents.

"You can see why the blacks steal," said one old man, ex of Rhodesia. He'd been captured by the Germans at Tobruk. "In the POW camp at Breslau we worked in the post office—stole everything in sight. Only natural under the circumstances." He flipped his cigarette out onto the lawn, the way everyone does in South Africa. There's always someone to pick up the butts.

"The only reason blacks have bones in their skulls is to keep their ears apart," said a startlingly ugly old lady just as the maid, with expressionless face, was passing the cocktail weenies around.

"Now, wait a minute. . ." I said.

"Well, of course *your* blacks have white blood." The ugly woman shook her head. "I've never understood how any man could be attracted to a black girl," she said, helping herself to several miniature frankfurters and looking right through the very pretty maid. "That kinky hair, those fat noses, great big lips . . ."

I would be drummed out of the Subtle Fiction Writer's League if I invented this scene. The old woman was not only ugly with the ugliness age brings us all but showed signs of formidable ugliness by birth—pickle-jar chin, mainsail ears and a nose like a trigonometry problem. What's more, she had the deep frown and snit wrinkles which come only from a lifetime of bad character. All that day I'd been driving through KwaZulu, through the Valley of a Thousand Hills in the Natal outback, driving through little villages where the Zulu girls, bare-breasted to show their unmarried status, were coming to market. Burnished skin and dulcet features and sturdy little bodies like better-proportioned Mary Lou Rettons—I had fallen helplessly, fervently, eternally in love thirty or forty times.

And the South Africans drink and grow resigned to fate, at least the younger ones do. At a dinner party full of junior business executives, the talk was about the olive-colored South African passport that most countries won't accept as a travel document. "We call it the 'Green Mamba,'" said an accountant, "because you can't take it anywhere."

The guests discussed countries the way people their age in Manhattan discuss unfashionable neighborhoods where they might be able to find a decent-sized apartment.

"We're looking at Australia," said an estate agent.

"Oh, Christ, England, I guess," said a law clerk from Tom's office. "My grandmother is English."

"The 'Florida option' is what most people are thinking about," said an assistant hotel manager. "Same weather, strong economy, and that's where everybody else goes when their governments fall apart."

They didn't talk about money or careers. They didn't even talk about apartheid as much as we do.

"If the United States were serious about fixing the situation here," said the law clerk, "all they'd have to do is give every young professional in South Africa a green card. Nobody would be left." At least nobody they knew very well.

"When you don't work with people and you don't live with people, you don't know them," said the accountant. "Just the help."

And the help's attitude, lately, has been, as they put it, "shifting."

"Who can blame them?" said the law clerk.

"They say it's those of us who've been moderates," said the estate agent, "who'll have our throats cut."

"What about the Afrikaners? Do you blame them?" I asked.

Helpless shrugs all around. "A lot of us are part Afrikaans," said the assistant hotel manager. And he told a Van Der Merwe joke, the South African equivalent of a Polish joke, about an American, an Englishman and Van Der Merwe the Afrikaner. They can each have a wish. All they have to do is run off a cliff and shout their heart's desire. The American runs off the cliff and shouts, "Gold!" A pile of gold bars appears at the bottom of the cliff. The American falls on top of it and he's killed. The Englishman runs off the cliff and shouts, "Silver!" A pile of silver coins appears at the bottom of the cliff. The Englishman falls on top of it and he's killed. Then Van Der Merwe runs off the cliff, but as soon as he gets over the edge he looks down and yells "Oh, shit!" A huge pile of shit appears. Van Der Merwe lands in that and walks away unscathed.

Those Afrikaners drink a lot, too, though it looked like just plain drinking as far as I could see. I spent an evening in a dirty little bar in a farm town called Humansdorp in the Cape Province. At first I didn't think the locals even noticed I was there. Then I realized they had all been speaking Afrikaans when I came in, but, after they heard me ask for more ice in my whiskey, they switched their conversations into English—still not saying a word to me. The bartender regaled one customer with the details of a practical joke he'd played, putting cayenne pepper in somebody's snuff. The rest of the bar was trading stories about bad and foolish black behavior.

A kid who'd just gotten back from his two-year army hitch was saying that Namibian girls smear menses mixed with mud all over their bodies. (For all I know it's true but no wierder than some of the ingredients I've noticed in my girlfriend's shampoo lately.) Somebody else said he kept building houses for his farm families, and they kept tearing holes in the roofs to let out the smoke from their cooking fires. There was concerned clucking over the neighborhood black teens. After they're circumcised they're supposed to spend a month alone in the bush, but instead they spend it begging beside the highway. Finally one of the Afrikaners turned to me and asked about sheep farming in the United States. By that time I'd had enough to drink to tell him, although I don't believe I know which end of a sheep you're supposed to feed.

Then everyone wanted to have a chat. "Was it difficult figuring out the South African money?" (There are 100 cents to the Rand.) "Did people try to deal [cheat] you around here?" "Does America have a lot of blacks?"

"I want to go to America," said the young ex-soldier, "to see how you do it."

"Do what?"

"Get along with the blacks."

What a strange place America must be—land of sanctuary for all beleaguered oppressors, with simple money and endless sheep-farming opportunities, where blacks behave somehow because they've got white blood. Mike Boetcher, the NBC correspondent in Jo-Burg, told me his baby's nurse, a beautiful girl of nineteen, wants to go to Harlem "because everybody is young and rich there" and because no one in Soweto has enough cows to pay her bride price. Mike said he tried in vain to tell her most guys in Harlem don't have a lot of cows. And in the Transkei "homeland" I talked to a black divinity student who'd visited America. "The most wonderful place," he said, "so wealthy and beautiful and with perfect racial harmony."

"What part of America did you visit" I asked

"The South Side of Chicago."

I was pretty drunk myself by the time I'd been in South Africa for three or four weeks. Not that I'm not usually, but there was something white African in this bender. I was fuddled. My head boiled with clichés. I was getting used to being confused. I was getting used to hearing the most extraordinary things. From this Irish couple who'd been living in Africa for three decades, for instance. "There hasn't been apartheid here for years," said the wife.

"One of the problems is that that word was invented," said the husband.

I was becoming South African—used to having people all around me all the time doing everything for me and not doing it well.

I went in to dinner at my resort hotel in Mosselbaai, on the spectacular Big Sur–like "Garden Route" along the coast between Port Elizabeth and Cape Town. I'd had my six or eight whiskeys with the Irish couple in the lounge and was ready for one of the elaborate, big, bland and indifferently cooked meals that constitute South African cuisine. The restaurant was turned out in red plush and crisp linen. Candles glittered in cut-glass sconces. But when I sat down at my table there were three teaspoons, two water glasses, one dirty wine glass, no forks, no knives and no napkin.

"I need a dinner fork, a salad fork, a knife and a napkin," I

said to the waiter, who stared at me in dull suprise and then headed
out across the dining room at the speed of a change in seasons. His
feet were sockless below the tuxedo pants and he was standing on
the backs of his shoes with just his toes stuffed into the unlaced
oxfords.

He returned with another spoon.

"I need a knife, a fork and a napkin!" I said.

He came back twenty minutes later with the water pitcher and
filled my wine glass.

"LOOK HERE," I said, "DO YOU SPEAK ENGLISH?"

He thought about that for a long time. "Oh, yes." He disappeared and came back in half an hour with one more water glass.
"Is the master ready to order?"

He was without recourse, voteless, impoverished, unproper-
tied, not a legal citizen in his own nation, yet he had me reduced to
a paroxysm of impotent drunken rage. I left him a huge tip and ate
my chicken with a spoon.

It's always hard to see hope with a hangover, nowhere more so
than at the butt-end of this continent in a country that's like a
nightmare laundry-detergent commercial—makes whites whiter,
coloreds brighter. They're building themselves a gigantic Cin-
erama, Technicolor Ulster here. And the troubles in Ireland have
been going on since my own relative Tighernan O'Rourke, prince of
Breffni, had his wife stolen by Diarmuid MacMurrough, king of
Leinster, and O'Rourke got so mad that MacMurrough had to call
on Henry II of England for help. That was in 1152. I think we can
expect the same swift and decisive resolution to the problem in
South Africa.

Divestment and sanctions—I guess those are the big answers
proposed in the States. Well, economic sanctions sure nipped the
Russian Revolution in the bud, made the Ayatollah Khomeini's
Iran fold like a hideaway bed and put Chiang Kai-shek right back
in power on the mainland.

The whole time I was in South Africa I only talked to one
person who was in favor of sanctions and that was the divinity
student in Transkei who'd visited the South Side of Chicago. He
cited biblical example ("When the Pharaoh hardened his heart,

169

God had to find another way"), but he also told me the Bible requires polygamy. So I'm not sure whether he was in earth orbit or not. Of course, there were a lot of people I didn't talk to. The comrades, busy performing "the necklace"—that is, putting flaming car tires around people's necks (actually, down over their shoulders in order to pin their arms to their sides)—were hard to chat up. And I never bumped into Bishop Tutu. Most of the blacks I did talk to would be considered, by South African standards, middle class, even sellouts—Uncle Bantus. They told me "political power grows from economic power." They saw sanctions as hurting one of the few black chances to get a leg up the ladder.

I have no idea whether they were right or wrong. But when I was in Ulundi, the administrative capital of the Zulu tribal lands, I was hanging around, drinking beer and talking to people, and a young political organizer leaned over to me and said, "It's really very simple why we are against sanctions. If we have money, we can buy *guns*." So maybe we should factor that into our next U.S.-Out-of-South-Africa rally.

The South African government's own solution, the homelands, is a hideous joke. I traveled through the Tswana tribal homeland, Bophuthatswana, in the north; KwaZulu in Natal where the Zulus refuse to accede to "independence"; and through the two Xhosa homelands, Transkei and Ciskei along the Indian Ocean. They're all the same. Everyplace is littered with windowless huts that you couldn't tell from latrines if there were any latrines to tell them from. The garden plots look like Grateful Dead fan beards. People are dumped into these rural wastes, far more people than the land can support. So the men have no choice but to go off to the rest of South Africa and work as "foreigners." The homelands are on the worst land in the country, scorched foothills and prairies on the verge of desertification. Raw trenches of the red African soil have eroded in webs across the pastures. Every foot of ground is overgrazed.

The tribal economic system, like that of ancient Europe, is based on cattle. (The word "pecuniary" comes from the Latin, *pecus*, "cattle.") The cows aren't often eaten or sold or even milked. They are the bank account, the measure of the clan's and the family's wealth. They're also an ecological nightmare in these cramped precincts.

I used to have eight head of Hereford beef cattle at my place back in the States. I asked some people in Ulundi what kind of wife these would get me.

"Oh," said one, "probably a girl who's lived in the city for a while and had a couple of kids."

"But," I said, "these are pure-bred Polled Herefords, going a thousand pounds or more."

"No, no, it's like Rand notes, it's the *number* of cows that counts."

I did see one homeland that worked, beautiful and severe bushveldt taken back from Boer farms and restored to its natural state with blesbok and gemsbok and springbok boking around all antlered and everything and herds of zebra—art deco on the hoof—and packs or gaggles or whatever-they're-called of giraffes (an NBA of giraffes would be the right term). This was, however, a homeland for the animals, the Botsalano Game Park in Bophuthatswana.

Tom Mills and I were riding in a Land Rover with his wife and two kids when we came right up beside five rhinoceri—four really enormous gigantic ones and a calf that was pretty tremendously huge itself. It's not easy to describe the effect that the first sight of a wild rhino has on a not very brave author from Ohio. It's like taking your four-year-old on a surprise visit to the Mesozoic era. I felt a vaulting thrill combined with some desire to start crying and crawl under the jeep. Tom, in what I felt was an extremely foolhardy move, turned off the engine.

"There are two kinds of rhinos," said Tom. "White rhinos are fairly docile. They don't usually bother you. But black rhinos are very nervous and aggressive. They'll charge."

"These rhinos are gray," I said.

"White rhinos and black rhinos are actually about the same color," said Tom.

"How do you tell them apart?"

"White rhinos have a square upper lip. The black rhino's is pointy."

I looked at our rhinos. Their upper lips were square, in a pointy sort of way. "How else do you tell them apart?"

"I forget."

The rhinos, who are very nearsighted, finally noticed us. They cocked their heads in this Godzilla way they have and began to amble in our direction. A rhinoceros ambles at about 60 mph. There was a moment of brief—but nonetheless high—drama while the Land Rover engine went ugga-ugga-ugga before it caught.

The rhinos made South Africa more depressing, if that's possible. The big game is disappearing from Africa. Most Africans have never seen a rhino in its natural state (which is a state of mild pique, I believe) any more than we've seen the prairie black with bison. And, to be fair, the white South Africans are the only people on the continent returning any land to the wild. Whatever's going to happen in South Africa will be bad for the rhino, too. And rhinos only occasionally kill for fun and never go to the U.N. afterward and say they did it because of American imperialism or communist subversion.

We drank as much as usual that night, sitting outside the tents with Botsalano's game warden. While baboons goofed off in the shrubbery and frogs sounded in the water hole like ten thousand little boys with sticks on an endless picket fence, Tom's wife Sally talked about her father, an Edinburgh grocer who'd come out to South Africa when she was a little girl. "He was looking for a healthier place to raise a family, where my sisters and I could grow up with more of a future than we'd have in Scotland."

The game warden told how the leopard was coming to extinction in South Africa. The leopards used to be hunted as trophies, mostly by Americans and Englishmen. Any farmer who had a leopard shot on his land received a trophy fee of several hundred Rand. So whenever a farmer had a leopard around, he was careful to preserve it until some rich guy came looking to decorate the rumpus room. Even if this cost the farmer a few lambs or calves, it was worth it. Then the animal rights people, the "bunny-huggers" as the warden called them, got legislation passed forbidding the import of all spotted fur, including stuffed heads, into the U.S. and the U.K. Now the farmers just shoot the leopards—mothers, cubs and everything—as pests. "So fucking bloody much for good intentions," said the warden.

A couple days later, driving with Tom in his Mercedes sedan through the perfectly empty Sunday streets of Jo-burg, I put it to him about South Africa. "There aren't *that* many Afrikaners. What,

three million *vs.* two million English and other real Europeans?
And you guys control the economy, almost all the major industries,
right?"

"Mostly, yes."

"You've got the money. You've got forty percent of the white
vote. And you've got twenty-four million blacks, coloreds and
Indians who'd back you up. What's keeping you from taking the
Afrikaner National Party and snapping its spine like a chopstick?"

"That's just not how the English are, you know," said Tom.
"Most of us aren't very political."

"A couple of Chicago ward bosses and you'd have this country
in your pocket."

"I suppose people think it wouldn't be cricket."

I'd never heard "wouldn't be cricket" used seriously before.
Interesting what "cricket" means if you think about it—boring,
insanely complicated and riddled with snobbery and class.

We'd pulled onto the N-3 freeway. Jo-burg's office towers
shone behind us. Flat-topped artificial hills from the gold mine tips
rose in the distance. I was staring out the window at South Africa's
admirable highway beautification when we came over a rise, and I
caught a glimpse of what was beyond the screen of trees and
shrubs.

Thousands of tiny, slatternly huts were pressed together in a
jumble stretching for miles. And every one of those hovels seemed
to be on fire. Smoke drifted in an ominous smudge across the
highway. "Riots!" I thought, trying to fasten my seat belt for the
high-speed evasive driving we'd have to do through hordes of angry
comrades who would, no doubt, come roiling across the freeway at
any moment, stones and firebombs in hand.

"If you look over there," said Tom, "you can see Alexandra.
It's one of our older black townships."

Maybe he hadn't noticed it was on fire. "Isn't it on fire or
something?" I said.

"That's from the cookstoves. They don't have electricity."

And then Alexandra slipped back behind the decorative land-
scaping and was gone.

Tom and I had been out that afternoon shooting doves again
with Connie the Greek car dealer. We were shooting near Sharp-

ville, site of the famous 1960 massacre, a sleepy farm town, nobody's picture of a killing ground. All around were huge Afrikaner grain spreads, completely up-to-date and identical to big mechanized American farms except they weren't going bankrupt—thanks, in part, to worldwide bans on selling grain to South Africa. But out in the middle of these homesteads, invisible from the pretty country roads, are the people who work the land. Their one-room, cinderblock, tin-roofed shacks are set in the fields with wheat growing right up to the doors—not even room for a garden, just a communal well in a muddy dooryard. There were half-naked kids all over the place. We took some of the kids along to run after the dead birds and pluck and gut them—"curly-headed retrievers," the South Africans say. The kids got a Rand apiece, about fifty cents, U.S., plus cigarettes. One of the boys, who said he was fifteen but looked an undersized twelve, was fascinated by Tom's Mercedes. He'd never been in a car before. Tom and I gave him a ride up and down the dirt track by his home. The boy kept sniffing and poking at the air conditioner vents. "*Where* does the cold air all come from?" he asked.

"Um . . ." said Tom and looked at me.

"God, I don't know," I said. "Something gets heated and that, uh, makes it cold." So much for the educational benefits of superior civilization. Tom flicked the electric sun-roof switch to change the subject.

The kid watched the roof panel slide back and forth. "Now I've seen everything," he said.

Tom had a client named Gilead, a man of sixty or seventy who'd started out selling coal from a sack in the black townships and was now one of the richest men in Soweto. Save for a bit of melanin, Gilly was the image of my Irish grandfather—close-cropped hair, a build like a Maytag's and fingers thick as my wrists. He even had the same gestures as my grandfather, pulling on the old-fashioned pointy lapels of his banker's stripe suit, then planting his thumbs in the pockets of his vest and toying with the thick watch chain that ran across his belly. Gilly's skull bore four or five large hatchet scars from the gang quarrels of his youth. When I first met him, in Tom's office, he was telling about one of the stores he owns being "off-loaded" by the comrades.

"The gangs, they set up at either end of the street, you know. They are just boys, some no more than ten years old. Some of the boys come into your store and buy a pop. Then they throw the bottles around to create their diversion and begin to empty the shelves. And you just stay quiet if you don't want to be necklaced."

"Yes, but *you* weren't in the store when that happened," said Tom.

Gilly began to laugh. "No, I was not in there the first two times it happened."

"Well, he was in there the third time," said Tom to me, "and he chased them down the street with his pistol."

"Oh, ho-ho-ho-ho," Gilly laughed and rocked back in his chair as though the comrades were the best joke in the world. "When I was young, ho-ho-ho-ho, there were guns everywhere in the townships. And these little fellows, all they've got are stones."

"You know what we have to do," said Tom when Gilly'd left, "we have to get Gilly to come out to our house for dinner and bring his wife and some of his friends. It would be interesting for you to talk to them."

But the riots in Soweto kept anyone from getting in or out after dark and, even in the daytime, there were too many barricades and stonings to bring the women along. So Gilly and three of his black friends, young men in their twenties, came to an afternoon *braai*, a barbecue, at Tom and Sally's house. A Christmas-week strike had begun in Soweto that day and Gilly, Bob, Carswell and Nick arrived in a rusted Datsun, although Gilly owns a BMW.

We all sat on the patio for a stiff twenty minutes while the Mills's maid peeked around the doorpost with an expression of intrigued disapproval. But then a few beers were had and the steaks and the *boerewors* sausages began to spatter on the grill, and one more of the hundred thousand endless discussions of South Africa's "situation" began.

The strange thing is that when I look in my notes now, if I cover the names, I can barely tell who said what or if the speaker was black or white. Carswell, Bob (and me, I guess) favored one man, one vote. Gilly, Nick, Tom and Sally felt Tom's idea about property qualification had merit. There was a general denunciation of the Group Areas Act, which dictates where what race can live, and of U.S. sanctions, too. "Politics is dirty," said Carswell and

there was unanimous disparagement of President Botha and Winnie
Mandela. Everyone agreed moderates would come to the fore if
they just had a chance. Bob described, with considerable anger,
how the riots and strikes in Soweto were controlled by anonymous
pamphlets and unsigned ads in the *Daily Sowetoen*. He blamed
outside agitators, just like the Reagan White House does. "They
call you up in the night," said Carswell, "and ask what size tire
would fit you."

"We need more black police and black army forces," said
Nick. Nick, Bob and Carswell had small children and were furious
about the black school boycott. They said the ANC leaders were
pushing a public-school strike while the leaders' own children were
being educated in private schools. They feared, they said, "the
intentional creation of a black underclass." Of course, there's one
of those already but, anyway, everyone praised capitalism for a
while and Bob made a poetic appeal for whites to stay in South
Africa, although perhaps he was just being polite in response to the
hospitality.

Then Nick said something that shocked me, and that I could
see suprised Tom and Sally. "I'm angry that South Africa is singled
out," he said. "Why should Senator Kennedy come here and tell us
our troubles? We're not the only country in the world where bad
things happen."

"I have just this one fear," said Carswell. "Attack from the
outside—South Africa has no friends."

After the meal Gilly waxed historical and told a horrifying
story about seeing three men crucified by the Spoilers gang in
Alexandra in the 1940s. "One man was still alive, nailed up to this
post. He was screaming but his mouth was dry and no sound came
out. I will never forget it."

"What are you guys going to *do*?" I asked Nick, Bob and
Carswell. "How are you going to get rid of apartheid?"

"Such meetings as this are valuable," said Carswell, as
though something had been accomplished that afternoon.

"That was a real eye-opener," said Tom when Gilly and his
friends had left.

"Incredibly interesting," said Sally. "We've got to do that
again."

And it dawned on me—they'd never had black people as guests in their house before.

"We've seen Gilly and his wife at office parties," said Sally. "And there are black and Indian students at the kids' schools. We've seen the parents at school functions."

We were going to the Fletchers' house that night for dinner. "Let's not say anything about this," said Tom. "I'm not sure how Bill and Margaret would feel about it. They're a little old-fashioned about some things."

"Yes," said Sally.

But at one that morning when we were all good and drunk and passing around the Afrikaner Witzend brandy, Tom couldn't resist. "You'll never guess what we did this afternoon," he said to Bill and Margaret. "You know my client Gilly, who owns all the stores? Well, we had him and some of his young friends out to a *braai*. They had some extraordinary things to say. It was a real eye-opener."

"Incredible," said Bill. "What a great idea. We ought to do that, Margaret. With some of my subcontractors. That's a great idea."

"We really should," said Margaret.

I had the most peculiar feeling in my woozy haze. I was present at the birth of a fundamental, epochal realization of human fellowship. But I was sure the birth was coming too late to save the baby.

I'd walked Gilly out to the Datsun when he was leaving Tom's house. And he took me by the arm and said, "Apartheid is the evil thing. Apartheid must just stop. If those laws are removed, no more policemen will be needed." He glanced toward Tom and Sally. "They all know it's wrong."

I said, "They don't seem to know how to get rid of it."

"They know," said Gilly. "They just don't want to give up the advantage they have on the black man."

"Is it too late?" I said.

"What man does man can fix."

Maybe. On my last day in South Africa I drove through Soweto—probably not a good idea for a person as putty-colored as myself in a shiny red rent-a-car. Also, it was illegal. No white person is allowed to go there without government permission. Even white police and soldiers don't enter Soweto unless the "situation" gets so out of hand they think they have no choice. But I'd been in South Africa for a month and had not met one white person who'd been there. It's just outside Jo-burg, a huge adjunct taking up the whole southwestern quadrant of the city's outskirts. But I hadn't talked to any white person who'd ever even seen Soweto.

And then I couldn't find the place. A city of two million people and when I looked at my rental car map it wasn't there. I drove around the N-1 beltway and there were no signs, no exits marked Soweto. I got off in the southwest and headed in what I thought must be the right direction. I took a couple of gravel roads, navigating by the sun. Finally I saw a Soweto sign, the size that might say "PICNIC AREA 1 MILE." And on the other side of a hill was Soweto, as big as the San Fernando Valley, a vast expanse of little homes.

It was not such a terrible-looking place, by Third World standards. It was littered and scruffy and crowded, but most of the houses looked like what you'd see on an American Indian reservation. Each modest dwelling was set on a small plot of land. There was electricity and no raw sewage stink.

Soweto was almost rich as riches are measured in Africa. And there was plenty of economic power here for political power to grow out of it if that were the way things worked in South Africa. But it wouldn't have mattered if each of those houses had been Graceland. People would be just as oppressed. South Africa is one of the few places I've ever been where things are not a matter of dollars and cents.

I locked my car doors, adjusted my necktie and drove through the place in a sweat. Soweto is like discovering arithmetic. It is an epiphany about what "83 percent of the population" means. Until then I hadn't *seen* the blacks in South Africa, not really, not even in the overpopulated homelands. Now they pressed in on every side in the slow jam of bicycles, trucks and foot traffic. I hoped I had something in my wallet, some leftover receipt from a United Negro College Fund donation or some damn thing to save my pink ass when the comrades got to me. Everyone was staring in my windows. Everyone in the crowd was looking at my pale, stupid face.

And then I saw that they were smiling. And here and there was a happy wave. There was laughter from the little kids. I drove through Soweto for nearly an hour without so much as a bad look tossed in my direction, let alone rocks or firebombs.

Maybe I'd caught them by surprise and they didn't know what to make of me. Maybe they thought I was so crazy to be there that it was funny. I didn't know.

Months after I got back I was giving a lecture on journalism at some little college in the middle of Pennsylvania and I told the students about driving through Soweto. One of them came up to the lectern afterward. She was from Soweto, an exchange student. "Don't you know why the people were smiling and waving at you?" she said. "They thought you were great."

"But why?"

"It's *illegal* for you to be there. How did you ever get in?"

"I don't know. I was lost. I came in through some back roads."

"The government isn't letting anyone in there and when people saw you, that you had managed to get in some way. . . . They figured you must be somebody good, an organizer, or from some international group, that you would even be there."

"Even though I was white?"

"*Because* you were white."

There *is* some hope for South Africa, for the souls of the people there anyway. I mean, personally, if I'd lived my forty years in Soweto and I saw some unprotected honky cruising down my street on a Saturday afternoon, I would have opened that car like an oyster and deep-fat fried me on the spot.

Through Darkest America: Epcot Center

· ·

MAY 1983

At Epcot Center the Disney corporation has focused its attention on two things greatly in need of Disneyfication: the tedious future and the annoying whole wide world.

Once the future promised weekend tours of Jupiter, 200-mph Pontiacs shaped like tropical fish and happy robots making every kid's bed. The world beyond our shores was a wonderland of oddball plants and animals, peopled by folks in interesting colors who lived in Taj Mahals and trees. Today the future is a quagmire of micro-chips. They'll connect your television to somebody's typewriter, and, if you can't score a million at Donkey Kong, you'll be out of work. Meanwhile, the rest of the world has become a jumble of high-rises, from which pour mobs of college students headed for our embassies with kindling and Bics.

Mickey, Donald, Goofy to the rescue! Give us hope! Give us joy! Give us funny mouse ears, anyway, to wear while we man the ramparts of civilization.

Alas, it's not to be. Walt is dead. And, after a couple of hours at Epcot, you'll wish you were, too.

P.J. O'Rourke
. . . .

Epcot Center is one element in the vast central Florida complex where Disney is attempting to remedy America's chronic leisure surplus. The whole is twice as large as Manhattan Island. Epcot itself is almost the size of Central Park.

Five big American corporations sponsor pavilions in the "Future World" half of Epcot Center. I was expecting wonders. I'm a fan of big American corporations. At least, I used to be. I thought they embodied that true basis of the American character: utopian greed. Their vision of the future always combined mercantile rapacity with such courageous lack of common sense—"Hey, Dad, can I have the keys to the auto-gyro?" I guess I'm out of date.

Instead of miracles, each pavilion has a mechanical ride that whisks you through darkened scenes full of robots which have even less personality than human actors. Every ride seems to begin with cavemen and end in a video game where a recorded voice asks you to face the challenges of tomorrow. I thought that's what we're paying these corporations to do. In between the automat Neanderthals and the tepid splatter of strobe effects is the briefest, most bowdlerized, most fact-free possible exposition of something that has something to do with something the corporation vends. It's non-education in the guise of un-entertainment, and there's not even a good sales pitch to excuse it.

The Bell System's "Spaceship Earth" is, I suppose, the best of the lot. You're trundled around inside the immense whiffle ball that's Epcot's trademark and exposed to *tableux morts* showing glimpses of communications technology from mud to the modern day. The last scene is a nightmarish vault filled with blasting, flashing television screens. I thought this brought the point home nicely that it doesn't matter how elaborate a communications system is when there's nothing to communicate.

General Motors has something called "The World of Motion" that should properly be titled "Ride the Wild Ironies." In the first place, they propel you through their robot show in a form of mass rail transit. And the tram cars are all too much like current GM automobiles—small, slow and made out of plastic. Also, the ride keeps coming to a halt, caught in some mid-exhibit traffic jam. Furthermore, General Motors tries to make its history of transporta-

181

tion comic at a moment when the U.S. auto industry is just not a laughing matter.

It's interesting to see what the members of a corporate board can agree upon as funny. At GM, funny is round, puffy faces and great big behinds—though other out-sized body parts will do. We're shown a cave family with very swollen feet. (They had to *walk*, you see.) And there's a group of caravan travelers being overcharged by a fellow with a huge hooked nose. I hope no one thinks this is anti-Semitic, not after all the trouble GM went to making 15 percent of their robots black whether black people belong in the scenes or not. (No, there aren't any out-sized male parts visible.)

Exxon's "Universe of Energy" tends to the peculiar rather than the humorous. There are no markings on the entrance doors. You mill around outside the Exxon monolith until they agree to let you in. Then you're made to stand in a large, dim hall while an incomprehensible film montage about wind and sun and rain and strip mines is shown on a wall. Another such montage is endured inside a theater. When it ends, the blocks of theater seats start moving around in a most disconcerting way. After two or three minutes of mechanical confusion, the seats locomote through a short tunnel filled with clock-work dinosaurs. The dinosaurs are depicted without accuracy and much too close to your face.

One of the few real novelties at Epcot is the use of smell to aggravate illusions. Of course, no one knows what dinosaurs smelled like, but Exxon has decided they smelled bad.

At the other end of Dino Ditch the seats rearrange themselves and there's a final, very addled message about facing challenge-hood tomorrow-wise. I dozed off during this, but the import seems to be that dinosaurs don't have anything to do with energy policy and neither do you.

If you have the right attitude, these exhibits are swell. They're Tilt-O-Whirls for intellectuals. They excite all kinds of thrilling mental terror about the banality of American thought, electrify you with horror at the myopia of corporate perspective, and create marvelous suspense as you consider what's in store for our society now that we've lost not only our visionary capacities but even our simple avarice. I mean, why can't you buy a Mickey Mouse phone in the Bell pavilion?

Maintaining the right attitude is a chore, however, and one I abandoned after the intensely stupid Kodak "Journey Into the Imagination." Epcot Center is a family attraction, so I didn't expect to see the things that occupy my own imagination. Still, Kodak could have done better than this jumble of redundant Jules Verne machine parts blowing colored bubbles through chemistry-set tubing and dangling crude unicorn cutouts from the walls. The nation that produced Mormon theology, Edgar Allan Poe and the Reagan Administration's economic policy deserves more.

There is supposed to be an interesting 3-D movie somewhere at Kodak, but I was desperate to get out of the place. It was twenty degrees hotter inside than it was in the midday sun. Like the rest of the buildings in Future World, the Kodak pavilion's sleek functionalism is for strictly decorative purposes. Even a company with as little imagination as Kodak should know better than to have a greenhouse roof in Florida.

The remaining pavilion is sponsored by Kraft. It's called "The Land," and I can't tell you what goes on in there. I stepped inside and didn't see anything made from an organic substance. This included their food. I didn't go on the ride for fear they'd make me eat some of it.

All these exhibits seem more involved with literal than figurative tomorrows. They're as up-to-date as next Monday. Visiting Future World is like opening a Chinese fortune cookie to read, "Soon you'll be finished with dinner."

The other half of Epcot Center is called "World Showcase," and it consists of nine national pavilions arranged around a phony lake. An objective look at the world as presented here results in these conclusions: Earth is made of cement painted to look like different parts of Los Angeles, and its salient feature is overpriced gift shops.

"Mexico's" gift shop is housed in a vividly bogus Mayan temple. The sales floor is supposed to represent a Mexican marketplace. Seeing a Mexican marketplace portrayed as clean, quiet, safe and expensive is, somehow, as alarming as seeing a pyramid of human skulls in downtown Kansas City.

A clean, quiet, safe and expensive "Germany" is, on the other hand, soporiferously convincing. For a moment I thought I *was* in Germany. I left as quickly as I could.

"Italy" has so little to do with things Italian that I wonder if maybe this isn't some kind of revolving exhibit that, on other days of the week, is labeled "Belgium," "Seattle" and "Sydney, Australia."

The only interesting pavilion is mainland China's. They used some real wood and real ceramics in their reproduction of an ancient Peking temple. And they have a pretty movie about China's big, weird landscape. Political points are deftly made—"How wonderful it must have been when *everyone* could first enter the Forbidden City." But I'm not sure I want to live in a world where Exxon needs to take lessons from the Chicom hordes who murdered our boys at the Yalu. Also, their movie is shown in 360 degrees, which assumes we white devils have an extra set of eyes on the back of our ears.

"America" has accurately horrible food and inaccurately horrible young people dressed as members of the Continental Congress and singing "Turkey in the Straw."

I don't know why Mickey Mouse isn't in the "France" exhibit. You see him all over Paris where he is considered an existential figure of stature equal to Camus or Jerry Lewis. But it was worth Epcot's $15 admission ticket to see a glass of "lait" on a French menu.

"Japan" has the best gift shop.

"Canada" is surely indulging in a bit of good-natured self-mockery with a national display so dull that its centerpiece is a one-quarter scale replica of the Chateau Frontenac, a second-rate luxury hotel built in Quebec City in the 1920s.

I picked up one of the toys for sale at the "United Kingdom" pavilion. I leave it to your imagination where it was made.

With Epcot Center the Disney corporation has accomplished something I didn't think possible in today's world. They have created a land of make-believe that's worse than regular life. Unvarnished reality would be preferable. In fact, it might be fun.

"United Kingdom" could feature green-haired teenagers wearing diaper pins through their lips and spray-painting swastikas on the fake bull's-eye pub windows. "France" could be manned by snarling Parisian *garçons* bullying the naive tourists into ordering peeled mice in heavy cream. "America" could be the very stretch of

highway through Kissimmee, Florida, that leads to Epcot's gates—
a thousand Dairy Queens, RV parks, pee-wee golf establishments,
and souvenir stands selling cypress knee clocks and shellacked
blowfish. All the Mexicans next door could be trying to sneak in.
We could buy cars from General Motors, gas up at Exxon and drive
over to the Bell System where, if they have any sense, they'll give
us free whiskey so we'll make nine-hour phone calls to old
girlfriends in Taos. When we've spent all our money doing this, we
could go to Kraft and get free government-surplus cheese-food
substances. And, if Disney still wants to make Epcot Center
futuristic, they could do so by blowing the place up with an atom
bomb.

Among the Euro-Weenies

APRIL–MAY 1986

The Europeans are going to have to feather their nests with some-body else's travelers checks this year. The usual flock of American pigeons is crapping on statues elsewhere. Sylvester Stallone canned the Cannes Film Festival. Prince won't tour this side of the sink. The U.S. Junior Wimbledon team is keeping its balls on the home court. And Trans-Atlantic rubber-neck bookings have taken a dive. Some say it's fear of terrorism. Some say it's Chernobyl fallout. Some say it's the weak dollar. But all of that ignores one basic fact. This place sucks.

I've been over here for one gray, dank spring month now, and I think I can tell you why everyone with an IQ bigger than his hat size hit the beach at Ellis Island. Say what you want about "land of opportunity" and "purpled mountains majesty above the fruited plain," our forebears moved to the United States because they were sick to death of lukewarm beer—and lukewarm coffee and lukewarm bath water and lukewarm mystery cutlets with mucky-colored mushroom cheese junk on them. Everything in Europe is lukewarm except the radiators. You could use the radiators to make party ice. But nobody does. I'll bet you could walk from the Ural Mountains to the beach at Biarritz and not find one rock-hard, crystal-clear, fist-sized American ice cube. Ask for whiskey on the rocks, and you get a single, gray, crumbling leftover from some Lilliputian puddle freeze plopped in a thimble of Scotch (for which you're charged like sin). And the phones don't work. They go "blat-blat" and "neek-neek" and "ugu-ugu-ugu." No two dial tones are alike. The busy signal sounds as if the phone is ringing. And when the phone rings you think the dog farted.

All the light switches in Europe are upside down. The electrical plugs are terrifying with nine or a dozen huge, nasty prongs, and you'd better wear rubber boots if you come within a yard of them because house current here is about one hundred thousand volts. Not that that makes the appliances work. This electric typewriter I'm pounding, for instance—I'd throw it out the window but it's one of those silly European windows that, when you push it open from the right, comes around from the left and smacks you in the back of the head.

The Europeans can't figure out which side of the road to drive on, and I can't figure out how to flush their toilets. Do I push the knob or pull it or twist it or pump it? And I keep cracking my shins on that stupid bidet thing. (Memo to Europeans: Try washing your *whole* body; believe me, you'd smell better.) Plus there are ruins everywhere. The Italians have had two thousand years to fix up the Forum and just look at the place.

I've had it with these dopey little countries and all their poky borders. You can't swing a cat without sending it through customs. Everything's too small. The cars are too small. The beds are too small. The elevators are the size of broom closets. Even the languages are itty-bitty. Sometimes you need two or three just to get you through till lunch.

It's not like the Europeans have been very nice hosts either. The whole month here has been one long shower of shit about America, just because we took a punch at the Libyans. There were huge demonstrations in Germany, Italy and Spain. In West Berlin twenty thousand young bucketheads turned out. In Barcelona a group of protestors vented their fury on that symbol of American imperialism, a McDonald's. In London thousands of peace-

mongers blocked the main shopping thoroughfare of Oxford Street,
staging sit-down strikes and throwing bottles at the police. Thousands more Brits came out to holler in Manchester, Cardiff and
Glasgow and at the military bases on the Clyde and in Oxfordshire.
According to various opinion polls, 66 percent of the British
deplored our behavior as did 75 percent of the West Germans, 32
percent of the French and 60 percent of the Italians. In Belgium a
friend of mine was stopped on the street by a policeman and told he
should be ashamed to be an American.

The cover story of *Time Out*, London's equivalent to *New York*
magazine, was OVER ARMED, OVER EAGER, OVER HERE. A
British TV comedy program showed a puppet skit with President
Reagan as the Jordanian who tried to blow up an El Al airliner and
Mrs. Thatcher as the dim-bulb pregnant Irish girl duped into
carrying the explosives. *The New Statesman* ran an editorial explaining how U.S. defense policy can be understood only in light of
American football. "Defense, to the average redneck," it said,
"means hitting your opponent hard before he sees the ball." An
article in the magazine *New Socialist* said that in the U.S. world
view "non-Americans are simply not people," claimed that, "To be
President, you have to be mad or an actor," and asked itself, "Does
not the United States need a hostile relationship with the Soviet
Union to contain discontent at home. . . ?" Another article in the
same magazine began, "It is the United States which is clearly the
greatest evil to peoples seeking just rights of self-determination."
(*New Socialist* is not, by the way, some nut-fudge fringe publication
like it would be in the States. It's the official organ of the Labour
Party.) As *Paris Match* put it, *"Le point de vue européen était
différent et tous nos responsables plaidaient pour une action plus
discrète."* Whatever that means.

Actually, the only *discrète* people I've met here were Libyans,
the employees of Libyan Arab Airlines in Paris, who never referred
to our rocketing and bombing each other as anything but "this
difficult situation."

I was talking to the Libyans because I never wanted to go to
Europe in the first place. I was headed for Tripoli. It was a dream
by-line: "From our correspondent on the Line of Death." But daily
life kept getting in the way. Taxes were due. I owed a 4,000-word

story to *Gerbil and Pet Mouse Monthly.* My girlfriend was restive. She pointed out I'd forgotten Christmas and that when I'd taken her out for New Year's, I'd taken her out in the backyard to blow off M-80s under the garbage cans.

I set to work with a will, emptying checkbooks, wrestling accountants, interviewing small rodents, scouring the bargain bin at Cartier's. By Monday, April 14, I had everything paid, written, kissed, made up and in the mail. My safari jacket was packed, my tape recorder loaded. I zipped shut my official foreign correspondent duffel bag, fixed myself a drink and flipped on the eleven o'clock news. "BOOM!" My friend Charles Glass, ABC-TV's Middle East correspondent, was holding a telephone receiver out a window of the Grand Hotel in Tripoli. "We're not sure exactly what's going on," shouted Glass at the phone. I was. Those weren't the Nicaraguan *contras* out there pounding Mad Mo, the terror-bombing Sheikh of Shriek. "It would appear that the United States has launched a military action against Libya," shouted Glass, trying to sound grave. But you could hear the boyish enthusiasm creeping into his voice the way it always does when a reporter manages to get himself right smack dab in the middle of something god-awful.

I could have cried. I did cry. I threw things. I took the first plane to Paris.

Paris had the nearest Libyan Embassy or People's Bureau or whatever they're calling them. It looked like military school the way I'd pictured it when my parents used to threaten to send me there. I made four trips to this forbidding crib before somebody there told me the only way I could get a visa to go to Tripoli was to go to Tripoli.

I went back to my hotel and got on the worthless, static-filled French telephone. Air France wasn't flying to Libya just then. British Airways definitely wasn't. Swissair was coy. Maybe they were, and maybe they weren't. I finally got a reservation on Lufthansa, rushed to their office and handed over a thousand dollars worth of funny-colored French bumwad. The ticket agent said, "You have a visa?"

"My visa is waiting for me in Tripoli."

Holidays In Hell
....

"We cannot take you to Tripoli without a visa."

"I can't get a visa without going to Tripoli."

"You can get a visa in Tripoli?"

"Right."

"But we cannot take you there."

"Why not?"

"You don't have a visa."

You can always reason with a German. You can always reason with a barnyard animal, too, for all the good it does.

I didn't figure an American would be very welcome on the Libyan flag carrier at the moment, unless he wanted to travel naked and in a muzzle. But it was worth a try. I went to the Libyan Arab Airlines office on the Champs-Elysées. There were half a dozen Libyans inside. I picked out a young one behind the counter and began explaining with many worried hand gestures how I had been told by my editor, of a very important magazine, to go directly to Libya no matter what and now I was stranded in this faraway country among foreigners and could not seem to get to Libya by any means, etc. "Oh, my goodness," said the young man, "and right now there is this . . ." He paused and considered the delicacy of my feelings. ". . . this difficult situation."

I'd hate to have to explain this to anyone who was on the *Achille Lauro*, but Arabs are the sweetest-natured people on earth. To meet an Arab is to gain a devoted friend. If you even make eye contact with an Arab, you've got a pal for life. "Would you like some coffee?" said the young man. The other Libyans pulled up their chairs and offered cigarettes. But there was one, with sharp clothes and an equally sharp face, who eyed me narrowly. He said, "What kind of journalistic story is it that you wish to do?"

Well, he had me there. I'd never given it a thought. I just figured, what with guns going off and things blowing up, there'd be plenty of deep truths and penetrating insights. Tragedy and strife produce these things in boxcar lots, as any good reporter knows. Also, I wanted a chance to wear my new safari jacket. You really

190

look like a twink if it isn't adequately dirty and sweat-stained.
"Uh," I said, "I'd like to do a *cultural* piece. ("Cultural piece" is a
key phrase for foreign correspondents. It means you aren't going to
poke into any political leader's Luxembourg bank account or try to
find out if his wife has ten thousand pairs of Maud Frizon pumps in
the palace basement.)

"There is a great lack of understanding between the Arab
world and the United States just now," said the young man behind
the counter.

"There sure is," I said.

"Why do *you* think this is?" said the sharp dresser.

The truthful answer would have been, "Because one by one
and man to man Arabs are the salt of the earth—generous, hospitable, brave, wise, and so forth. But get you in a pack and shove a
Koran down your pants and you act like a footlocker full of glue-
sniffing civet cats." We're a frank people, we Americans. But not
quite *that* frank. I decided to blame it on Paul Newman.

"It's because of *Exodus*," I said. "*Exodus* was a very popular
movie in the United States. Ever since this movie all Americans
think everyone in Israel is kind and good and looks like Paul
Newman."

"Hmmmmm," said the Libyans. It made sense to them.

"I will call my uncle," said the sharp dresser. "He is an
important man at the embassy in Rome."

"I will call the embassy here," said someone else.

"I will book a flight," said the young man behind the counter,
and he got me more coffee (The only decent coffee I'd had since I
left New York, by the way).

The Libyan Arab Air people squared everything with the
Ministry of Information in Tripoli, got me a ticket for that Friday,
and told their airport manager at Orly to take me under his wing.
All to no avail, however. Come Friday, the French government
decided to expel four Libyan diplomats, and I was bumped off the
plane.

In the meantime, I was stuck in Paris. A lot of people get all
moist and runny at the mention of this place. I don't get it. It's just
a big city, no dirtier than most. It does have nice architecture
because the French chickened out of World War II. But it's sur-

rounded by the most depressing ring of lower-middle-class suburbs this side of Smolensk. In fact, one of these suburbs is actually named Stalingrad, which goes to show that the French have learned nothing about politics since they guillotined all the smart people in 1793.

French women, whether pretty or not, all walk around with their noses in the air (and pretty big noses they usually are). I guess this is what's meant by their "sense of style." Where did this sense of style thing get started? The French are a smallish, monkey-looking bunch and not dressed any better, on average, than the citizens of Baltimore. True, you can sit outside in Paris and drink little cups of coffee, but why this is more stylish than sitting inside and drinking large glasses of whiskey I don't know.

I was exhausted the night I arrived and couldn't think of any place to go except Harry's New York Bar. Harry's is a 1930s hangout left over from the days when Hemingway used to stop in while taking a break from pestering large animals, such as his drunk friend F. Scott Fitzgerald. At least the drinks at Harry's aren't microscopic. I had three and called for the "carte de menu." I'd forgotten that Harry's doesn't serve food.

"We do *not* serve food," said the waiter, cocking a snook. There was a ferocious pause, "except hot dogs." Thus, on my first night in this capital of international gastronomy, I dined on two hot dogs and five Scotches.

The next night I called my girlfriend who was back in the States and, no doubt, happily contemplating the sterling silver Elsa Peretti refrigerator magnet I'd bought her to make up for Christmas. She's spent a lot of time in Paris. "Where's a good place for dinner?" I asked.

"There's the Brasserie Lipp on the Avenue St. Germaine," she said, "or La Coupole in Montmartre."

"Not La Coupole," I said. "I've been there before. That's the place that's crowded and noisy and smells bad and everybody's rude as hell, isn't it?"

"I think you just described France," she said.

Actually, it was Brasserie Lipp I'd been to before. I remembered the minute they stuffed me behind a hankie-size table between the pissoir and a trolley full of sheep cheese. I ordered steak, and they brought me sauerkraut.

Nobody's French is *that* bad, not even mine. But Parisians never deign to understand a word you say in their own language, no matter how loud or often you pronounce it. They insist on speaking English until you wonder if the whole thing is a put-up job. Maybe they just take a couple of years of Frog Talk in high school like the rest of us and can no more speak French themselves than they can make ice cubes.

I also went to the Louvre. Big deal. The "Winged Victory" of Samothrace looks like somebody dropped it. And the "Mona Lisa" has a sheet of bulletproof glass in front of it, covered with smudgy nose prints. Besides, I think if something is going to be as famous as the "Mona Lisa," it ought to be bigger. Do not, however, miss the Peter-Paul Rubens Unabashed Sell-Out and Philistine Sycophant Room on floor two. In 1622 Queen Marie de Medici commissioned Rubens to paint about two dozen Greyhound bus–sized canvases celebrating every moment of her worthless life. The series runs from Queen Marie's birth, attended by all the hosts of heaven, to her marriage to the King of France when they invited every figure in ancient mythology including Io the cow. These paintings take win, place and show in the international hilarious fat girl derby.

At least the French weren't rioting about American imperialism. In fact, it was hard to tell *what* the French thought about our little experiment in Libyan bomb tag. (You're "it," Muammar, and no taps back.) The French official position was all over the map. It was "a question of national sovereignty" one day and "we weren't consulted in advance" the next. Then it was "we don't approve of such methods" followed by a hint that they would have approved of such methods after all if we'd only used bigger bombs. The French are masters of "the dog ate my homework" school of diplomatic relations.

French unofficial position, that is, the opinion of taxi drivers, bartenders, the concierge at the hotel and those old women they keep in the bathrooms, was no easier to figure out. I'd ask and get a nudge, a smirk, pursed lips, shrugged shoulders, knowing rolls of the eyes, waved hands, knit brows—the whole panoply of Froggy visual ticks.

Maybe it *is* fun to sit outside in Paris and drink little cups of coffee. You can watch the French grimace and posture. And then you can guess what they're saying to each other.

"I think, Antoinette, for me the croissant has the aspect existential. It is bread, the staff of life, but no? And yet, there is the paradox marvelous. Because the bread itself, it is a lifeless thing. Is it not true? We must order croissants."

"No, no, no, no, Jacques. To think as this is is to make the miscomprehension of the universe, its nature. To order the croissants would be an act inconceivable. An action of the most bourgeois type . . ."

Who gives a shit what the French think.

After I was kicked off the plane to Libya, I went to visit my friend in Brugge, the one who was under instructions from the police to be ashamed. We spent the weekend looking for fun in Belgium, which is an isometric exercise. That is, it's a strain and you get nowhere.

A hotel desk clerk gave us the name of the one local hot spot. It was called "The Korral" or "Sixes Gun" or some such bogus American moniker like they put on everything over here when they want you to think you're going to get something un-European, like a good time. It was a crowded place where they played French rock and roll (which sounds like somebody's chasing Edith Piaf around the old Peppermint Lounge with an electric hedge trimmer).

My friend was trying to explain that you don't put sweet vermouth in a martini when a little scene caught my eye. Standing by the door was a Belgian greaser, a young hard guy with a modified skinhead haircut, dressed all in black and carrying a motorcycle helmet. He was running through all the usual teenage tough-kid postures and checking out the room to make sure all the other kids understood how unconcerned he was with their opinion. Perched on a railing in front of him, with her legs wrapped around his butt, was an adorable blonde girl about sixteen years old. She was kissing and nuzzling her cool beau, who would peck her briefly then swig his beer and check the room again.

In the breast pocket of her blouse the girl had a little toy stuffed rabbit. After another offhand kiss from her boyfriend, she took the rabbit out, held it in her hand and whispered in the boy's ear. I couldn't hear what she said and they were speaking Flemish anyway, but I could tell what was going on:

P. J. O'Rourke
· ·

"I want a real kiss."

"Yeah, okay."

"Now the bunny wants a kiss."

"Knock it off."

"The bunny wants a kiss soooooooo bad."

"Come on, knock it off."

"If the bunny doesn't get a kiss, *somebody's* going to be very cross."

The greaser kid scoped the room with mean but panicked eyes. Then he kissed the bunny.

On Monday I went to the U.K. to make one more attempt to get to Libya before I started kissing toy bunnies myself. I got a reservation on Lufthansa again. I figured I'd just lie, show them my old Lebanese visa with a lot of Arabic squiggles on it. Germans respond well to lies. At least, they always have historically.

Then I went to the ABC News bureau in London where they had a phone line open to the Grand Hotel in Tripoli. I talked to my old Lebanon buddy, ABC video editor George Moll.

"Get your ass down here!" said George. "This is great! And bring some salami, okay? And cheese. And potato chips and pretzels."

"And cigarettes!" said a voice in the background. "A carton of Marlboros."

"Two cartons!" said another voice. "And a carton of Salems and chocolate bars and Cokes!"

"And bring pita bread!" said George.

"Pita bread? What the hell do you want with pita bread? You're surrounded by Arabs," I said. "You can't get pita bread?"

"You can't get *anything*," said George. "And for chrissake bring booze!"

"How can I do that? They'll kill me."

"Naw," said George, "they'll just rough you up. Anyway, they won't catch you. It's easy. Just get a six-pack of soda water, the little bottles, the kind with the screw tops. And fill them up with vodka

195

and screw the tops back on and put them back in that plastic collar thing."

"Are you sure you should be telling me this over the phone?"

"If they can't make pita bread, what the fuck do you think their phone taps are like?" said George. "So, anyway, what's happening?"

"Nothing much," I said. "It's raining. And everybody's yelling at Margaret Thatcher about the F-111s and. . . ."

"Not up there," said George. "I mean, what's happening down *here*? They won't let us out of the hotel."

Loaded with three times the European Economic Community's import limit on tobacco and foodstuffs and stinking like a delicatessen, I got as far as Frankfurt. Then a telex came through from Libya that all foreign journalists who could count higher than ten were expelled.

Back in London—tired, discouraged and a little drunk—I called an old girlfriend from college. She and I had been through a lot together back when the U.S. was taking a punch at the Vietnamese and I was the one blocking the streets and screaming about American imperialism. (Morality was so much simpler when I thought the government was trying to kill *me*.) This girl is married now, with a family. So it wasn't anything, you know. . . . I mean we'd hardly seen each other since she moved to England fifteen years ago. I just longed for a friendly face. (Where do they keep the motels in Europe, anyway?)

"You're bloody *mad!*" she shouted. "All you Americans are *mad*! All you want to do is put McDonald's all over the earth and start World War III!"

And this from someone who was born and raised in Great Neck, Long Island. Well, if I was going to get barked at, it might as well be by a person who does it for a living. I went to see Meg Beresford, general secretary of the Campaign for Nuclear Disarmament.

In England, even the peace movement has a bureaucracy, and the CND is the central organizing body for all those demonstrations the Brits are always having against cruise missiles, Polaris submarines, atomic power plants and other things that can or do blow up. In England, everything has a musty old tradition too. It was the

CND who, nearly thirty years ago, devised that semaphore of Nuclear Disarmament initials, the ☮ . Thus, the "footprint of the American chicken" is really a European invention.

Meg told me that the phones at CND had been ringing off the hook on the day of the air strike and that the demonstrations against the raid had been highly spontaneous. She said the air strike was "a foolish way to try to deal with terrorism" and that people in England had "a feeling that Libya is rather a small actor" in the terror pageant and that the effect of the raid "will be to bring terror to our streets."

What I didn't understand, I said, was the emotional intensity of the demonstrations. Big civilized countries had been launching punative raids on misbehaving weedy little native powers since . . . . Well, at least since the Redcoats shot up Lexington and Concord.

Meg said that when the F-111s were launched from English soil, the British realized for the first time "what those bases were for."

This made the British sound a little thick.

Meg claimed the apparent attempt to kill Qaddafi himself had upset people, "like watching one of those John Wayne movies."

When a European mentions John Wayne, you know you're going to get an earful.

Meg admitted there was "resentment at American culture." She said, "Western democracies feel there is nothing immoral about spreading that kind of system, spreading Western-style democracy." She paused. "McDonald's everywhere."

Will somebody please tell me what's the matter with McDonald's? It's not like the Europeans don't line up by the millions to eat there. Maybe McDonald's food isn't the best thing for you, but roasted goose liver smooshed up with truffles isn't either. And has anyone ever smoked a joint and had a "*pâté de foie gras* attack"?

"There is," said Meg, "at the back of the American psyche the feeling that the American way is the best."

As opposed to what? As opposed to living in seedy, old, down-at-the-heels England with an eighteenth-century class system and seventeenth-century plumbing? Or as opposed to lining up for pita-bread ration cards in a half-assed African sandlot run by a fanatical big mouth with a dish towel on his head?

"What do you think we *should* be doing?" I asked Meg.

"Sitting down in a really serious way to solve the Middle East problem is what Reagan should be doing."

"What if it won't solve?" I said. "I know the source of this terrorism is the Israeli-Palestinian problem. And that's a place where two wrongs don't make a right. But it's also a place where two *rights* don't make a right."

"The Palestinian problem has to be treated in a much more serious way," said Meg.

The Europeans are great ones for solving problems by taking them more seriously.

She said there was a need for a "definite Middle East policy that's not involved with violence." (Which would be a first in three or four thousand years.) "Something," said Meg, "that other European countries with more experience and understanding could get involved with. . . . The U.N. has to be the place where these things ultimately get solved."

I mean, the U.N. has done such a bang-up job on the Iraq-Iran war, for instance, and the Pol Pot holocaust. They've really got things straightened out in Namibia and Afghanistan too—with the help, of course, of those European countries with more experience and understanding.

I don't mean to pick on Meg Beresford, really. She is obviously a decent person and committed as all get-out to international niceness. But she herself said, musing on the booze-addled States-side Micks who give the IRA guns and money, "If the U.S. feels morally justified in bombing Libya, Britain should feel justified in bombing the U.S."

"Damn right," I said. "Any dumb potato-head who's dragged those rotten ancestral quarrels to his new home in America deserves no better than to get a British laser bomb targeted on his south Boston bar." (That is, assuming the British *have* laser bombs, and assuming the British have the capability to launch a trans-Atlantic air strike without U.S. aid. Which they don't.)

I left CND even more depressed than when I'd arrived. Not over anything Meg said, it's just that why are all high-minded causes so dowdy? The CND offices were an earnest muddle of desks and cubicles and unpainted bookshelves with piles and stacks and quires and reams of those mimeographed handouts that swarm around all do-good organizations like flies on cattle. The better the cause, the worse the atmosphere. And what cause could be better than saving the whole of mankind from nuke vaporizing? You could bottle the dumpy glumness at CND and sell it to . . . well, to the English. London is a quaint and beautiful city—if you stick to the double-decker tourist buses. But the CND offices were out in the East End, in the aptly named district of Shoreditch. Dr. Johnson said, "When a man is tired of London, he is tired of life." But these days he might just be tired of shabby, sad crowds, low-income housing that looks worse than the weather and tattoo-faced, spike-haired pin brains on the dole.

Meanwhile, the Soviet Union was trying to poison half the world with its Chernobyl atomic power plant. But was anybody blocking Oxford Street or calling Gorbachev's energy policy "a game of cossacks and rabbis"? It just didn't seem fair.

I decided to go to West Berlin. Berlin was close to the scum cloud of cesium, iodine and other isotopes that will light up your thyroid and give your kids three heads. Maybe I could make some sense of the Europeans in this isolated, beleagured and slightly radioactive outpost of freedom. And maybe I could peek over the Iron Curtain and get a look at what we've been protecting these Euro-weenies from since 1945.

That wasn't hard. The boundary between East and West is shockingly apparent from the air. The plane descended to 9,500 feet, the permitted altitude through the air corridor to Berlin, and there it was—a thick streak of raked-dirt minefield following, with painful accuracy, the medieval zig-zag border between the kingdoms of Hanover and Prussia.

There was a slide-show change in the landscape. Crisp paved highways turned to muzzy gravel roads. The little towns were suddenly littler. Surburban sprawl evaporated. The distinctive fish-bone patterns of parking lots disappeared. The lush, ditzy quilt-work of private farmland gave way to big, rational, geometric collective fields, where the crops looked thin and the furrows were harrowed T-square straight with no concession to contour plowing.

The constraints, the loss of liberties were visible from nearly two miles up.

Upon landing the scenery changed back. Suddenly you were in the world again, at least the slightly fussy, slightly tiresome European version of it.

It was May Day, and when I checked into my hotel, I asked the desk clerk if there were any big Red doings scheduled.

"Yes," she said, "in the Platz der Republik there is always a large program."

"Where's that?" I asked.

"Oh, just down the street."

"In *West* Berlin?"

"Oh, yes."

"Don't they have a big May day thing in *East* Berlin? I mean, this is the main communist holiday."

"No, I don't think so," said the desk clerk, "not so much over there. The demonstrations are usually on this side."

The Platz der Republik is a wide, grassy square near the Brandenburg Gate. The "large program" was a sort of political fair put on by one of West Berlin's left-wing trade-union organizations. There were no pony rides or ferris wheels, but there was food, beer, a bad rock band singing memorized American lyrics and a hundred booths and tents filled with haymows of those high-minded mimeographed leaflets. The booths seemed like the world's worst carnival games. "Hurry! Hurry! Hurry! Hit the clown on the nose, and win three hundred pounds of literature denouncing U.S. intervention in Nicaragua and a 'Ban NATO' button!"

It was fascinating to wander among the posters and banners and displays of elaborately captioned photographs and be absolutely ignorant of the language. German, to me, looks like what worms do under rocks. There were lots of photos of dirty and tired-looking workers, but I couldn't tell if they were exploited victims of capitalist oppression or heroic comrades struggling to build the joyful new world of socialism. The dead babies in blast wreckage were definitely victims of capitalist oppression. They just didn't have a Kievish look about them. In fact, I saw no reference to Chernobyl. It had been almost a week since the accident started, and the plume of loathsomeness sprouting from the Ukrainian steppe had, that very day, reached its greatest extent. But there were plenty of poster-paint cartoons of Uncle Sam with dog fangs. Usually he was gnawing on someone foreign-looking.

And fifty feet away was the Berlin Wall.

West Berlin is the city that Iggy Pop once moved to because New York wasn't decadent enough for him. I was expecting at least *Cabaret* or maybe *Götterdämmerung* performed by the cast of *La Cage Aux Folles*. Forget it. We bombed the place flat in WWII, and they rebuilt it as a pretty good imitation of Minneapolis. The downtown hub of West Berlin, the Europa Center, is a perfectly modern business/shopping/entertainment complex. As a result, the hot tip for an evening of merriment is to cruise the mall. Furthermore, they serve you bologna for breakfast.

On Saturday there was finally a demonstration in West Berlin protesting the Chernobyl mess. Eight or ten thousand people participated, but this was only half the crowd that rallied against the Libya strike. None of the placards or banners even mentioned Russia by name. And the whole thing was a thoroughly spiritless affair.

Everyone gathered in the Europa Center in front of the Aeroflot airline office. A couple of chants were begun, but nobody took them up. Then the crowd marched. It marched a mile out toward the Technical College, a mile down toward Adenauer Platz and a mile or so back toward downtown, where it petered out in some obligatory speech-making. Apparently this was a standard route. On the way, the crowd passed the American cultural center, which was blocked off by tall wire-mesh barricades and a tripe cordon of riot police. There was nothing in the least anti-American about this demonstration, but the authorities seemed to be worried that the protestors would turn and storm the cultural center from pure force of habit.

As I slogged along, bored and footsore, I talked to the English-speakers in the bunch. They said it was a shame I'd missed the Libya demo. That one was much more interesting.

"How come?" I asked.

They got all excited and told me West Germany was "a colony of the United States." They told me the La Belle discotheque terrorist bomb that killed an American soldier in Berlin was probably a set-up. "Perhaps this bombing was necessary to bomb Tripoli." And they told me . . . Shit, they told me all sorts of things. Basically, they told me off.

I'm sorry. I quit. I just don't have the stomach to go through my sheaves of scribbled notes and piles of garbled tape cassettes again just to shake out three more quotes about what a sack of bastards Americans are.

The day before I left Berlin, I ran into a dozen young Arab men on the street. They were trotting along, taking up the whole sidewalk, accosting busty girls and generally making a nuisance of themselves. One was beating on a snareless drum, and the others were letting loose with intermittent snatches of song and aggressive shouts. They descended on me and loudly demanded cigarettes in German.

"I don't speak German," I said.

"Are you American?" said one, suddenly polite.

"Yes."

"Please, my friend, if you don't mind, do you have a cigarette you could spare?"

I gave them a pack. "Where are you from?" I asked.

"West Beirut," said the drum beater.

"I've been there," I said.

"It is wonderful, no?"

Compared to Berlin, it is. "Sure," I said. They began reminiscing volubly. "What are you doing here?" I asked.

"Our families sent us because of the war. We want to go back to Beirut but we cannot."

I told them I guessed I couldn't go back either, what with the kidnapping and all. They laughed. One of them stuck out his middle finger and said, "This place sucks."

"You should go to America," I said.

"There is only one bad thing about America," said the drum beater. "They won't let us in."

Back in London, I was having dinner in the Groucho Club— this week's in-spot for what's left of Britain's lit glitz and *nouveau* rock *riche*—when one more person started in on the Stars and Stripes. Eventually he got, as the Europeans always do, to the part about "Your country's never been invaded." (This fellow had been

two during the Blitz, you see.) "You don't know the horror, the
suffering. You think war is . . ."

I snapped.

"A John Wayne movie," I said. "That's what you were going to
say, wasn't it? We think war is a John Wayne movie. We think *life* is
a John Wayne movie—with good guys and bad guys, as simple as
that. Well, you know something, Mister Limey Poofter? You're
right. And let me tell you who those bad guys are. They're *us*. WE
BE BAD.

"We're the baddest-assed sons of bitches that ever jogged in
Reeboks. We're three-quaters grizzly bear and two-thirds car wreck
and descended from a stock market crash on our mother's side. You
take your Germany, France and Spain, roll them all together and it
wouldn't give us room to park our cars. We're the big boys, Jack,
the original, giant, economy-sized, new and improved butt kickers
of all time. When we snort coke in Houston, people lose their hats
in Cap d'Antibes. And we've got an American Express card credit
limit higher than your piss-ant metric numbers go.

"You say our country's never been invaded? You're right, little
buddy. Because I'd like to see the needle-dicked foreigners who'd
have the guts to try. We drink napalm to get our hearts started in
the morning. A rape and a mugging is our way of saying 'Cheerio.'
Hell can't hold our sock-hops. We walk taller, talk louder, spit
further, fuck longer and buy more things than you know the names
of. I'd rather be a junkie in a New York City jail than king, queen
and jack of all you Europeans. We eat little countries like this for
breakfast and shit them out before lunch."

Of course, the guy should have punched me. But this was
Europe. He just smiled his shabby, superior European smile.
(God, don't these people have *dentists*?)

Thirty-six Hours in Managua —
An In-depth Report

....

SEPTEMBER 1987

There are probably more fact-finding tours of Nicaragua right now than there are facts—the country has shortages of practically everything. Nonetheless, everyone's going, every senator and representative, the entire pet shop full of '88 presidential candidates, every church-group bake-sale committee and Mush-R-Us liberal coalition. I see that even Mayor Koch is planning to go, probably looking for new kinds of mismanagement to be used in New York City.

Well, I wasn't about to be left out. I wheedled my way onto a weekend trip sponsored by the National Forum Foundation, a conservative think tank founded by former Vietnam POW Senator Jeremiah Denton and headed by the senator's son Jim. The Forum Foundation has been taking bipartisan delegations of congressional staff members to Nicaragua. The theory is, I guess, that congressional staff members haven't been listening to their own campaign promises for years and are therefore not insane yet. If you take staff members, they might see something. Whereas if you take congressmen themselves, they'll probably think they're back in their home districts and promise to quit committing adultery.

Anyway, my staff delegation (or "StaffDel," as these things are called) was made up of young men and women whose bosses were potential swing votes on the *contra* aid question. The staffers were in their middle twenties, earnest, bright and dutiful. On the plane to Managua they studied State Department briefings and Congressional Research Service reports, scoured books pro and con about the Sandinistas and filled note pads with neatly lettered questions to ask anyone who'd stand still. I drank.

Is Nicaragua a Bulgaria with marimba bands or just a misunderstood Massachusetts with Cuban military advisors? Beats me. Personally, I like the kind of research you can get your hands on, the kind you can heft. That is, I like to do my principal research in bars, where people are more likely to tell the truth or, at least, lie less convincingly than they do in briefings and books. But I hadn't even made it to the bar in the Augusto C. Sandino Airport when Nicaragua began researching itself and in a palpably hefty way. To get into the country, you have to change sixty U.S. dollars into Nicaraguan cordobas. Jim Denton went to the exchange window with $480 for our group of eight and came back with 4,080,000 cordobas, which filled an entire Adidas gym bag. In 1979, in the last days of the utterly bankrupt Somoza regime, the "corb" was fifteen to the dollar. Now the official rate is 8,500 to 1. On the black market you can get 14,000.

Somebody has definitely let a dialectical materialist loose in the Nicaraguan monetary system. You probably have to take economics over again two or three times at Moscow U. before you can make cash worth this little. And free enterprise had disappeared from Sandino Airport (if enterprise is the word for what goes on at Latin ports of entry). There were no taxis, no guys trying to snatch your luggage, no touts, no beggars, no shoe-shine boys, no Indian urchins selling you Mayan relics from Taiwan, no nothing but runty teenagers in army uniforms staggering around morosely under the weight of AK-47s. (Amigos, if you'd get with the right superpower block, you could have M-16s. They're four and a half pounds lighter.)

We drove to Managua in a U.S. embassy van with bullet-proof

windows. It was early Friday evening but downtown was nearly empty. The traffic was mostly East German IFA trucks full of soldiers. Our Nicaraguan driver said IFA stands for *Imposible Frenar A tiempo*, "Impossible to Stop on Time." The few private cars were shambling down the vacant streets trailing smoke. Hardly a one had both headlights working. Many of the streetlights were also out. There were still a few commercial billboards, stained and faded. But there were lots of brightly painted new signs with pictures of workers and peasants—chins, guns, gazes and what-not uplifted. And the Sandinista Front initials, FSLN, were spray-painted on all vertical surfaces.

A few cantinas and cafes were open, but the people inside them just seemed to be standing there. We passed a Japanese car dealership with one car on the lot. Broken mechanical things seemed to be piling up at intersections. Factory yards were high with weeds. I opened the van door to find out if music was playing anywhere. It wasn't. And one thing that I saw was truly shocking. Nicaraguans were in line at bus stops—long, orderly, silent lines. Latins don't queue up for anything, let alone quietly. It's *contra*, as it were, everything in the culture. Imagine Lutèce serving a Bartles and James wine cooler. Imagine British soccer fans applauding politely when Milan scores. Imagine the Supreme Soviet conducting business in bikini underpants. Something, I realized, was deeply, deeply wrong in Nicaragua.

Now, a lot of people tell me this gray and depressing atmosphere is a product of the civil war, that Nicaraguans are on short rations and under tight discipline because they're in a struggle to the death with vicious mercenaries supported by massive U.S. covert aid. These are the same people who tell me the *contras* are completely ineffective, have no chance of winning and have squandered all the cash they get from America on big houses with swimming pools in Miami. I don't know. I'm not a liberal so I have a poor grasp of stuff I don't know anything about. I have, however, been in places where guerrilla wars were being fought—El Salvador, the Philippines and Lebanon. Those places weren't like this, and East Berlin, Poland and Russia were.

But let's be fair. Maybe Nicaragua isn't really communist. Maybe it's just going in for the "Communist Look." You know, the

way you can get a "Turbo Look" Porsche 911 with the air dam and
the fat tires and the big whale-tail spoiler in the back but without
the actual turbo-charged motor—sort of a life-style, fashion-
statement kind of thing. Some Albanian-trained decorator probably
came over to our luxury hotel, the Managua Intercontinental, and
pulled up all the carpets at the corners, spread dust and mildew in
the rooms, rubbed the chrome off the sink fixtures, broke the
shower heads, made the bar service surly and complicated, and
took all the comic books, sexy *fotonovelas* and copies of the *Miami
Herald* out of the hotel newsstand and replaced them with biogra-
phies of Fidel Castro and the works of Lenin. "Today's tourist . . .
goes back to his air-conditioned hotel and orders haute cuisine,"
read the brochure from the government tourist agency called *Intu-
rismo,* as in the Russian *Intourist.* "Friday Special—Festival de
Hamburguesas" read the menu in the lobby.

We met our first Sandinista that same night, General Secretary
of the Foreign Ministry Alejandro Bendaña, who mentioned that
he'd rather be out dancing at the street festivals (which I saw no
sign of) and said he assumed we would, too. Tsk. Tsk. There but
for lack of international understanding . . . Bendaña oozed self-
confident charm. His clothes were nattily rumpled, he bummed
cigarettes and, having gone to Harvard, he spoke better English
than we did. He was full of enthusiasm for the Central American
Peace Pact, the Arias Accord. Bendaña vowed Nicaragua would
comply—unilaterally if need be—with all of the Accord's requirements, though he had to look in his briefcase to see just what those
requirements were.

In a fit of bonhomie, Bendaña then hinted the government
would soon allow the one opposition newspaper, *La Prensa,* to
publish again, permit the Catholic radio station to resume broad-
casting, free some political prisoners and announce a partial
cease-fire with the *contras.*

"The revolutionary process," said Bendaña with real heat,
"does not require having a newspaper shut down, does not require
having a radio station shut down, does not require eliminating
political parties. Those measures go against the grain of the revolution!" By the look on the faces of the StaffDel members, I'd say it
had occurred to them that Bendaña worked for a revolution that

didn't require those things but had done them anyway. The aides had some major questions, which Bendaña parried like an amused and slightly absent-minded Northwestern football coach defending his team's record against Michigan and Ohio State.

"The revolution has made mistakes," said Bendaña. "We are prepared to put the Cubans on a boat tomorrow."

I liked the guy—a bad sign. People I like shouldn't be allowed anywhere near government. I know my friends. They'd borrow the Soviet Hind helicopters for picnics, seduce Rumanian gymnast nymphettes and tell every gaggle of visiting Americans exactly what they wanted to hear, just like I would. "Some believe the Nicaraguan revolution was on a Marxist-Leninist track. We don't see it that way," said Bendaña.

This hardly jibes with what Bendaña's Sandinista *compañeros* have been saying.

". . . Marxist-Leninism is the scientific doctrine that guides our revolution," announced Defense Minister Humberto Ortega in a speech to the Sandinista military in 1981.

"You cannot be a true revolutionary in Latin America without being Marxist-Leninist," Interior Minister Tomás Borge told *Newsweek* in 1984.

For years now you've been able to count on the Sandinistas for William F. Buckley fodder, for Reagan-electing quotes:

> We are not going to be so naive as to accept a civic opposition, because that doesn't exist anymore.
> —President Daniel Ortega, quoted
> in *The Economist*, 1986

> Our friendship with Libya is eternal.
> —Tomás Borge, quoted in *The Washington Post*, 1986

And my personal favorite:

> They [*La Prensa*] accused us of suppressing freedom of expression. This was a lie and we could not let them publish it.
> —Nelba Blandón, Interior Ministry
> Director of Censorship, quoted in *The New York Times*, 1984

I guess the big question is, are they kidding? Are the Sandys pulling our leg when they say this stuff? Or are they goofing on us when they say they're going to allow unfettered elections and freedom of speech? Should we believe what they've said before? Should we believe what they're saying now? Or should we sit by the algae-choked swimming pool at the Managua Intercontinental and drink two dozen beers brought to us by a waitress who can no longer legally be tipped and has turned as efficient and willing as the average Budapest customs official?

The next morning we went to meet with the leaders of the Nicaraguan Permanent Commission on Human Rights, who were not nearly as full of pep as the General Secretary of the Foreign Ministry. In fact, they were a depressing bunch.

Nicaragua has two competing human-rights commissions. Human-rights commissions seem to go forth and multiply in places where a human right hasn't been seen in years. The Permanent Commission on Human Rights was founded in 1977 to deal with the heinous crimes of the Somoza regime. In those days the commission defended a number of people who later became Sandinista leaders, including the present Interior Minister (and head of the DGST secret police) Tomás Borge. Now the Commission has its hands full dealing with the heinous crimes of its former clients. "They called us communists before. Now they call us counter-revolutionaries," sighed Executive Director Lino Hernandez.

We sat in a drab and cluttered boardroom. An ancient, wounded air conditioner sputtered and 40-watt light bulbs winked as Managua underwent its daily electricity shortage.

Hernandez and his commissioners presented us with a neatly organized horror of figures and cases. The Commission has been tallying about one hundred and thirty "severe violations of human rights" per month. Each complainant must provide identification and be fingerprinted and otherwise get serious about his or her allegations. The commission estimated there were about seven thousand political prisoners in the country not counting between thirty-five hundred and forty-five hundred former members of the Somoza National Guard, mostly enlisted men serving jail sentences of up to thirty years for having backed the wrong horse.

According to Hernandez, most of the political prisoners are *campesinos* accused of giving some kind of aid and comfort to the *contras*. "Attempts against the state" is the cover-all charge. The *campesinos* are usually grabbed by the military and always handed over to the DGST, which stands for "General Department of State Security," just as KGB stands for "Committee of State Security"— another one of those commie fashion statements. The prisoners are held incommunicado under less than delightful conditions and interrogated with the usual Latin American light touch. So far, said Hernandez, only one political prisoner, the head of a labor union, had failed to sign a confession. Not bad, out of seven thousand.

After confession and about nine months of waiting around in jails without counsel, the guilty parties are tried by a "People's Anti-Somoza Tribunal," made up of two Sandinista-block committee members and one lawyer from the Sandinista lawyer's association. The regular Nicaraguan court system has no jurisdiction over these trials. No copies of charges or confessions are made available to lawyers, press or defendants. "If a person is under control of State Security, all we can do is ask and wait," said Hernandez.

"And despair," piped in another member of the Commission.

The StaffDel scribbled furiously, taking down names and numbers, probing each statement, asking for more precise translations. I doodled. I was drawing little pictures of mobile homes. It must have been something subconscious to do with "workers' paradise." I was drawing the workers' paradise we have back in the States—cars up on blocks and broken toys in the crabgrass and a nasty dog chained to the satellite dish. These workers' paradise things just never seem to pan out.

Hernandez and the Commission members looked exhausted. Hernandez himself had just gotten out of jail, where he'd been put for observing an anti-Sandinista protest. Maybe they were all lying. But to what end I can't imagine. All sorts of other lies are available that would be easier and more profitable to tell.

After the Permanent Commission of Human Rights began reporting Sandinista human-rights violations, the Sandinistas set up their own human-rights commission, the National Commission for Protection and Promotion of Human Rights, the CNPPDH. One of its members is a U.S. nun, from the Agnesian order, named Mary Hartman. She has spent twenty-five years in Nicaragua and bears *no* resemblance to the character once played by Louise Lasser.

P. J. O'Rourke

Sister Mary Hartman, carrying a large Souvenir of Cuba key ring, ushered us into the CNPPDH headquarters, which looked like it had once been someone's middle-class house. The walls were decorated with Sandinista slogans. "I want this to be a dialogue," Hartman said and then didn't shut up for forty-five minutes. She was an intense, fidgeting, tall and alarmingly skinny woman with hatchet face and lantern jaw. She spoke against the United States with considerable venom, tacking a disconcerting little north woods "huh?" to the end of each sentence. ". . . violators of international law, huh?"

One of the StaffDel members asked Mary Hartman about the unusually high rate of confessions among prisoners appearing before the People's Anti-Somoza Tribunals. Hartman said it was only 95 percent. "I don't find that surprising," she said. "Because they were captured, huh?"

"You mean," said the staffer, "that because the government has them in custody, it stands to reason that they're guilty?"

Hartman answered by saying there are only fourteen thousand *contras*. Six thousand of them are ex-Somoza National Guardsmen, and the rest are "kidnapped or fled and then were somehow convinced to fight or something."

"This afternoon," said Jim Denton, "we're going to talk to a group called Mothers of Political Prisoners."

Mary Hartman said the group was funded with U.S. money and that many of the mothers were not women of good character and that they had been bribed "with things like Camel cigarettes, huh?"

"No doubt you've investigated hundreds, if not thousands of these cases," said Jim. Hartman nodded vigorously. "Could you give us specific cases where the mothers had been bribed or were otherwise found to be untrustworthy?"

Hartman said she could, she certainly could.

"Well . . ." said Denton.

"I don't have the files right with me, huh?"

"If you could give us just one or two specific cases, even just the names," said Jim. "That way we'll be able to respond to these women this afternoon, when they complain to us about how their chidren are being treated."

"I've investigated many, many of these cases," said Hartman.

211

"Actually," said Denton, "just one would do."

"Why, yes, I have one right here," Hartman looked at a pile of file folders on a desk and pulled one off the top. She searched through it, but it seemed to be the wrong file. "Nicaragua has an excellent record on speech, assembly and property rights, huh?" she said.

"But could you give us one example of unreliable or suspect testimony from one of the members of the Mothers group?" said Denton.

Hartman's eyes darted momentarily to the spot where she'd laid her souvenir key ring. "I can't right now, huh?" she said. "My office is locked."

The StaffDel members had never seen a whole bunch of Mothers of Political Prisoners before, which group—as such groups usually do—also included wives, girlfriends, sisters, grandmas and diaperless, dirty-faced, crying infant children of Political Prisoners. It wasn't something that exactly brightened the StaffDel's day. Or mine. I peeked at this angry, indignant and impoverished assemblage and slid for the door. There is a certain look these women have—a mix of love lost and one atom of hope that *you,* because you're an American and clean and well-fed and rich, can somehow help. They are all over the world, those ladies, in South Africa, the Middle East, Indochina, Russia, Northern Ireland, Cuba, Chile—all bearing the same expression and all coming at you singly or in groups, publicly or on the sly, as the political climate of the time and the place allow. What possible damned thing can you say to them? The only real answer would be to load up and start shooting dictators, juntas, ayatollahs, politicians and, of course, every communist you can get in your peep sights because the commies are the top-seeded players in the twentieth century political prisoners cup match. But the Congress of the United States doesn't approve of anybody doing this sort of thing anymore, especially not when accompanying a congressional staff delegation and, besides, I didn't have a gun.

The StaffDel emerged from the Glum Mums confab looking like they'd been in an emotional Cuisinart. From there we were all stampeded into a meeting with the anti-Sandinista civil opposition. Actually, in our thirty-six hours in-country, we met with three groups of opposition politicians plus an opposition priest and an editor from the muffled opposition newspaper. After the real human-rights commission and the other human-rights commission and the mothers and the general mess in the streets, we should have been ripe for propaganda picking. We should have come back to the States loudly parroting the opposition line. The trouble is, I don't think any of us can remember what it was, not even the most dutiful of the note-takers. My own notes from the civil opposition meetings look like one of those cocktail napkins where you've written a drunken, coked-up, middle-of-the-night, brilliant movie idea. "Fr last 150 yrs Nic sit. nt ben conumdrs t. Nic people advismisng any pol. stabil," I have one opposition figure stating. These guys were so boring that I'm amazed they haven't all been hired as George Bush speech writers.

Each member of the opposition had a long rhetorical set piece blaming all of Nicaragua's past troubles on American intervention and all of Nicaragua's present troubles on a lack of it. This was always followed by a detailed account of the quarreling and infighting among the opposition parties, which seem to divide and multiply faster than salmonella bacteria in warm tuna salad—Liberals, Liberals With Hats, Christian Democrats Under 5'9", Conservatives Who Sing In The Shower, etc., etc., etc. Only the priest was amusing. He talked about S. Brian Wilson, the U.S. peace activist who got run over by a munitions train. "I wish the peace groups in the United States would also demonstrate in Red Square," said the priest, "and see if they don't run a train through there."

At least the priest had been an anti-Somoza fighter. He had a couple big scars across his skull, courtesy of Somoza's National Guard. The Sandys *did* fight Somoza. You can't take that away from them. After forty-five years of the Somoza family's sordid bloodsucking and murderous buffoonery, it was the Sandinista front, not the civil opposition, who pulled the plug. And in 1980, when Anastasio Somoza had bolted and was living the life of a rich swine in Paraguay, it was probably a Sandinista operative who put a bazooka shell through the window of his armor-plated Mercedes limousine and sent the fat bastard to hell in small pieces. But it's one thing to burn down the shit house and another thing entirely to install plumbing.

The real argument against the Sandinistas isn't made by the

civil opposition or the human-rights do-gooders, much less by the
contras or Ollie North or the Great Communicator his own dumb
self. The real argument is made by invisible chickens. There are no
chickens, no chickens at all in the Eastern market, the largest
market in Managua.

It doesn't matter what kind of awfulness happens in Latin
America—and practically every kind of awfulness does—there are
always chickens. No Peruvian mountain village is so poor that you
can drive through it without running over a chicken. No Mexico
City slum is so urban but dawn comes in with rooster crows as loud
as Los Lobos live in your breakfast nook. No oppression is so
thoroughgoing that there's not a cockfight on Sunday with the loser
fried up, *¡muy gusto!*, with the feet still on. But there were no
chickens in Managua.

And there was plenty of nothing else besides. In the vast
market sheds, the government-allotted stalls with government-
determined prices were empty. In the spaces between the sheds
vendors had set up illegally with scanty piles of bruised fruit and
little heaps of rice and maize. Every now and then, the vendors
said, officials from the Interior Ministry cleared them out. For
misunderstanding the Labor Theory of Value chapter in *Das Kapital*, I guess. Some people had tried to make something, anything,
to sell—crude kitchen utensils pounded out of old tin, charcoal
braizers made from cut-down mortar-shell cases, lumpy toys
hacked from palm wood and pathetic clay whistles in the shape of
birds, colored with something cheap and greasy that came off on
my hands. Others displayed rags and old clothes that might as well
have been rags. Many black marketeers really had nothing for sale.
Spread on the ground in front of them would be a dozen washers,
some screws and a broken light socket. Yet there was plenty of
money visible, fists-full of bank notes, which the dispirited crowd
handled like so much toilet paper. I take that back. There's a
shortage of toilet paper.

A pretty teenage girl asked me to marry her without seeing my
face. (Of course, somebody has pointed out that that's the only way
a pretty girl *would* ask me to marry her, but even so . . . .) I had
my thumbs hooked in the back pockets of my jeans, and the girl
came up behind me, tapped the little crown trademark on my

budget-model Rolex and asked our translator, "Will this guy marry me?" A little later I got a rotten onion thrown at me. I wheeled around, but there was nothing to see except a crowd of impassive faces.

"What was that about?" I asked the translator.

"Oh," he said, "somebody thought you were an *Internacionalista*, one of those Americans or Europeans who come down here to help the Sandys."

If Manauga had been gloomy by night, it was positively funereal in the sunshine. There were more of the orderly, silent lines—one outside every store. The soldiers had caught that People's Republic trick of going zany when anyone takes out a camera. *"Prohibido! Prohibido!"* yelled some AK-waving dork when one of the StaffDel tried to take a picture of a tree in the *Parco Central*.

I didn't think you could wreck a Central American country. I thought they came prewrecked from the time of the fall of classical Mayan civilization in 900 A.D. I didn't think you could make things any more depressing than they are in, say, El Salvador or the slums of Colon, Panama. But the Sandinistas had done it. And the Nicaraguans were losing that big, rude, cynical Latin American laugh. They were starting to get the dry humor of perfect despair that the Poles and Czechs and Russians have. We would pass by a burned-out factory, and our driver would say, with deadpan face, "This belongs to the people now."

I decided I could learn something from the Russians myself. The Russians have been dealing with communism longer than anybody else, and they know what to do in the face of it. They get shellacked.

That night there was a dinner at the American ambassador's house. "The hell with the bunch of them," I told a deputy assistant political officer who had the misfortune to be seated next to me, "let's invade." This is called *Double Foreign Policy on the Rocks*.

"That's what the Sandys say we're going to do," I explained. "And that's what the peace creeps back home say we're going to do, too. So, what the hell? Sure, there'll be a worldwide outbreak of anti-Americanism. But how much *more* anti-Americanism can there be than what we've got already? Tell me that! And some of the Nic-os will probably bitch—complaining about Yankee imperialists while they apply for VISA cards and open Tower Video franchises and begin eating again. But, shit, if we're going to have the Marines run U.S. foreign policy, let's do it right. Better than having them sneaking around the National Security Council and testifying in front of Congress wearing their goddamned marksmanship medals. Whaddya say?"

I don't remember exactly how the deputy assistant political officer responded, but I don't believe that he absolutely flat-out told me no.

Through Darkest America, Part II: The 1987 Reagan/Gorbachev Summit

· ·

You can imagine my excitement at being right there, my personal self, intimately present at this actual moment of eventhood. There I was, eye-witnessing the arrival of Mikhail Gorbachev in the United States of America.

I mean I watched it on TV—me and most of the other seven thousand reporters covering this combined summit conference, missile kissoff and Soviet-American love-in. There was some kind of media-pool screw-around that you had to sign up for eleven years in advance to really go to Andrews Air Force Base, or really go to the White House, or really go anywhere else. As a result, only a few hundred reporters ever laid eyes on the Big Glasnosky. The rest of us were stuck in the windowless sub-basement grand ballroom of the remarkably ugly J. W. Marriot Hotel, in the *Reagan-Gorbachev Summit International Press Center* (or "Press Pit" as it was called), where we crowded around the half dozen Sony monitors and gaped at *CNN*. One Japanese TV crew even pointed their camera at the screen and vidoetaped the video of the occasion. So—in case you'd ever wondered where reporters get their news—they get it the same place the rest of us do, from television.

"Mongolian Cluster Fuck" is the technical term journalists use for a preplanned, wholly scripted, news-free event. A summit conference is as interesting as a second cousin's wedding. Some stuff goes on that we might like a peek at, but it goes on behind locked doors. What we get to see is the bride and groom walking down the aisle.

Anyway, here was Gorbachev. He's young (well, young*ish*) and handsome (in a Fred Mertz sort of way) and highly charismatic (by old, fat Politburo standards). He got off the plane with his wife, Raisa—who everyone agreed is very lifelike—and strolled down the red carpet pumping mitts with everybody in sight. Gorby did not kiss the ground. Otherwise, it was more or less the same arrival ceremony that the Pope got. I'm beginning to wonder about America's love affair with foreign authority figures. Did we put an ad in the newspaper or something?

> Naughty, naughty nation
> seeks European autocrats
> for heavy P R. No gays.
> Send foto.

Gorbachev made some VERY SIGNIFICANT REMARKS, the contents of which I'm sure I'll remember in a minute. Ditto Secretary of State George Shultz. Then the Gorber and his little Raisa Bran hopped into the hilarious Soviet Zil limousine, which looks like a double-wide Studebaker Lark, and booked.

Tom Brokaw, Peter Jennings, Dan Rather and the rest of Punditry, Inc., immediately went on the air to explain WHAT IT ALL MEANS, and I would gladly do the same except I was sick the week we studied this in journalism school.

It was to be a short visit for the G-shevs. More than four days in the U.S. and Raisa's VISA card bill would shatter the fragile Soviet economy. There was time only for a bun fight or two, a couple of fireside chats about whether the Russians should screw the Afghans or let the Afghans screw themselves, and, of course, the WE HAVE SEEN HISTORY MADE TODAY signing of the INF treaty—a treaty that makes the entire world safe for the other seven billion atomic warheads the U.S. and the Soviet Union have pointed at each other.

Only one way to cover a story like this, and make that a double, bartender, please. *American Spectator* reporter Andy Ferguson and I took ten or a dozen Stolichnaya practice shots at the Washington Press Club and lit out for the Vista Hotel, where more than a hundred Soviet journalists were bunked. We figured we'd join them in some tabletop cossack dancing and in singing bawdy songs and then get them to spill the beans about what they'd like to do to the Jewish *refuseniks* if nobody was looking.

But when Andy and I got to the Vista, somebody had shut off the funski valve. It had never occurred to us that the Kremlin's new anti-booze campaign would apply to journalists. Now, *that's* a human-rights violation. The commie agitprop artists were all being herded into a buffet dinner without so much as an aperitif. Andy and I tried to blend into the crowd but were given away by our neckties. The Sovs are becoming reasonably Western-looking, about like the Munsters, but they still lag in necktie technology and wear dirt-and-lint-colored polyester stripes the width of a bedspread. "No reception! Is only dinner!" said a guy in a large suit who I don't think checks spelling for *Pravda*. "They are only eating. Do not American reporters eat?" he joshed (a genuine example of KGB humor).

Well, in our case, actually, no. We drink. So we waited in the lobby bar. But, as soon as the buffet was over, the Soviets trooped into the hotel elevators and disappeared, sealed off by a line of U.S. marshals. Maybe they were just anxious to get back to their rooms and finish Gorbachev's hot new best-seller, *Perestroika*—a real page-turner with fabulous plot, deft characterizations and a surprise ending I won't reveal here.

Indeed, everybody in Washington was acting like a wet trench coat. Picture being stuck anyplace with seven thousand reporters, let alone seven thousand *sober* reporters telling each other WHAT IT ALL MEANS.

You can always measure how important something is supposed to be by the amount of solemn, earnest, boring behavior it involves. I guess the INF treaty is supposed to be pretty darn important because the whole press corps was tiptoeing around D.C. like they'd just farted in church. And network talking heads were swelling with self-regard, gaining two or three suit-jacket sizes an hour. After all, if a pretty darn important thing is going on and you're someplace near it, you must be pretty darn important yourself. In case anybody missed the point, flacks were wearing their summit press-credential necklaces everywhere, too—not tucking them in a pocket as usual but letting all the little plastic cards hang outside their Burberrys like kindergartners sent home with notes to mother pinned on their snowsuits.

On the morning of THE SUMMIT: DAY TWO, Gorby was put through several kinds of pomp and circumstance on the White House lawn. Reagan was all smiles for this first Communist dictator in history to have a hug-a-bear nickname. Then the pair of them went off to "grok," or whatever superpower leaders do.

Raisa took a tour of Washington at 40 mph in a convoy of nine armored limousines—which, if you think about it, is the smart way to see an American city. (In case you've been in Antarctica or something and haven't heard enough summit trivia, Raisa's measurements are 38, 27½, 38—this according to European television, which is the source of many of journalism's most colorful, though not necessarily truest, facts.)

Myself, I went across the street to Lafayette Park, where America's Goo-Goo Clusters and Moon Pies traditionally gather to demonstrate. Here I found Buddhist drummers who, I think, were drumming in favor of the treaty but wouldn't stop drumming long enough to say. A homosexual group demanded that leftover ex-missile money go to AIDS research. Hare Krishnas were lobbying for the right to bother people in Russian airports, too. Eritreans wanted whoever it is who's in Eritrea to leave now. Some sixty peace activists seemed miffed because this arms deal came from guys in suits instead of people marching in Central Park. And one three-man organization with signs in Russian advocated the return of major-league baseball to the District of Columbia.

On the sidewalk in front of the White House, a large, angry

crowd of people from places like Poland, Vietnam, the Ukraine, Afghanistan, Latvia, Lithuania, Estonia, Hungary and Czechoslovakia were pointing out that the Soviets know how to cause trouble the regular way, no H-bombs required.

An even angrier crowd of Jewish activists was getting itself arrested at the Soviet Embassy. The Czars spent five centuries trying to chase the Jews out of Russia. Now the Soviets won't let them leave. This is something the Russians should just make up their minds about.

It was a bit of a shock to see the Soviet flag flying all over Washington, even though a lot of people in my family think that's what's been going on since the first FDR administration. Reagan's right-wing ex-pals were also not enthusiastic about that red dishrag. They want to know, "Is the Gipper *channeling?*" That is, they assume Ron is a conservative Republican, at least in this incarnation. But perhaps he's gone into a trancelike state, and creatures from the spirit world are speaking through him—Eugene McCarthy, maybe.

Such die-hard Bolshi-haters put the kibosh on a proposed Gorby address to both houses of Congress. Congress already has plenty of dumpy bald guys who hardly speak English addressing it, said the right-wingers, with some justice.

But nyet-sayers were a minority. Gorby fever raged in the capital, especially among Establishment liberal types such as the ones who fill your TV screen every night at seven. These people were tripping all over each other about how reasonable, convincing and just plain friendly Splotch-Top is. They were even praising the dread Ron for having Spot over to visit.

This was a bit of a mystery since Communists and Republicans both hate liberals. Reagan believes liberals should be deported to Russia, and Gorbachev believes they should be sent to Siberia. The two sides are in perfect agreement on this point. But you know how liberals live in the past. Maybe they think good U.S.-Soviet relations will put a stop to Hitler and Mussolini. Or maybe the liberals feel that, if we're headed into a period of economic fuck-ups, we'd better get tight with the folks who wrote the book on fucking up economies. (Vid. *Das Kapital*.) Whatever,

there's probably no truth in the rumors that Gorby will head the '88
Democratic presidential ticket. Constitutional difficulties about his
not being born in the U.S. are one drawback, but the real problem
is that Gorbachev's soft on trade sanctions and favors government
deregulation of industry.

MOMENT TO REMEMBER: THE HISTORIC SIGNING came at two
P.M., Tuesday, December 8. It's a straightforward deal. Reagan
needs something to keep his second term from being reviewed like
a Madonna movie, and Gorbachev wants to save bucks on military
expenditures. The Soviets are sick of surviving on bread and lard.
They'd like to have a more Westernized lifestyle with croissants and
lard instead.

It seems like an all-right treaty to me. The Soviets have to give
up 693 missiles, and we have to give up only 154. All the atomic
warheads will be destroyed. That will create nuclear waste, which
is good because, this way, even if disarmament proceeds to its
logical conclusion and atomic weapons are completely eliminated,
anti-nuke protestors will still have something to demonstrate
against and won't be unemployed.

On the other hand, it's not a *great* treaty. Ron got the Redskis
to sit down and talk butterball by being tough and filling Europe
with cruise missiles and so forth. Maybe he should have been
really tough and nuked Leningrad. The Soviets might have signed
away the whole ranch if he'd done that. Also, the commies are the
only people on earth who think Star Wars will work. If they're that
gullible, maybe we should have held the summit at Atlantic City
and let them lose all their missiles playing Keno.

Oh well, it's not as though either side really needs many
warheads. A couple dozen apiece would do the trick. The Russians
could have some aimed at Japan, so if we act up they can destroy
our economy. We could have some aimed at *The Village Voice*, so if
the Russians misbehave, we can kill a lot of communists.

After the treaty signing many VERY IMPORTANT THINGS happened, all of which I scrupulously followed in every painstaking
detail on the giant-screen TV at the Kit Kat Klub. Make that a
triple, please. This is another technical term journalists use:
"Covering a story from Mahogany Ridge."

P. J. O'Rourke
. . . .

Tuesday night, the Gorbachevs had dinner at the White House and Mikhail kissed Van Cliburn a lot. Wednesday, Gorby met with congressional leaders and discussed whether the Soviet Union is an Evil Empire or just like the United States or both. Later that day The Gorb met with a delegation of American intellectuals, led by John Denver. Raisa went to tea with Nancy. If body language is anything to go by, they got along like two cats in a sack. Raisa had to sit through the whole Just Say No routine but managed to resist the temptation to shove the First Lady's face into a plate of cucumber sandwiches.

On Thursday Gorb-O breakfasted with George Bush, but George just spent the whole meal buried in *The Wall Street Journal,* grumbling about bond prices. Barbara says that's the way he always is in the morning.

And, of course, Ronny and Splotch had a whole bunch more meetings, which seems to make everyone feel warm all over. I can't think why. The last time an old, sick, addled American president (Roosevelt) sat down with a Soviet leader who'd had great press ("Uncle" Joe Stalin), half of Europe was given away.

Mexican Border Idyll

· ·

OCTOBER 1986

I just came back from a month on the Mexican border, where I personally captured three illegal aliens. This saved the United States a lot of money in welfare, social services and unemployment benefits. Therefore, each of you owes me 50¢. Unless, of course, you happen to be illegal aliens, in which case you owe me a kick in the ass. Thoughtful-type readers—the kind who worry about the morality of the whole issue—may be confused about whether to send me money or wring my neck. I'm confused myself. A month on the border would confuse anybody.

It was in Laredo that I captured my aliens. I didn't mean to capture anybody. I just got over-excited, temporarily forgot I was a journalist and started acting like a law-abiding citizen.

I was riding around town with a very affable young border patrol agent named Howard Adams. His job for the evening was to keep "illegals" from hopping the midnight freight to San Antonio. A radio call came in saying three aliens had been spotted slipping into an equipment pen next to the rail yard.

224

The pen was a link-fenced half-acre filled with couplers, wheel trucks and other giant, rusty train junk. The moment we pulled through the gate, two young men hopped out of the scrap iron. Adams ran them down while I trotted after him, trying to take notes, get my flashlight to work and not bark my shins on things. The illegals got as far as the fence, examined its height, shrugged and surrendered.

Adams locked these two in the car and went looking for the third. I followed him as he ducked behind a derelict semi-trailer. He shined his flashlight underneath and said something in Spanish. There was a wiggling in the gloom. A rather plump adolescent had managed to squeeze himself into the trailer suspension, into a six-inch gap between the axle and bed. He squeezed himself out, shrugged, and Adams marched him to the car. I peered underneath, jiggling my defective Everready, trying to see how somebody could fit in that miniscule space. Somebody could, I guess, and with room to spare, because when the light finally came on, there was another somebody staring at me. He had pushed himself even further back above the axle.

"Howard!" I shouted. "I found one more. Is there something that I'm, like, supposed to say to him?"

"Say, 'Vamos!'" yelled Howard.

"Uh, vamos," I said. The fellow crawled out and stood next to me, shrugging a great deal.

I looked back under the trailer to see how in the hell two people could possibly fit in that space and shit, there was a third guy as squashed as filet of sole. I was beginning to feel like the circus cop arresting all the clowns in the miniature taxicab. "Come on, vamos yourself," I said, and when he did, there was yet another goddamned kid packed in behind him. I had them all shrugging in my flashlight beam by the time Adams got back to the trailer.

"Me compadre es periodista," (My friend is a journalist) said Adams. The illegals nodded their approval. That they'd been busted by somebody with no power to do so and no business doing it and who, on second thought, wished he hadn't, seemed to bother nobody but me. One of the Mexicans said something, and Adams translated. "This is the eleventh time he's been caught in two weeks."

Illegal-alien traffic is so heavy at Laredo that there's no time to take people back to the border one by one. A school bus with chicken wire over the windows is parked by the freight yard until it's full. It made three trips to the border that night, by no means a record.

There was a lot of singing and laughing on the bus. The prisoners leaned against the chicken wire and traded jokes in Spanish with the border patrol agents. I talked to one of the women agents. "They're going up to get construction jobs in San Antonio, Dallas and Houston," she said. "Mostly they're young men. They'll send for their families later. We see a few women and children through here, and we worry about them because the trains are so dangerous. There was one family with two beautiful little girls. We caught them three times.

"We haven't seen them for a while," she added with a slightly wistful tone. "I guess they finally got through."

Adams took me to the freight yard where the train was being made up. It was terrifying in there. Switch engines were moving the stock around in the dark, and the sidings were so close together there was only a shoulder's width between the rumbling boxcars. Shapes and shadows appeared in our flashlight beams as illegals darted through the crashing machinery. I saw one roll himself across the rail bed between moving wheels, trying to get out of our way.

At the depot a railroad detective showed me photographs. In one picture a man, about twenty, had been cut into five distinct pieces—two legs, a head, a torso, one arm. His eyes were open. He died so quickly there wasn't much blood. "It happens two or three times a week," said the detective. "Sometimes in the yard and sometimes out on the line. The wets are all afraid of snakes. They sleep on the ties because they think snakes can't get between the rails."

When the train was ready to pull out, we went to the last switch onto the main track. As the locomotive moved through, dozens of Mexicans dashed out of the shrubbery and tried to grab hold of the gondolas and flat cars. Most of them fell back. The train was moving too fast. The illegals already on board whistled and waved. When the train was gone, Adams and the other agents rounded up the stragglers. One illegal said, "Will you drive around a little and look for my friend. He'll need a ride to the border."

"Oh, for chrissakes," said Adams and began scouring the neighborhood.

The boundary between Mexico and the United States is two thousand miles long with few natural barriers. It's just an imaginary map doodle through a bunch of scrub. There isn't even a linguistic gulf since the majority of people on both sides speak Spanish. But this ill-patrolled and undefended frontier is the one place on earth where a fully developed nation collides head-on with the filth and chaos of the Third World.

The burghers of northern Europe have Italys, Greeces and Yugoslavias between them and true want. The Japanese are a sea away from the needy Filipinos and Chinese. Even Russia has its own dirtball provinces of Kazakhstan and Uzbek to give it some distance from the hordes of Asia. But in North America the poor and benighted stand with noses pressed against the candy-store window, from the yacht basins of San Diego to the yahoo party beaches of South Padre Island.

A walkabout on the border raises all the big, ugly, stupid questions of the twentieth century: What makes a Mexico a Mexico? What makes a United States a United States? And what the hell are we supposed to do about it?

The Mexicans have another question: Why stay where money isn't when you can go where money is? A question they answer with their feet. And the U.S. Border Patrol doesn't have much of an answer to that. Manolo Ortiz, PR chief of the Immigration and Naturalization Service's Southern Regional Office, told me that in 1968 the Border Patrol nabbed 128,000 people trying to sneak into the U.S. In 1984 it was one million. And last year's total was almost twice that. Ninety-seven percent of these folks are Mexican, and, though two million get caught, between two and four million don't. That means at least a couple Clevelands worth of Mexican citizens gate-crashed our country last year.

"We only have 3,200 agents in the entire Border Patrol," Ortiz said. "All it amounts to, really, is controlled illegal entry."

An agent in Ortiz's office put it this way: "We could stand on the border with linked arms, and they'd still get across."

Ortiz took me to meet the INS Southern Regional Commissioner, Stephen H. Martin. Martin is a prominent businessman from Louisiana, active in Republican politics, but not too full of gas for a federal appointee. "Our mandate," said Martin, letting a little of that gas out, "is to protect the border and to protect all the people along the border regardless of nationality."

Ortiz, who had a better sense of humor, said, "There's a fence on the international boundary in El Paso. It's called the 'Tortilla Curtain.' Aliens were cutting themselves going through the holes in it. So the government built a flimsier fence."

"What causes all this illegal immigration?" I asked. Here was a *real* stupid question, but it's a stupid world.

"Economics," said Martin, looking as if he'd been asked a real stupid question.

"Okay, then, why is Mexico so poor?"

For the next month I asked everybody on both sides of the border this question. The only answer I got that made any sense was from an El Paso bartender. He said, "You know, this old Texas boy and this Mexican were having an argument, and the Texan says to the Mexican, 'How come you-all are always mad at us and blaming America for everything and so on?' And the Mexican says, 'You stole half our country. And not only that, Señor, you stole the half with all the paved roads.'"

There are a lot of other stupid questions that I asked, too. In McAllen, Texas, I asked Silvestre Reyes, chief of the Border Patrol division that covers the boot toe of Texas, if we should use the military to seal the border.

"The border is dangerous enough, without bringing a war-time mentality to it," he said and made a face. "That's an obvious conflict in philosophy to use our military against a peaceful ally."

In San Antonio I asked Deputy Southern Regional District Dirctor John A. Abriel what would happen if we *did* seal the border.

"Some congressmen have said if the border was sealed off we'd get a revolution in Mexico," he said. Abriel looked tired and harried. He looked like a man facing a question so big and so stupid that it might need a big, stupid answer.

"But maybe," he said, "sealing the border would give Mexico impetus to reform."

"Is the United States," I said, "using its border as some kind of political safety valve for Mexico or something?"

"I wouldn't throw that theory down the drain," said Abriel. "I have a similar gut feeling." And he gave me another load of horrible wetback statistics.

"Look," said Abriel, "illegal immigration is not *malum en se,* not evil in itself. We sympathize with the illegals. We empathize. But the bottom line is the taxpayers expect protection, expect enforcement of the immigration act. I think it was President Taft who once met with an old Indian chief and asked the chief if he had any words of wisdom for the president of the United States. The chief said, 'Watch your immigration laws.'"

In McAllen I went out on night tour with two supervisory patrol agents, Travis Johnson and Benny Greenfield.

Both were Texans in their forties.

Greenfield was a tall, laconic, cowboyish man who dipped snuff as most agents do, lest a cigarette give them away on stakeout. Johnson was shorter and very kindly mannered, with a chuckle that might be called giggling in a man with less dignity and no gun.

We drove to a low dyke near the Rio Grande, overlooking half a mile of fallow bottom land. There are electronic sensors planted along the U.S. bank of the river, old Vietnam War equipment, the same sensors that were used to stop traffic across the DMZ and down the Ho Chi Minh trail. And you remember how well that worked.

The sensors are monitored in the sector HQ, where an operator had radioed Johnson and Greenfield. There had been two "hits" below the dyke. Greenfield had a pair of binoculars, and Johnson was trying out an experimental infrared scope that made him look like he was wearing a nineteen-inch television around his neck. "Most of the illegals are good fellows," said Johnson. "You'll see, we kid around with them." Although they didn't much, that I saw.

The agents scanned the darkness until Greenfield said, "Yep." Then Johnson handed me the infrared scope.

It showed heat as light so that the warm soil and grass glowed faintly. Coming through this luminescent hay were two brilliant, featureless silhouettes, looking like aliens indeed, like *Close Encounter of the Third Kind* aliens. It made me wonder, for a moment, how many nine-eyed refugee-oids from collapsing-white-dwarf-stellar systems are out there in the Milky Way.

"They'll head for the brush," said Greenfield. To our left, the front slope of the dyke was covered with trees and undergrowth. Johnson went down to the foot of the levee, and Greenfield and I walked along the top and lay down in the grass at the edge of the shrubbery. A few minutes later, we could hear the illegals crashing through the sticks and leaves.

Immigration may be a moral quandary. But, at the moment, it was lots of fun too. I almost forgot the thumb-sized mosquitoes and the fact that I'd plopped down in what seemed to be a patch of fish-hook plants. The noise came directly at us. It sounded as though the illegals would step out of the bushes onto Greenfield's head. And the first one almost did. Greenfield let him walk between us so that we were, the three of us, as close together as people in a cash-machine line. As the second illegal came out of the woods, Greenfield jumped up.

The second man did a back dive into the greenery. But his friend seemed too startled to move. Greenfield took him by the arm, and the fellow sighed and shrugged.

When the first illegal had been locked in the car, we went through the strip of brush, just like you do to flush grouse. Greenfield pushed up the middle. I walked along the top of the dyke. And Johnson took the edge of the field. It was a moonless night, and cattle were grazing everywhere. I walked into a cow and scared the socks off myself. Meanwhile, the second illegal disappeared, a "got-away" as they're called.

We went to another crossing point, which Johnson said was a local favorite. There was a long, sandy road running down to the river between sugarcane fields. The infrared scope picked out two tiny bright dots, and we hid in the cane until an old man and a boy walked by. Greenfield and Johnson grabbed each by an elbow.

Neither protested. They shrugged as they were patted-down for weapons and put in the backseat cage with their countryman.

These three desperados had been caught red-handed. Their crime? Looking for work. If they'd pulled the caper off, they would have scored less than minimum wages in conditions not fit for farm animals. But they'd been nabbed. Now they'd have to face the music. Their punishment? Greenfield and Johnson would take them to the nearest international bridge and let them go home.

"What do you do if they run away?" I asked Greenfield.

"I chase them."

"What if you can't catch them?"

"I let them go."

"You don't shoot them?"

Greenfield looked shocked. "What for? They're trying to make a living. They're not criminals." He thought that over. "They're just breaking the law."

The next day I drove an hour and a half north to Falfurnias, with assistant chief patrol agent Juan A. Garcia, to look at a highway checkpoint. We pulled over a couple miles short at a rest stop. "If somebody's carrying illegals," said Garcia, "they'll stop here and make them walk around the checkpoint to be picked up on the other side. It's a long walk."

We went over to the fence behind the rest stop to "cut sign," as the Border Patrol calls tracking. The land was dry, baked scrub, hot and flat as a griddle for fifty miles in every direction. "That business about Mexicans being close to the land and never getting lost and being able to withstand thirst and heat forever is non-sense," said Garcia, whose own parents had come over when nobody minded.

There were plenty of footprints at the fence, mostly cheap men's sneakers. But mixed with these were fresh prints from a woman's high-heeled shoes and from a small child's sandals. We followed the tracks a hundred yards into the scrub. Those high heels must have pinched like a thumb in a car door. And how far did the kid get before it started to bawl? "We'll check for them at the drag," said Garcia.

The drag looked like a wide dirt road crossing the highway

between the rest stop and checkpoint. But it was raked daily so that
any tracks across it would show. We drove for two miles along the
drag without any sign of the little sandals or the high-heeled shoes.
"They've gone wide into the brush," said Garcia. "Sometimes we
spot them because of the vultures."

At the checkpoint the patrol agents had just caught a young
man, an illegal, with four pounds of marijuana in his pickup. They
opened the package for me, and I sniffed it. It was really forty-
toke, am-I-high-yet? Tampico ditch weed. I'll bet I wasn't the only
person in the room who felt like a dick nodding over the gravity of
this crime. The dope had been hidden in a hole cut through the
floorboard behind the pickup's seat. A section of sheet metal had
been carefully sawed out and put back in place with auto-body
filler. Then it had been sanded, spray-painted and covered with
carpet. The Border Patrol agents were mystified about why anyone
would go to so much trouble over four pounds of stems and seeds.

"Maybe it's a test run," said one of them.

"Or maybe it just shows how bad things are in Mexico,"
Garcia said to me while we were driving back. "The Mexican
minimum wage is $3.21 a day. Unemployment is 50 percent."

When we were about thirty miles from McAllen, Garcia spotted four illegals standing under a tree on the other side of the
highway. They weren't hard to pick out. They were each carrying a
little plastic grocery bag, usually the only luggage an illegal has.
They wore shoddy jeans and dusty, cotton plaid shirts. And they
were thin, the way only very rich Americans and very poor non-
Americans are. We were in an unmarked car, and when Garcia cut
through the median strip to get to their side of the road, the poor
ignoramuses stuck out their thumbs.

Garcia patted them down and put them in the backseat. Then
he got a snub-nosed revolver out of his briefcase and slipped it in
his pants pocket. The illegals were all from the same little town
near Reynosa. The oldest, who looked well past middle age, was
forty-three. Two others were in their mid-twenties. The youngest
was eighteen. They'd come across the river somewhere, they
weren't sure where, between McAllen and Brownsville at ten
o'clock the previous morning. They'd been walking ever since. It
was three P.M. when we picked them up. They said they'd come out

on the highway because they were hungry. "Why don't you interview these guys," Garcia said. "See what their lives are like?"

I asked them how much money they had, Garcia translating.
One said one thousand pesos. Another said five hundred. The
eldest had four hundred. That was a little over $2.50 among them.
The youngest had nothing.

"Where did you expect to find work?" I asked.

"Wherever," said the eldest. He told me he had eight children. He'd been to the United States three times before. The two
guys in their twenties had each been twice. This was the first time
for the youngest. When they'd been here in the past, they had
worked on ranches, mostly picking fruit and vegetables.

"How long did you hope to stay?"

"As long as there was work," said the eldest. He had been
here for two months the last time. Usually he got $2.75 to $3.00 an
hour with room but not board.

Garcia told them I was a *periodista* who worked for a magazine
called *Rolling Stone, "Piedra Rolar."* They all thought that was a
very funny name for a magazine. They were still chuckling about it
as Garcia escorted them to the pedestrian walkway across the
border.

Not everything that comes over the Rio Grande is quite this
benign, of course. Since Don Johnson and Philip Michael Thomas
cleaned up south Florida, Mexico has become the main drug route
into the U.S. There's also a lively trade along the border in
"OTMs"—"Other Than Mexicans." These are aliens who get smuggled for a price out of South and Central America, China, Korea,
India, even Poland. OTMs are routinely robbed by "Border Rats,"
gangs who commit their crimes in the U.S. then slip back to
Mexico. The Mexican illegals are robbed, too, though there's little
enough to take from them. And the Border Patrol has the highest
casualty rate in the line of duty of any U.S. government uniformed
service.

I went on a drug stakeout with one of the agents from the
McAllen sector. "The smugglers are armed, and they will shoot,"
said the agent, who was carrying a Heckler and Koch MP5 submachine gun. After hiding his patrol car, he and I stood alongside a
road about a mile from the Rio Grande. Between the road and the

river was a huge mesquite thicket. "The joke along here," said the agent, "is that you can stop your patrol car anywhere on this road, blink your headlights three times, and the smugglers will run out and jump in your backseat by mistake." He'd no more said that than a car came down the road at about three miles an hour. We hit the dirt.

The car was a convertible with two flashy Latin girls in it, radio turned up loud. It rolled to a stop not twenty feet from us. "This is it," whispered the agent, and he belly-crawled forward, moving fast and soundlessly, until there was just one ragged shrub between him and the car. He could almost reach the door handle. I followed, more in the fashion of a trout across the bottom of a rowboat. I could see the agent slipping a clip into the MP5.

I tried to muffle my frenzied breathing by shoving my face into the ground. But that only got dirt up my nose, so I had to muffle my frenzied sneezes by shoving my face further into the ground, which got dirt between my chattering teeth. This went on for thirty minutes. So did the legion of bug bites.

Finally, the driver turned off her radio.

Giggling voices filled the night air.

"Antonio es muy simpatico."

"Sí, sí, cómo no, y Roberto es muy generoso."

We had been pinned down for a half-hour by an all-girl heart-to-heart. The driver gunned her engine, and the two young ladies drove away to their disco date.

But what does this tomfoolery look like from the other side? Not so snappy and dramatic, I'm afraid. I rented a car and drove along the south side of the border, from Matamoros on the Gulf of Mexico to Tijuana on the Pacific. It was what TV news cameramen call "cut to obligatory squalor." The overfed white reporter goes around stuffing his microphone—or, in my case, pencil—in people's faces.

"Just how poor are you?" "Mind if I look around in your hovel?" "Say, you wouldn't happen to have any kids that are a little more crippled or anything, would you?"

Anyway, it's a mess over there. To tell the truth, it isn't a worse mess than the Brownsville section of Brooklyn or downtown Detroit. But it's a different mess. Even in the best parts of Nuevo

Laredo or Juárez, the pavement is coming to bits. There's garbage all over the place. The buses and trucks belch smut. Buildings are being made from such bum materials that it's hard to tell if the construction is going up or coming down. In fact, neither. Since the oil bust and foreign-debt crisis a couple of years ago, most Mexican building sites are just sitting there.

The individual poverty was grim-o. But it was the corporate, the commonweal poverty that jerked the senses. Mexico isn't just squalid homes. It's squalid industry, squalid infrastructure. No adequate capital investment has ever been made in Mexico, not even by capitalists in the machinery of their capitalism. The whole country looks like it's run by slum landlords. Especially the bathrooms.

There aren't many sewage treatment plants in Mexico or, for that matter, many sewers. Even septic tanks are a luxury. Mexico is a nation of cesspools, of holes in the ground. You can't put toilet paper in a cesspool; that clogs it. So all the used toilet paper goes in wastebaskets or, more often, cardboard boxes on the bathroom floor. Except people forget, and half the toilets in the country are overflowing. I think public rest rooms are crucial to understanding a culture. Look at the street-side pissoirs of France, the ancient water closets of Britain, the ceramic relief palaces of the United States. But don't go to the john in Mexico unless you plan to learn more than you want to know.

Besides bathrooms, I figured I'd also better go see some politicians. If you're looking for fleas, you have to lie down with dogs. When I got to Juárez, across from El Paso, I went to the local headquarters of PAN, the National Action Party (the acronym means "bread" in Spanish). PAN would be the opposition party if there were such a thing in Mexico. But the ruling party, the PRI, has won, by this means or that, every presidential and gubernatorial election since 1929. PRI stands for "Institutional Revolutionary Party," a name that manages to include most of mankind's bad ideas about governance. PAN occasionally wins a municipal election.

PAN HQ was a large building in one of the better commercial districts. But all the windows were broken, and the walls were defaced with spray paint.

I arrived in the middle of a press conference—as boring a

thing to sit through if you don't know the language as it is if you do. When it was over, instead of running for the bar like American reporters, some of the journalists stayed and argued vehemently with the PAN spokesmen. They were employees of the government-controlled papers and TV stations. Imagine Peter Jennings giving you grief on the air and then sticking around to tell you President Reagan thinks you're a shit, too. When all the reporters had finally left, I asked Juan Torres, the pissed-off looking president of the PAN Juárez committee, my favorite question:

"Why is Mexico so poor?"

"Corruption!" said Torres. "We are in a sea of corruption! There has been nearly sixty years of the same party! Because of that political party, we have not become an economic power."

"What should the U.S. do about illegal Mexican immigration?" I asked.

But Torres had had enough for one day. "The U.S. can do what it likes," he said and handed me off to PAN committee member Pepe Marquez.

Marquez spoke very quickly, as though the Mexican social disaster might overtake us at any minute and we'd have to hightail it across the Rio with the rest of the wetbacks. He, too, blamed everything on the PRI, throwing in many statistics about how the Mexican government controls 75 percent of business and industry and 80 percent of agricultural land and so on—the kind of facts and figures responsible reporters dutifully copy down and all readers blithely skip. In the news trade, this stuff is known as *"MEGO,"* short for "My Eyes Glaze Over."

Marquez noticed that I was beginning to snooze. He paused, trying to figure a way to put his case succinctly. "If the government was given the desert to manage," he said, "there would be a shortage of sand."

"Is there something the United States should be, you know, doing?" I asked.

"The Mexican government," said Marquez, "is kept alive by the United States agreeing to bank loans."

Interesting that our administration, so sis-boom-bah about anti-communism, is footing the bill for their administration which sounds pretty communistic.

"Well," I said, "how'd your windows get broken?"

"A group of leftists did it, the CDP, the Committee for Popular Defense."

"Did they attack the PRI offices too?"

"They never attack the PRI."

"Why'd they hit you and not the ruling party?"

Marquez gave me one of those world-explaining, whole-body Latin shrugs, an educated version of the shrugs I got from the illegals on the border. "The CDP, they are *supposedly* against the government."

I drove south out of Juárez, across the beautiful edges of the Sierra de la Magdalena mountains, through the prairie scrub of northern Chihuahua State and into vast rolling hills, green and well-watered and empty. A Cleveland a year, full of would-be immigrants, could be built out here for decades.

In Chihuahua City the Institutional Revolutionary Party was setting up a press conference, too. President de la Madrid would address the media the next day in an enormous hotel ballroom, full of comfortable chairs, buffet tables, red velvet draperies and putting-green-size Mexican flags. I asked the party officials for a PRI spokesman, and they got me an appointment with Arturo Ugalde, the Chihuahua state director of economic development.

I had an hour to kill so I went sightseeing. There was a beautiful eighteenth-century colonial baroque palace on the main plaza. Father Hidalgo, the leader of Mexico's revolt against Spanish rule, had been imprisoned here until his execution in 1811. The walls of the palace courtyard were covered with murals painted by Pina Mora in the early sixties. They depicted, in heroic style and with villainous content, the entire history of Mexico. The *literally* heart-wrenching Aztecs were shown sacrificing people and skinning them alive. Then came the dirtsack Conquistadors, with dim Montezuma mistaking Cortes, of all people, for a god. Then Catholic missionaries converting the Indians to death.

Father Hidalgo figured large, murdering Spanish civilians and getting the stuffing kicked out of his revolution in its only pitched battle. Mexico didn't become independent for another decade, not until the local Spanish aristocrats declared it independent because the government back in Spain was getting too liberal. This was faithfully depicted as was the period of bloody chaos from 1821 to 1848, the period of bloody chaos from 1858 to 1867 and the period of bloody chaos from 1911 to 1920. (Artist Mora was forced to use every conceivable variation of the determined peasant with up-raised face holding a gun in the air with one hand.) Also portrayed was Benito Juárez, the "Abraham Lincoln of Mexico," who freed the Indian peons but accidentally destroyed their livelihood by letting communal land fall into the hands of speculators; the comic opera emperor Maximilian, installed by Napoleon III because Mexico defaulted on French bank loans (Citibank take note); and dictator Porfirio Díaz, who sold the country's natural resources to foreign companies for peanuts and gave press swine William Randolph Hearst a 2.5 million-acre ranch in Chihuahua as a thank you for good newspaper PR. In the middle of all this was a cluster of pale, slightly vampiric-looking characters in blue uniforms carrying a frightening and complicated flag full of stripes and things. They were taking California, Arizona, Nevada, Utah, New Mexico, and Texas away, Rt. 66 included.

I drove to Ugalde's office in an industrial park on the edge of town.

"Why is Mexico so poor?"

Ugalde hemmed and hawed a while about the Mexican economic system and then blamed it on the Indians. "We never," said Ugalde, "had the saying 'the best Indian is a dead Indian.' I will put it this way: We have three types of people. People in the south of Mexico, they want. People in the middle, they think. People in the north, they work."

What he meant was the south has the most Indians. And in the middle, Mexico City, the intelligentsia make their Indian heritage a point of pride. But in the north of Mexico, people are mostly European. We weren't going to get anywhere with this line of reasoning.

I asked about Mexico's one-party system of government. What I have in my notes is: "Yr. gov.—fucked or what?" Though I'm sure I phrased that differently.

"If we had a perfect democracy—everyone votes, without any education—you could hardly expect anyone to win," Ugalde said, going all *glasnost* and Gorbachevy on me. "There will be five, six parties. Seventy million Mexicans want to be president, but only one can be. The PRI system has been the right people at the right time, avoiding dictatorship and political strife."

Then Ugalde pulled out a heap of charts and graphs that he said showed Mexico's rapid pace of development. "And the Japanese are coming soon," he said.

I told him I'd just spent a week with the United States Border Patrol, and I hadn't seen many signs of what you'd call rapid pace of development.

"People can go live in the U.S.," he said, as though it were a matter of whether to winter in Aspen or Palm Springs, "but it's hard. We are not so disciplined. We have to learn the laws and rules of living in a new place. There is a rigidity to the North. In Mexico we have an expression"—he gave me that wised-up shrug—"Everything is negotiable."

Ugalde sighed as though I'd made much more alarming allegations about the Mexican state of things than I had. "Mexico," he said, "is rich in raw materials but poor in resources of technology and of ways to use technology." In other words somebody stole the half with all the paved roads.

I left Ugalde's office and drove around the industrial park. It had been laid out in sectors like a spoked wheel. There were absolutely no buildings in the entire park, except Ugalde's little office suite. Grass was growing in the pavement cracks. And in the middle of the park, at the hub, there was an enormous welded-steel sculpture of Don Quixote tilting at a windmill.

So what's going to happen at our southern border? Is an enormous, terrifying, beaner tidal wave going to roll across our fair nation? Well, we don't have to worry about that. It already has. We've suffered a huge invasion of cheerful, hard-working, poor people, who grabbed all the shit jobs nobody else wanted and caused a fearsome outbreak of Tex-Mex yuppie restaurants.

We don't have a problem. It's the Mexicans who have the problem. And there are four billion other people in the world, most of them with even worse problems than the Mexicans have. Where are *they* going to go?

The Holyland—God's Monkey House

. . . .

You haven't really seen the Old City of Jerusalem until you've seen it at dawn on a Moslem sabbath while you're disguised as an Arab and accompanied by a guy who's probably with the PLO, plus two hulking press photographers in unlikely-looking Bedouin head-dresses, and all four of you are following the footsteps of Christ down the Via Dolorosa at a jog trot, running in and out of doorways dodging Israeli army patrols.

Old Jerusalem is a medieval city, not an adorably restored medieval city like Heidelberg, but a real one where you can smell the medieval sanitation and smack your head on the dirty, low medieval ceilings. The fortress-fronted, time-soiled limestone houses are built all over each other. The boulevards are steep, twisting, littered and as wide as a donkey. Some streets are roofed in stone; most have steps cut in the pavement, and they seem more like staircases in a crypt than city avenues. Lamps are few. Signposts date from the Ottoman Empire. Each shadow holds some sinister passage or dwarfish portcullis. The place is the original for

240

every game of Dungeons and Dragons. At dawn in Jerusalem, you could be in any century of human civilization.

The guy who was probably with the PLO, whom I'll call Ahmed, was smuggling me and my photographer friends Tony Suau and John Reardon into the forbidden precincts of the Haram esh-"Sherif, the Noble Sanctuary" enclosing the Dome of the Rock and the al-Aksa Mosque. Except for Mecca and Medina, these are Mohammedanism's most sacred shrines. Infidels are banned from the Haram's thirty-five acres on Friday, the Moslem sabbath, and this Friday the sanctuary was also being sealed by Israeli soldiers and Jerusalem police. There had been an ugly incident the week before. After midday prayers, some kids displayed the illegal Palestinian flag, burned the flag of Israel (and, of course, the U.S. flag, too) and threw stones. The Israelis responded with clubs and tear gas, and, at one point, actually tossed a gas grenade inside the al-Aksa Mosque. The result was some coughing and sneezing and lots of international indignation. Today the Israelis would be checking identity cards at the sanctuary's eight gates and letting in only respectable believers.

Tony, John and I had tried to slip into the Haram before the soldiers arrived. There was only one sleepy Moslem guard on duty at 6:00 A.M. at the Gate of the Tribes. We'd wrapped black and white checked *kaffiyehs*—traditional Arab kerchiefs—over our heads. But since I was wearing a Burberry trench coat and they were carrying thirty pounds of camera equipment, this wasn't much of a ruse. The elderly guard was having none of us. While we were arguing with him, Ahmed stepped out of a crowd of morning prayer-goers and took our part. (This happens all the time in the Middle East. No matter who you're arguing with or what you're arguing about, some stranger will always come to your defense. They're generous with their contention; you never have to argue alone in the Arab world.)

When he couldn't prevail on the guard, Ahmed took us home to a warren of ancient stone rooms (though the furniture was Danish Modern) and served us sticky tea and rolls and bread and coffee thick as syrup.

Several of Ahmed's knuckles were enormously knobbed and one of his fingers was bent at a sickening angle. There were scars around his wrists. He had been imprisoned by the Israelis for four years during the Seventies, he said, for "Palestinian activities" and again during the early Eighties for helping a friend repair a gun. He said he had been tied in a chair once for five days with a black hood over his head. "It was beautiful when they would take me away to beat me"—he gave us that big grin everyone wears in these parts when they talk about something grisly—"because then I could breathe and see."

Ahmed claimed there would be a demonstration at al-Aksa and that the journalists, the *sahaffi*, must be inside the mosque to see how Jews treat Moslems in this holy place. He led us through the Arab Quarter to the Via Dolorosa which runs parallel to the Haram's north wall. Then he opened an iron door near the *Ecce homo* Arch—the place where Pontius Pilate, saying "Behold the man," presented a flogged Jesus to the Jerusalem mob. We went through somebody's house, across roofs and down concealed spiral stairs with stone treads worn hollow by a thousand years of excapes and forays. It was a scene from an Indiana Jones movie except the stairs opened into someone's modern bathroom. We went out through the kitchen, down one more flight of steps cut into the Haram's wall and there, framed in a Byzantine Empire back door, was the Dome of the Rock—a big gold cupola rising from an octagon of royal blue tiles and set upon a vast stone platform like a bonbon on a deck of playing cards.

Burnooses were produced to conceal Tony and John's photo gear. I ditched my trench coat. And Ahmed showed us how to fasten the *kaffiyehs* properly with the *ukals*, the tasseled head-bands. Then we went, stiff with adrenaline, down the length of the Haram esh-Sherif compound, past guards and policemen and "fellow" Moslems. *"Walk comfortable!"* whispered Ahmed with some irritation. Tony's cameras were clanging under his lumpy robe. Israeli soldiers lined the sanctuary walls and helicopters swayed back and forth overhead.

The dim interior of the al-Aksa Mosque was the size of a large suburban house lot. There were no furnishings at all except luminous antique carpets spread two and three deep across the entire floor. Scores of columns, thick as automobiles, supported a roof so high it was nearly invisible. A few of the slippered worshipers knelt alone on prayer rugs; others gathered in small groups along the walls. For the next four hours Tony, John and I hid in these majestic shadows, wondering what the hell we were doing.

It was unlikely that the Israelis would let anything important erupt again in the Haram or overreact if it did. They'd taken too much flak about the mosque gassing. To put it in Protestant American terms: throwing a tear gas grenade into the al-Aksa Mosque on a sabbath was like attacking the Pebble Beach golf course with Agent Orange on a Sunday in June. So we weren't going to see much action. And we weren't really doing our jobs either. Outside the sanctuary, all through the Israeli-occupied territories of Palestine's West Bank and Gaza Strip, there were riots, retaliations, strikes, curfews, stonings, shootings, beatings, shoutings, whinings, and wild excuse-makings—the complete folderol of a Mideastern political crisis. Eager, ambitious reporters would have been out there interviewing the pants off everybody and filing serious, indignant yet balanced and thoughtful pieces. Instead, here we were dressed like ninnies and sneaking around in mosques.

However, dressing like ninnies and sneaking around in mosques is an important tradition among old Arab hands, dating back at least to 1853 when the explorer Sir Richard Burton dressed like a ninny for nine whole months and managed to sneak all the way into the holy Kaabah at Mecca. Like Sir Richard, T. E. Lawrence and others before us, we were trying to penetrate the soul of the Arab, trying to become one with him and fathom the Mystery of the East. It's just something you have to go through if you're going to be an old Arab hand, like eating a live guppy to get into Sigma Nu.

Shortly before noon, as the mosque was beginning to fill, Ahmed suggested that I go outside and mingle. I thought this was a little *too* P. J. of Arabia, especially since I look about as much like an average American jerk as it's possible to look and speak exactly two words of Arabic. But Ahmed thought I'd pass, thanks perhaps to a high school fist fight which left me with a Levantine nose. "If they start throwing stones," he said, "feel free to join in."

Pulling the *kaffiyeh* down over my forehead to hood my blue eyes, I walked outside into a milling crowd of two thousand Mohammedans. The crowd was all men and boys. Women pray separately in the Dome of the Rock. A few of the men were in church-going clothes but most wore jeans and sweaters like my own. My deck shoes—not a popular fashion item with desert peoples—were the only anomaly.

I didn't know quite what to do with myself, so I milled too. Fortunately the Arabs are also fond of lounging. And I lounged for a while—leaning against pillars, sitting on the edge of fountains, that sort of thing. Nobody bothered me; only a couple of small boys looked twice at my yokel face.

The men were chatting or walking alone lost in contemplation. Some strolled in pairs, holding hands. Then the *muezzin* called the faithful and suddenly I was the only person not facing Mecca. Not many O'Rourkes have ever bowed to Mecca, but I did and followed all the gestures and prostrations as best I could, half a beat behind the others, like singing along when you don't know the words.

There was a peculiar casualness to the worship. People ambled in and out of the mosque all through the service. It was God as an informal thing, but a serious informal thing, the way lunch is when you're hungry. A large part of the crowd stayed outside, listening to loudspeakers mounted on al-Aksa's portico, listening as though they were hearing something they were actually interested in, not a sermon or a scripture reading. I grew up in the prim and glacial ceremonies of the Methodist church—half grammar lesson, half drill inspection. It had never occurred to me that anyone might want to just come and *hang out* at a religious service.

This was no stick-on, decal God here, but a woven-in-the-cloth, blown-in-the-glass diety. In the Holyland, God comes with the territory. And though I don't suppose the Moslems would like to hear it, Israel, too, has God as standard equipment. After all, here it is, the State of Israel, with no other rationale for existence except a promise from God. I wonder what a Methodist homeland would be like—mandatory stay-pressed shirts, federal regulations about keeping feet off furniture and automatic death penalty for anybody with crab grass in his lawn.

There was, in fact, a demonstration after prayers, though not a very exciting one. Men came out of al-Aksa and yelled; women came out of the Dome of the Rock and shrieked. An Iman, a portly visiting president of the mosque in some West Bank town, was

hoisted upon shoulders and carried around the Dome. Dozens of
pocket-sized Korans were waved in the air. I demonstrated a bit
myself by milling around at a slightly faster pace than I'd milled
before.

True to Arab form, the demonstration immediately broke into
two quarreling factions: The group hoisting the Iman wanted to
keep a strictly religious tone of outrage to the proceedings; the
other group wanted to wave a small, homemade Palestinian flag and
scream at the Israelis. The soldiers along the walls looked tense,
and one platoon moved into the enclosure and stood along the edge
of the Dome's platform with weapons in array. But they didn't
interfere. A few young Moslems made feints at collecting stones to
throw but didn't follow through. With nothing to oppose it, the
demonstration died down in half an hour.

By the time Tony, John and I got smuggled out of the sanctuary, it was after three o'clock. Old Jerusalem was a very different
place in the afternoon. Israeli soldiers pried at locks with
crowbars, trying to force Moslem shopkeepers to end the general
strike that started in December while young Palestinian activists
darted through the marketplaces warning merchants not to open.
Arab boys of ten and twelve were picking up rocks and chunks of
cement and yelling encouragement to each other from the roofs.
Armored personnel carriers, filled with irritable-looking draftees,
squeezed along the few large streets. Islamic fundamentalists
barked over PA systems from storefront mosques. Greek monks,
Armenian priests, Catholic nuns and Coptic whatsits lumbered
around in full fig like parade floats. Ultra-Orthodox Jews plodded
by, wearing ridiculous beaver hats and making sour faces. Jesus-
addled German tourists strode overenergetically from one holy hot
spot to the next.

At dawn in Jerusalem, you could be in any century. But at
mid-afternoon, you know exactly what century you're in—the
twelfth, when everybody was bashing everybody over the head
about God.

The rock over which the Dome of the Rock is built is supposed
to be the altar where Abraham was going to sacrifice Isaac (until
Yahweh explained He was just kidding). David parked the Ark of

the Covenant here. And Mohammed is believed to have leapt into heaven with this rock as his trampoline. The hill the rock sits on—indistinguishable from the thousand other dumpy hills of Judea—is called Temple Mount by the Jews, Haram esh-Sherif by the Moslems and Mt. Moriah by the Christians. Solomon's Temple was here and the great Temple complex of Herod, destroyed by the Romans in 70 A.D. Thus the western wall of the Haram is the Wailing Wall of the Jews, who bemoan their fate on one side of it while the Moslems bemoan theirs on the other. The early Christians considered the place cursed because Jesus predicted the destruction of the temple (a safe enough prediction; the whole of Jerusalem has been destroyed more than thirty times). Score that round of theological debate to the early Christians.

In fact, I think it can be fairly said that *everything* in the Holy Land is cursed The Gaza Strip certainly is. I drove down there to take a look at the place where Israel's current batch of troubles began. The Strip is desolate and, at the same time, one of the most thickly populated places on earth. (Desolately overpopulated, cursed Holyland, blood-soaked home of the Prince of Peace—this region never seems to run out of oxymorons.) Gaza City has the same crowded poverty as Arab Jerusalem, but it's all new and made of cement. The land around it, the mere 140 square miles that make up this gigantic international sore spot, should be a place of gilt-sand beaches and graceful dunes dotted with palms and oasis wells. Instead it's Hell's Riviera with eight refugee camps housing a quarter of a million people.

The Palestinians in these camps were displaced by the 1948 war—the one Paul Newman and Eva Marie Saint won in *Exodus*. Since then they've been "temporarily" sheltered by the jack-off U.N.; ruled first by useless Egyptian bureaucracy, then by cold-hearted Israeli military fiat; ignored by the Western bloc; exploited by the Eastern bloc and just left there, like live bait in a geopolitical leg trap by their fellow Arabs.

In between the refugee camps are some ratty Arab farms (Palestinians, unlike Israeli citizens, do not get subsidized irrigation water). Also in between the camps are Jewish settlements. I have no idea why. The Jews have no biblical claim to Gaza except for some exploits of Samson's. ("Then went Samson to Gaza, and saw there a harlot, and went in unto her." *Judges* 16:1) The settlements are cheerless places surrounded by armed guards and barbed wire and featuring the usual dreadful Israeli architecture— a style that crosses the worker housing of Gdansk with the branch banks of Hollywood, Florida.

All the refugee camps had been put under curfew, which meant no one could stir outside the shack houses at any time for any reason. The curfew was lifted for only an hour or so a day, the time never announced beforehand. Even then only the women could go outside and get food.

I made my way into the largest of the camps, Jabalia, which houses fifty-two thousand people in what looks like, from a distance, a valley full of packing crates with electrical lines. Entering the camp was a less romantic business than getting into the al-Aksa Mosque and more dangerous, too. In the occupied territories, unlike Jerusalem, the Israelis were shooting people.

I crawled into Jabalia through a scraggly vineyard and spent an unhappy five minutes with my gut pressed to the sand, trying to look like a grape plant while an armored personnel carrier rolled along a nearby road. I visited an architect there, named Ali, who did not miss the irony of being an architect in a two-room cinderblock house with a corrugated asbestos roof.

I could see daylight all around the eaves in the eight-by-ten-foot living room. There was no heat, and a cold wind was blowing off the Mediterannean. Ali said the camp had been under curfew for seven days. The Israeli-controlled electricity had been cut off twice and at one point the water mains were shut for three days; people had to drink from rain barrels. The food in the camp stores had all run out, and the break in the curfew was not long enough for the women to walk into town and back. Money, too, had about run out, because of the Palestinian general strike and the fact that no one could get to work anyway. However, the United Nations was usually allowed to distribute food to children and nursing mothers once a day. And an informal smuggling network had grown up around the camp perimeters. Nobody was going hungry yet.

Ali counted himself lucky. There were only five in his family. Some people in the camp had households of ten or fifteen. I asked Ali's wife what she was feeding her kids. "Bread and tea for

breakfast," she said, "and tomatoes and vegetables that are smuggled." There was no meat or milk. She had no more said that than
Ali invited me to stay for dinner. You can't fault Arab manners. It
took ten minutes of diplomatic maneuvering to escape imposing on
their larder.

"Where are you from?" I asked Ali. Though, of course, since
he was only thirty-two years old, he was from nowhere. He was born
in the camp. But without hesitation Ali named a little village in
what's now Israel proper.

"My father goes to cry there. Nothing is left."

The press stands accused of holding the Israelis to higher
moral standards than it holds the other peoples of the Middle East.
That's not our fault. Moses started that. Are the Israelis treating the
Palestinians any worse than the Palestinians would treat the Israelis
if the sandal were on the other foot? Of course not. The Munich
massacre and hundreds of killings, bombings, hijackings, rocket
attacks and other mad-hat actions prove it. Unfortunately, morality
is not a matter of double-entry bookkeeping.

The Israeli-administered hospital in Gaza City, where Arabs
wounded in the rioting are treated, was a pile of shit. The floors
were dirty, the bathrooms were dirty and the little kitchens on each
floor were pathetic in their filth. The walls had been painted, a very
long time ago, in awful landlord colors. Damp marks spread across
the ceilings. Screens were missing from the windows and light
bulbs from the light fixtures. The hospital looked like the "colored"
waiting rooms used to look in bus stations down South. The doctors
were all Palestinian, but none of them would talk to me for fear of
Israeli ire. The patients, however, were pitifully eager to talk, as if
exposing their plight would make any difference in the dead-end
hatreds of this land. Maybe the Western powers will intervene, said
the Palestinians with forlorn hope. But we've done that before.
When Godfrey of Bouillon conquered Jerusalem in 1099 he slaugh-
tered all the Moslems and burned the Jews in their synagogue.

I went from bed to bed hearing dreadful stories. A fifteen-
year-old who looked twelve, and didn't have an eyelash's worth of
down on his upper lip, had been shot through the thigh bone an
inch below his balls. He said he had been bringing food home

when a soldier told him "come here." He did and got shot. He probably wasn't as innocent as that, but any grown man could have knocked this kid cold with a pancake spatula. The slightly larger boy in the next bed had an eye the size of a teacup and bruises like zebra stripes. He said he'd been detained by soldiers and beaten for thirty minutes. In a small room next door were four young men; all had been shot—in the chest; in the side; in the belly. Only one had been shot in the leg, the traditional shoot-to-wound target. In the ward across the hall was a ten-year-old with a bullet in his rib cage and a man and his teenage son who'd both been beaten senseless, they claimed, in a police station, and an old man who'd been beaten all over and had both his shins broken. And so on.

This is bullshit. This is barbarism. I've covered a lot of rioting and pushes-come-to-shoves, and there is no excuse for this kind of civilian-hammering by soldiers and police. Panamanian kids can throw a rock in a way that Palestinian boys, who are innocent of baseball, only dream about. The Panamanians have been rioting steadily since last July and only one rioter has been killed. Korean college students are the most organized and determined bunch of rioters on earth, and Korean riot cops are no bowl of Sugar Pops. But the Koreans have been at it since June 1987 and the death toll is only two.

A few days later Tony Suau and I got into a little riot, a riot-ette, in the Kalandia refugee camp on the West Bank several miles north of Jerusalem. This camp wasn't under curfew, but the Israeli army was running patrols through it and holding down intersections and generally acting like this was downtown Hue in the middle of the Tet offensive.

The enemy was horsing around in the side streets, giving each other nuggies and trying to figure out how to tie the *kaffiyehs* over their faces in a genuine fierce-desert-warrior way. They were twelve, thirteen, fourteen years old. I recognized their every move and didn't have to speak a word of Arabic to know what they were saying because this was Tommy, Larry, Gary, Wayne and me playing war in 1959, except for keeps.

Of course they were excited to find adult foreigners taking everything they were doing seriously. They delivered long speeches on patriotism as only pubescents can. I believe the equivalent translation would be, "My old man was on Iwo. . . ." And they showed us where to park our car so it wouldn't get hit with stones or rubber bullets.

We followed the kids through a maze of houses and passageways—another modern version of the architecture around the Haram—to an alley on a hilltop that commanded an Israeli control point. These kids are no future Dwight Goodens, but the rocks of Judea are excellent rocks, all pointy and jagged chalk limestone. And the kids get good distance with a run-up underhand throw like a cricket fast bowler's. Some of them also have the shepherd's sling David used on the Philistine version of André the Giant. The slings are as potent as a Whammo Wrist Rocket with a steelie in it—and almost as accurate.

The kids rushed down the alley, and the shop gates, parked cars and tin roofs at the Israeli-held intersection resounded with the merry bing and clatter of a Holy Land stoning.

At least the soldiers weren't firing much live ammo that week. Defense Minister Yitzhak Rabin had told them, "The first priority is to use force, might, beatings." And according to *The Jerusalem Post:* "Large numbers of troops are to be concentrated at each trouble spot, where they will fire rubber bullets, charge at the demonstrators, and try to get the leaders, whom they are to beat and detain." Or *try* to beat and detain since there was fat chance of laying hands on any of these high-speed, wily urchins.

The rubber bullets come at you with an untuned guitar-string twang and a whistle and hit the pavement and buildings in profound whacks. A couple of these projectiles bounced up by my feet. They're black cylinders about as big as the last knuckle on your thumb, heavy in the hand and hard as a shoe heel. I cut one open later. It had a steel pellet the size of a .45 slug inside.

The kids darted forward and back, jacked-up and grinning with the "drunk delight of battle" people used to get before it was discovered that war is horrible and wrong. The Israelis attempted a charge up the alley, but the kids held the high ground and the soldiers had no cover. Eventually the soldiers made an old man, who'd been driving by, get out of his VW van. They used the van as a rolling shield, pushing it uphill and zinging rubber bullets from behind. The kids (and me and Tony) made a tactical retreat.

I could understand why the Israeli soldiers were showing such anger and fear. It wasn't just the taunting, pesky boys armed with less than Neanderthal weapons. The whole Kalandia camp was alive with hatred. Moms and doddering granddads were shouting instructions from the house tops. "Jeeps are coming! A platoon is coming up this street! Over here!" Old ladies and little girls rushed out of houses and began throwing up barricades of trash barrels and paving stones they could barely lift. A pretty girl of twelve with an infant on her hip, whom we'd seen by the camp gate, was no idling baby-sitter. She was a lookout. She came running up the slope, baby aflap, saying something about troops with tear gas. Doors flew open and the half-pint Geronimos disappeared into labyrinthine Arab domiciles.

Again I was surprised by a peculiar ordinariness—hatred as universal, as simple, as much a foregone conclusion as God had been at the al-Aksa Mosque. It had never occurred to me that God *or* hatred could permeate people this way, let alone at the same time.

Tony and I drove on north and, near Ramallah, caught up with another Israeli patrol just as it was entering the small Al Ama're refugee camp. There was a roadblock on the main street, a single burning truck tire. The Israelis get all exercised about roadblocks. They grabbed the handyman at the camp's U.N. office and made him pour water on the tire and pull it out of the road. None of the Israeli troops looked mature enough to trust with the car keys after dark. And all of them looked anxious with that particular anxiety of the stranger, the anomie modern fiction writers are always writing about except modern fiction writers think it takes place in lonely grad-school writing seminars.

The patrol's commanding officer was a captain, about thirty, and carrying, of all things, a pair of nunchakus—a dippy kung fu weapon made from a pair of sticks joined by a short chain. A crowd of cat-calling Arab boys had gathered down the street and stones began to fall in among us. The captain moved his patrol toward the boys. Tony and I tagged along. The soldiers had their gas grenades and Galil rifles ready. The boys vaporized.

The captain picked up the pace, trying to catch the kids and shake Tony and me. But, being in full combat gear, he could do neither. The soldiers were rude to us, as armed men invariably are. (And in the Middle East whoever's top dog at the moment is terrifically rude, just as he's terrifically courteous when he's shit-out-of-luck.) The Arab kids stayed always just beyond the next corner, while the soldiers ran faster and faster, around and back and up and down through the twisting streets, sweating like horses.

As the patrol approached an area, the pavement would be empty and all the houses shuttered and dark. As soon as it passed, the doors and windows opened and women and children poked their heads outside, laughing in happy malice. I saw a three-year-old boy step into the road and send mocking kisses at the Israeli soldiers' backs.

After forty-five minutes the soldiers gave up, winded. They returned to the entrance of the camp. By now there were some grudging smiles for Tony and me. The only soldier who seemed to speak English pointed at my notebook and said, "This they see and go wild."

"No, no," I said. "They see this," I held up the notebook— "and they only go wild two times. They see this," I pointed to Tony's Nikons, "they go wild ten times. They see TV"—I pantomimed a TV cameraman—"they go wild a *hundred* times!" The soldier laughed and translated for his buddies. They laughed, and gave us some dates and apricots from their packs. We gave them some cigarettes. Then we stood around shrugging amiably. "So much trouble . . . What can be done . . . Who knows . . ." with these young men who would have to live their whole lives in this mess.

When I'd been in front of the al-Aksa Mosque and everyone was bowing toward Mecca and praying, I prayed too. And I repeated that prayer when we left Al Ama're. Actually, it wasn't exactly a prayer. It was more a sort of chat with God. I said, "God, the next time you're looking for people, you know, to receive Revealed Truth and everything and be the Anointed of the Lord like the Christians and the Jews and the Moslems are, *please*, God, don't choose semiagnostic lapsed Methodists from Ohio. *Choose somebody else.*"

Epilogue: What Does the Future Hold In Store for Our Friends in Faraway Lands?

Like many people who've spent time absorbing the exotic sights, loud sounds and great big smells of the developing world and getting to know the special warmth and humor of its citizens ("Have a *Goodyear*," as the Soweto comrades said to the necklaced police informer on New Year's Eve), I can only wonder what the coming years will bring. What will happen to the "emerging nations" over, say, the next quarter of a century?

Personally, I believe a brilliant future awaits the Third World, a future filled with peace, prosperity, health and happiness, a future that the people of the Third World will reach, um . . . the moment they die and go to heaven. And, for a very large number of them that will be soon indeed, because they're dying like flies out there in Upper Revolta and Absurdistan.

This is the main thing the next quarter century will bring to the Third World—the same thing the last quarter century brought—lots and lots of colorful death. What with famine, war, genocide, sexually transmitted diseases and general dirty habits, we can expect the next twenty-five years to be a veritable festival of Malthusianism. Or semi-Malthusianism. Because the only thing that's going to exceed the astonishing, incredible Third World death rate will be its amazing, unbelievable, buglike rate of reproduction. By the year 2013 something like 3 billion people will be added to the earth's population, none of them in a place you'd care to have a second home.

Due to this actuarial wrestling match between mortality and screwing like bunnies, average age in the Third World will drop precipitously. By 2013 many Third World business and political leaders will be under the age of five. Thus government and economic matters will be conducted at approximately the same level of maturity and sophistication as they are now.

Of course, all underdeveloped countries will be military dictatorships. The army seems to be the only institution capable of keeping order in these lands. It does this by shooting all the corrupt and incompetent people, which in Uganda, for instance, turned out to be everybody. Usually, however, the corrupt and incompetent people the army shoots are army officers. This is why Third World military dictatorships tend to move, coup by coup, down through the ranks. Colonels overthrow generals, majors overthrow colonels and so forth until we get to Ghana's Flight Lieutenant Jerry Rawlings or Liberia's Sergeant Samuel K. Doe. The trend will continue. Soon Third World military dictatorships will be headed by Weblo Scouts and grade-school crossing guards.

Nonetheless, a rough political stability will have been achieved in some places such as Lebanon, Afghanistan, Angola, Peru and Sri Lanka, where insurgent terrorist groups will have multiplied until there is one for each living person.

The Indian subcontinent, much of Africa and parts of the Mideast will give up on the whole idea of independence and plead for reestablishment of the British Empire. "Please to come back Sahib English and snob us and get the Coca-Cola machine to work again," they will beg. But to no avail. Margaret Thatcher will be long out of office; the Labour Party will be back in power; and Britain will be a colony of Jamaica.

Ideologically, Marxism will continue to make enormous inroads in underdeveloped countries. After all, when you're living in hopeless poverty and filth and there's a political philosophy that offers you hopeless poverty and filth, it only makes sense to go with the flow. In 2013 *every* Third World country will be a member of the Communist Bloc. This should go a long way to destroying the new, hip, *glasnost* Soviet Union. The Soviet Communist Party chief (probably Olga Korbut) will find herself broke, confused, embroiled in a thousand local tribal wars and reduced to the same influence over international Marxism that Mayor Koch now has over New York.

Koch will be, thank God, dead by then. But not before having been elected secretary general of the U.N. The Ayatollah Khomeini, however, will still be alive and serving as president of the World Council of Churches.

Twenty-five years from now all religion will be fundamentalist religion, even the Church of England. Wild-eyed "Tutuist" Anglicans will riot in Anzania (formerly the Union of South Africa). They'll force people to play contract bridge at gunpoint and make unbelievers eat little sandwiches with the crusts cut off. No woman will dare appear in the street without a small, stupid hat like Queen Di's.

Zionism will still raise unaccountably powerful emotions in the Third World. And there will be continuing terrorist attacks and protest incidents in the Israeli capital of Riyadh.

Over the next two and a half decades the military balance will shift dramatically in favor of the Third World. We in the United States, the Soviet Union and China will have given up our nuclear arms because they didn't go with our shoes and took up valuable space that could be used to build vacation condos. In the meantime every Third World country including Fernando Po will have acquired the bomb. Unfortunately, they won't use their bombs on each other no matter how forcefully sensible people like ourselves argue for them to do so. They *will* use the bombs on us, or, at least, they'll try to. But every time they do they'll find five hundred or a thousand refugee families living in the missile silos and all the weapons-grade plutonium stolen to make glow-in-the-dark tourist knick-knacks.

On the financial front, most underdeveloped countries will

have economies based on breaking things, losing things and stealing. The resulting negative GNPs will be made up by World Bank loans—necessary in order to maintain low unemployment and inflation in the last of the remaining Western democracies (South Korea, Singapore and Taiwan). International currency will be the cow chip.

The Third World debt problem, however, will be solved at last as developing nations offer to "work off" their various loan defaults. The entire country of Bolivia will come over to your house and do the lawn.

This and other factors will make illegal immigration a continuing problem. But liberals will still resist passing laws giving the United States an official language. Many Americans, they'll point out, don't speak Spanish. Many speak Hindi and Urdu.

The Third World will be out of oil in 2013. But this will not cause economic dislocations since pollution by then will be such that all South American, Asian and African rivers will be flammable and can be burned as energy sources.

Another effect of pollution will be that all Third World wildlife that hasn't been eaten will be dead. There will be no more elephants, rhinos or lions except in zoos (where most college-educated people will also be confined). On the bright side, mutations caused by the disappearance of the ozone layer and high levels of carbon monoxide in the atmosphere will result in new forms of wildlife, such as fifty-foot boll weevils and mealworms the size of Amtrak trains.

Insects will be given a seat at the U.N., where they will vote with the Communist Bloc on most issues, especially the increase of farm subsidies in the U.S.

Third World nations will continue to gain influence in international organizations such as the Olympic Committee. As a result a number of new sports will be added to Olympic competition—street begging, student rioting and hostage murder (originally a demonstration event at the 1972 Olympics in Munich).

Another upbeat trend will be the gradual elimination of the international narcotics traffic. As the entire world becomes lethargic, larcenous, mentally disconnected and given to fits of violent rage, there won't be any need for drugs.

But other Third World health problems will persist, malnutrition being the worst because there will never be quite enough of it to eliminate the other Third World maladies. Public-spirited types will form Malnutrition-Aid organizations to raise money to take food away from the underdeveloped world's burgeoning mass of ignorant, crazy and ungovernable AIDS-fodder. But it will be too little, too late.

Bizarre diseases will continue to spawn in the developing countries. We're all hoping for one that kills only lawyers. And Third World values and aesthetics will also come to permeate the globe, causing a welcome respite from feminism and bringing spray paint to the fore as the principle medium of expression in literature and the arts.

But in the next quarter century the most dramatic change in the Third World will be the United States becoming a part of it. We are already well on our way. Many of our cities are indistinguishable, in large part, from Beirut. The manners, dress and grammar of our young people have a decidedly underdeveloped cast. And most of our intellectuals have belonged to "lesser breeds without the law" for ages. All we have to do now is elect a few more Democrats.

Z.